COMBAT
SHOOTING
with Massad Ayoob

Published by

Gun Digest® Books, an imprint of F+W Media, Inc.
Krause Publications • 700 East State Street • Iola, WI 54990-0001
715-445-2214 • 888-457-2873
www.krausebooks.com

To order books or other products call toll-free 1-800-258-0929
or visit us online at www.gundigeststore.com

ISBN-13: 978-1-4402-1857-6
ISBN-10: 1-4402-1857-9

Cover Design by Tom Nelsen
Designed by Dusty Reid
Edited by Corrina Peterson

Printed in the United States of America

 DEDICATION

This book is respectfully and appreciatively dedicated to
my brother and sister instructors.
The ones who trained me, and still do …
…the ones I've taught alongside…
…the ones I've trained…
…and the ones who came before any of us, but left artifacts to pass
on to us the precious lessons, often written in blood, that they had gathered
for us so we could pass them forward in turn.
I've put as many lessons from all of them as I could into this book.

Mas Ayoob
June 2011

CONTENTS
COMBAT SHOOTING

～ FOREWORD ～

first met Massad Ayoob in 1990, when I invited him to teach a two-day "Judicious Use of Deadly Force" seminar at a gun range where I worked. Little did I know that this encounter would change my life forever. Having already been trained in use of deadly force as a police officer and also as a police firearms instructor, I thought I was pretty well versed on the topic. Those two days though, where he dissected each and every aspect of the deadly force encounter, opened my eyes to a whole new way to look at the subject of use of deadly force in self-defense; that being to filter each and every aspect of teaching how and when to shoot, through the filter of the likely jury assessing whether or not your act was reasonable under the circumstances.

That year, not only did I take the aforementioned course, but I also took three other week-long classes from him, flying back to New Hampshire to complete the trilogy of LFI-I, II, and III, and along the way being asked by Ayoob to join the staff of the Lethal Force Institute.

When asked to write the foreword to this particular work of his, I must admit I was both honored and a little horrified. He was both my mentor and friend. Would I do him and this book justice? The good news is I don't have to, the work speaks for itself, and speaks volumes.

I asked for a pre-release review copy of the book, and upon reading it, the years of working with him on the range and in the classroom seemed to fly by in my memories. I could hear his words, and came to realize that this book, Combat Shooting with Massad Ayoob, was a compilation of his life's work to date, a history I am lucky to have shared with him for the past 20+ years.

The five different sections of the book, dealing with mindset, learning combat shooting, men we can learn from, competing as a way to sharpen your skills and choices that need making is a novel, but effective way to communicate the volume of information which an armed citizen should (and in many cases MUST) know before going armed in our society. Invoking the words of Jim

Cirillo, Charlie Askins and even Wyatt Earp drives home the point that modern day training for the deadly force encounter shares much of the same techniques and mindset that earlier generations of armed Americans successfully used to succeed in deadly force encounters. We are fortunate to have their exploits to study, and their words to heed.

Over the past decade or so, we in the business have heard the constant drum beat of the crowd who say that shooting in competition will teach you bad habits, and will likely get you killed. I agree with Ayoob and many of my contemporaries who have not only tried to quiet that voice, but also urge others to get involved in competing with a gun in hand. But, there is a point to the anti-competition crowd that is worth considering. If ALL you do is compete, and you learn how to run the gun under stress shooting a sport, then it is likely that under the stress of the gunfight, your body will naturally seek to relieve that stress by using familiar shooting techniques. That is why competition should not be your only training venue, but instead used as a test to see if your skills are honed and your techniques are sharp. Ayoob explains this concept admirably.

As a man grows older (I am in my mid fifties as of this writing), he starts to look back at his life and mentally reviews the worthiness of his many experiences, and plots his course for the remainder of his days. Twenty years ago, I took Ayoob on as a mentor in the business of teaching the how and when of using the gun for self-defense, one of the more intelligent choices I have made. I look forward to the next 20 years to see how the final chapters of this fascinating career play out, and hope to share a good portion of the next two decades with Mas, on the range, teaching, learning and competing.

Marty Hayes
Onalaska, WA

Welcome to these pages, and needless to say, thanks for buying the book. (Hopefully, that will be the only thing I say needlessly here.)

The topic is a broad one, and if the late editor Dan Shideler had assigned this book title to a hundred of us who work in the field, he'd have wound up with a hundred markedly different manuscripts. If you look at the six editions of Gun Digest Book of Combat Handgunnery that have been published over the years, you'll see that Jack Lewis and Jack Mitchell, Chuck Taylor and Chuck Karwan and I, all had different interpretations and ended up writing very different books under the same title. It's a broad subject, and a subjective one.

That's as much true on the readers' end as on the writers'. It's not all about mindset, though that's certainly part of it. Only one section on competition shooting? Yep, 'cause competition shooting is only one piece of the puzzle. Only three famous gunfighters profiled in depth? Yup, because that was all there was room for in a book that wasn't just analytical biography of been there/done that role models. Nothing on how to draw a pistol? Nope, that would be Gun Digest Book of Concealed Carry. What, no catalog of firearms? No, that would be Gun Digest.

Dan Shideler had wanted this to be a thinking man's book, with lots of quotes from thinking men. I've tried, in his memory, to make it so. An unexpected cardiac event took Dan from us before the book was fully underway, and his premature departure is in my opinion a loss to the entire shooting community. He had been a joy to work with on the first volume of Massad Ayoob's Greatest Handguns, and in his approach I saw his deep understanding of not only firearms, but this thing we've all come to call the Gun Culture. I miss him still, and hope that this book has turned out as he wanted.

I need to thank some other editors for permission to reprint here work I did originally for them. That includes group publisher Shirley Steffen and editor Linas Cernauskas at Harris Publications, which has published my annual Complete Book of Handguns since 1993; Roy Huntington, editorial director of Publishers Development Corporation and editor of American Handgunner, where I've been on staff for over 30 years; Jeff John, my editor at Guns, where I've served for a like period; Sammy Reese, who edits the PDC annuals; Dave Duffy at Backwoods Home magazine where I've been firearms editor for some 16 years now; and Bob Young, my editor at Black Belt. Without them, some of what you're about to read would be less fresh for relying on a much older memory of the events. Thanks also to Gail Pepin, who did much of the photo work with me, and Herman Gunter III, my tireless and sharp-eyed proofreader. And of course, thanks as well to Marty Hayes, one of the best trainers in the business and the founder of the Armed Citizens Legal Defense Network, for writing the foreword.

I started this book with the section on mindset, because that's where it all begins with the practitioner and therefore, is the core of the matter. Next comes a structured guide to learning combat shooting, because that's where the practitioner gains the ability to weave together the necessary elements of this multidimensional discipline. In the middle of the book we analyze the experience of three gunfighters who all "faced the elephant" more than once. It's striking how much they have in common, and on how many levels. Next is an introduction to the competitive element of combat shooting, and a rationale for why – though it's not complete training in and of itself – competition can be an extremely useful component of training, skill maintenance, and skill assessment. Finally, we close with some of the choices the serious combat handgunner has to make if they're going to get the most out of the whole endeavor.

I've left quotes as they were, and different writers, editors, and publications have different styles. Among the many quotes, you may see ".38 Spl." and ".38 Special," "bullseye" and "bulls-eye," etc. It's not my place to second guess another writer or editor's writing style, so I "played those as they lay."

There's the occasional website address for an organization or trainer, but I didn't put in a whole lot of those. They can change over time. Google can always find the current ones for anyone interested.

I hope, wherever he is, Dan Shideler is pleased with this book he assigned me to write. And I hope, wherever you are, you're pleased with it too. None of us knows when we'll actually need our skills in this discipline, which is why we need to keep them sharpened.

Stay safe,
Mas Ayoob
June 2011

AUTHOR WILL SHOOT AMBUSHER above with Simunitions .38, but not before being shot himself, in a force-on-force exercise at the National Tactical Invitational.

8

CHAPTER ONE

MINDSET

I n the word "gunfight," the operative syllable is *fight*.

John Steinbeck's classic quote, popularized by gunfighting instructor Jeff Cooper, was: "The mind is the weapon, all else is supplemental." Men have fought each other to the death since they dwelt in caves. All the gun did was expand the personal distance potential.

For decades, I've taught my students that the four priorities of surviving a violent encounter are:

1. Mental awareness and preparedness.

2. Proper use of tactics.

3. Skill in combatives, which includes – but is not limited to – the firearm.

4. Optimum selection of equipment to cope with the predictable threat.

Note that awareness and preparedness are taught together, even though at first blush they appear to be separate concepts. The reason for this is simple: they are two sides of the same coin, and the one without the other is useless. At Pearl Harbor on December 7, 1941, the awareness was there, but the preparedness was not. The blips on the radar screen were observed…but they were dismissed, and in minutes, one of the mightiest battle fleets on Earth was on its way to the bottom of the harbor.

Awareness begins with the realization that armed conflict with a violent human can occur. It does not require a high risk occupation; any of us can simply be picked as the next victim by one of the many predators that roam abroad in society.

Awareness encompasses alertness. There is no better way to quantify that than the color code, popularized beyond the military by the aforementioned Col. Cooper. He described four levels. In *Condition White*, one was totally oblivious to what was going on around him and likely to miss an early danger cue. A person in Condition White would be unprepared, slow to react, and likely to survive a homicidal attack only through luck factor or what I've come to describe as "schmuck factor." (With "luck factor," we survive simply because we were lucky. With "schmuck factor," we survive only because our attacker was an

SKILL WITH THE SAFETY EQUIPMENT is #3 priority. This qualification target was shot under time with S&W .44 Magnum Mountain Gun and Federal 180 grain/1600 foot-second hollow point.

even bigger schmuck than we were. Neither is a reliable strategy for survival.)Next up is *Condition Yellow*, which the Colonel described as a constant state of relaxed alertness. It simply means knowing what is going on around us at any given moment. If a friend said, "Close your eyes and describe who is within ten feet of you right now," you could do so. If a companion said, "Don't look at the GPS or the street sign, but tell me where we are right now," you could. Cooper made the point that a well-adjusted man or woman should be able to spend their entire waking life in Condition Yellow with no adverse psychological effects.

After an adult lifetime of trying to follow Cooper's advice and live in Condition Yellow (and passing his advice on to a great many students) I've come to believe that it's even better than the Colonel predicted. That is, it is not only without negative effect, it brings a positive effect. You may have started out looking for possible bad things, but your enhanced observation allows you to notice good things you were missing before. A common remark when I meet old students goes like this: "I took you seriously when you talked about 'casting out a sensory net' and Jeff Cooper's color codes of awareness. I've been looking for bad guys ever since. I haven't found many...but I've become a

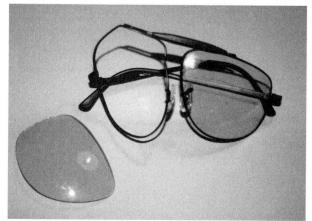

SAFETY, SAFETY, SAFETY. These shooting glasses saved the eyesight of a top firearms instructor in Idaho.

people-watcher. I notice the way the young lovers look at each other, the little boy playing with the puppy, the smile the passing grandmother gives her granddaughter...and thank you for that, because I was missing it before."

You know how people are always telling us to stop and smell the roses? I think the corollary is that when you're actively looking for thorns in the bush, you can't help but smell the roses.

The next notch up on the color code scale is *Condition Orange*, a heightened alertness that occurs when we know something is (or may be) dangerously wrong. At this point, we actively focus on gathering intelligence to determine exactly what that potential danger is. We are looking and listening and analyzing. We are particularly monitoring things like avenues of access and egress (for us, or for potential opponents), and looking for cover – cover that we can take, *and* cover an opponent may be hiding behind in ambush.

At the top of the Cooper scale was *Condition Red*. This was armed encounter level: the moment of truth.

It is time for a brief digression. It is said that when Jeff Cooper was a young Marine j/g in the Pacific Theater during WWII, the USMC had already developed a color code that had five levels. In that particular framework, Condition White meant something like "Safe at Base." Condition Yellow was the alertness one would have on patrol. Condition Orange was an intensified level when something led the Marine to believe that contact with the enemy was imminent. Condition Red was one or more enemy soldiers in sight, and at the top was a fifth level: Condition Black, or combat in progress.

I've always felt the latter, five-level version of the color codes made more sense in the domestic sector, for the

armed private citizen as well as the law enforcement officer, as distinct from military operations. In this Condition Red, we are confronting someone who more likely than not is a dangerous criminal. It escalates to *Condition Black* when that individual actually attacks.

The continuum as related to the gun is as follows. A person totally in Condition White might not even want to be armed. One does not have to be armed to be in Condition Yellow, but if one is armed, one should definitely be in that state of mental awareness. The homeowner hearing the burglar alarm go off, or the police officer receiving a radio call to respond to an armed robbery in progress, should instantly escalate to Condition Orange. They don't know the exact nature of the danger or the exact "face of the enemy" in question, but they are aggressively looking for those things. At this point, the gun may or may not be drawn depending on the totality of the circumstances, but the firearm should most certainly be instantly available. In Condition Red, we have spotted the potentially lethal gunman, and it is probably now appropriate to take him at gunpoint – an act that would be felonious aggravated assault if done without just cause. Condition Black is a lethal assault in progress: the opponent is trying to kill or cripple you, or kill or cripple someone you have a right or even a duty to protect. It is at that point that we unleash deadly

CHOICE OF GEAR is fourth down on the list. Lead hollow point .38 Special "FBI load" proved a good man-stopper with both snub-noses and 4" service revolvers.

SAFETY IS A CONSTANT CONCERN in all forms of combat shooting. A carelessly overpowered handload blew up this heavy frame Smith & Wesson .357 Magnum Highway Patrolman.

force, and actually open fire.

In Colonel Cooper's code, developed by a wartime Marine who killed enemy soldiers with his sidearm in both a hot war and a cold one, it made sense to combine Conditions Red and Black into a single Condition Red, and that the circumstances would determine whether we shot our opponent or not. That makes sense in military combat, when one's very mission is to shoot and neutralize enemy combatants on sight.

In domestic society, it doesn't work that way. Cop or "civilian," you are far more likely to be in a situation where you need to take someone at gunpoint (Condition Red), than you are to be in a situation where you have to shoot someone (Condition Black). On the witness stand, we'll be cross-examined as to what our standards and our state of mind were at the time we fired the shot or shots in question. Topping the spectrum with a single "Condition Red" allows a lawyer with an unmeritorious case to argue, "So, this Condition Red thing, you're telling us that capturing a man at gunpoint without bloodshed, or killing him…that's all the same to you, and doesn't make any difference?"

The five-color system allows the person who was forced to fire to delineate a documentable standard that shows he or she could indeed distinguish between the two situations, was able to determine that this was a "shoot situation" instead of a lesser "gunpoint situation," and credibly explain and authenticate why.

PREPAREDNESS

Awareness allows you to see the danger coming in time to do something about it. Perhaps, ideally, you may avoid it entirely if you are not bound by an occupational oath to "ride to the sound of the guns" and confront and contain the threat.

Preparedness encompasses some of the elements that follow. Preparing by learning and practicing tactics. Preparing by developing skill in hand to hand combat as well as with your weapons, both lethal and "less-than-lethal." Preparing by determining beforehand the best tools for managing the most predictable threats, and acquiring those tools, and the skill that makes them effective.

But within the framework of this topic, preparedness goes farther than that. It encompasses the realization that the use of deadly force in self-defense may have unpleasant legal, social, financial, and psychological effects. The few seconds of the fight itself will be the worst possible time to realize this, because until one has come to terms

PEERS LEARN FROM ONE ANOTHER. Author, left, with LE training authority Dave Spaulding at Montgomery County, Ohio police academy. Both served for years on firearms committee for American Society of Law Enforcement Trainers.

with it, one is likely to hesitate to use that level of force. That means that the winning combatant is, all other things being equal, likely to be the one who has most certainly determined beforehand that he or she can handle that aftermath.

And, the history of combat tells us, it is likely to be the one who knows what he or she is fighting for.

Loren Christensen completed a distinguished career on a big-city police force, working one of its highest-crime areas for much of that time. He is also a lifelong martial artist and trainer. For his book "Warriors: On Living with Courage, Discipline, and Honor," he asked several of us to write on various topics in the field of human conflict. My contribution was as follows:

WHY WE FIGHT[1]

It is not enough to teach a practitioner *how* to fight. It is essential to teach him or her *why*. History is replete with ragtag patriots who kicked out of their homelands hardcore professional soldiers who had invaded them, a history we Americans celebrate every Fourth of July. Skill and knowledge aren't enough. There's that thing called "motivation."

The warrior skills, truth to tell, are so involved that they can become their own *raison d'etre*. Why else would martial arts be a sport that creates a lifestyle, and why else would combat shooting be something practitioners do in a competition arena for their primary avocation? Let's admit the dirty secret: learning to fight, with or without a weapon in hand, can be *fun*, and sometimes the fun and the self-esteem of achieving a certain skill level can become the tail

13

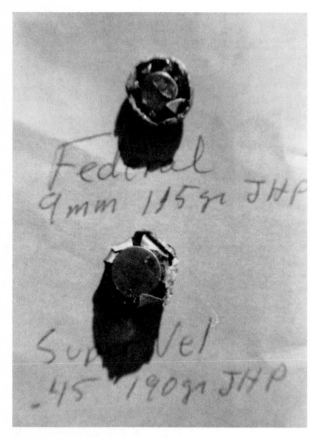

BY THE 1970S, ammo technology had improved dramatically. Federal 9BP 115 grain 9mm, top; Super Vel 190 grain .45 ACP, below, both removed from animals they cleanly killed.

that wags the dog. When that happens, the result can be a national champion *karateka* or pistol competitor…but not necessarily the best prepared warrior.

If you have been in this business long enough, you have come across the person who looks you in the eye and says, "I'd rather die than kill my attacker." If you get that from a cop or soldier, your duty is to remove them from The Job, because they're obviously not ready to perform it. When you hear it from an ordinary citizen, you have a little more room. My answer has always been, "That's okay, because it's your life…isn't it?"

They normally answer "Yes." Fine so far. Then I ask them the litmus test question.

"Tell me something. If that same guy you'd rather die than kill was standing over your baby's cradle, holding a knife, ready to sacrifice your child to Satan – what would you do then?"

When you ask that question the answer comes boiling up out of them in pure reflex, before they can think about it, more than nine times out of ten. "I'd kill him!"

Then I pause for a moment, to let them reflect on what they've said, and ask them the final self-probing test question: "What's the difference?"

We know the answer to that question. We know it because we have stood at the precipice of Death and looked down into the abyss, and it is a knowledge we have an ethical obligation to impart to those we teach.

The answer is, there is no real difference at all. Death is The Great Separator. Whether it is the parent who dies, or the child, either way each is lost to the other forever more, at least upon this earth.

You reading this, you who have been there at the edge of the Darkness and looking into the Void…remember. Did it not happen – at that moment, or very shortly thereafter – that you thought of your loved ones? How long did it take for the realization to hit you that you almost didn't see your children grow up, almost lost your last chance to say good-bye to your parents?

This tells us something, something we need to share with those we teach in the art and science of survival of violence. Hold that thought, and let's look to some analogous concepts to see how they fit in.

THE MANY ELEMENTS

The survival disciplines are multi-dimensional, and each inter-related discipline can be a life-long study in and of itself.

A conflict involving lethal force is, by definition, a near-death experience for the survivor. We can learn a great deal about how to face imminent death by studying not just combat survivors, but all survivors of near-death events.

Virtually all of us contributing to this effort are familiar with the splendid work done by Dr. Alexis Artwohl when she was police psychologist for the Portland Police Bureau, as published by her and her colleague Loren Christensen. Few are aware of a corollary study done in the early 1990s by Dr. John Woo, Chief of Psychiatry at the University of California, Irvine.

While the Artwohl study focused entirely on officer-involved shootings, the Woo study was geared to the perceptual phenomena of near-death survivors at the time of their incidents, and covered a broader spectrum. I came into it when Dr. Woo approached me to arrange interviews with Lethal Force Institute graduates who had survived gunfights. They would join a much greater body of research participants who had survived falls from high places, automobile collisions, train wrecks, plane crashes, near-drownings, sudden and cataclysmic medical emergencies, and other immediately life-threatening situations.

The same phenomena I had been studying, writing, and teaching about since the 1970s were all there when I read the results of the Woo research. Tachypsychia, the sense of everything going into slow motion. Tunnel vision. Auditory exclusion, or "tunnel hearing," and more. But Woo's study asked about one question that I had never thought to ask the gunfight survivors I interviewed. I wanted to kick myself when I realized the oversight.

The question was, did you experience a sensation of "your life flashing before your eyes" at the moment you looked Death in the face?

A significant number of the participants in the Woo study had experienced exactly that. It's something we've all read or heard about. "My life flashed before my eyes." It's a perception so common that almost everyone who has experienced it uses virtually those exact same words to describe it.

Since learning that, I've made a point of polling my own students when we talk about the altered perceptual phenomena which occur in violent encounters. I ask how many have heard of the "life flashing before the eyes": virtually all have. Then I ask how many have experienced it themselves, and in a class of any size there usually are at least a couple.

And then I ask one more question, a question so obvious I've never heard anyone ask it in these discussions: *"What were the images?* You were twenty, thirty, whatever years old; there wasn't time for all of it. When you thought you were about to immediately leave this world, what were the images that computer between your ears thought were so important they had to be reviewed for one last time?"

The answers have been strikingly uniform. I'm still waiting for one of them to tell me, "I flashed back to the cutest gal I ever picked up in a singles bar," or "I saw myself back at the podium receiving my life achievement award."

No, every single one of them told me that the images they saw when they looked at their imminent demise were the faces of their mothers and their fathers and their lovers and their sons and their daughters.

And the lesson from all those flashing lives is this: the people we love are our *raisons d'etre*. Our reasons for being. The ones for whom we fight.

EXAMPLES

Medical literature is replete with examples of "surren-der death," patients who shouldn't have died from what ailed them but did, because they simply "gave up." And any experienced trauma doc, ER nurse, or paramedic can describe cases of the opposite. The patient who was torn apart by outside trauma or rotted away by disease from inside who managed to stay alive long enough to accomplish something important.

We've all heard the stories of the little granny lady who manages to lift up the car that is crushing her grandchild. No one ever mentions that she tore loose every muscle in her back and suffered two or three compression fractures of the spine. It suffices to know that superhuman physical ability is there on tap, triggered by supernormal need to act.

I tell my students of two police officers in Ohio. Terry, a county deputy, remembers being down on his back, being stomped into the parking lot of a roadhouse by a veritable giant. Kicked in the groin, battered about the head and almost fading out of consciousness, unable to breathe because his ribs were broken, he was ready to let go. "It wasn't just the pain," he told me much later. "It wasn't even the humiliation of being beaten. A big part of it was despair, looking at the faces of the people I was dying to protect. They had their faces to the window, watching me get kicked to death, and not a God-damned one of them was willing to come out and help me."

Terry paused and added almost in a whisper, "And then I saw in my mind's eye, as if I was there, my two sons standing at my grave."

The witnesses inside the roadhouse saw something close to a miracle then. One of them told an investigator later, "The deputy climbed the big guy's body."

They saw a hand rise up and grab the big man's jeans, and another reach up and clutch his belt. One of the sheep inside had at least called 9-1-1, and when the responding deputies arrived, Terry was on top. The big man's eyes had rolled back in his head, and Terry was somewhere else behind a face covered with blood and grime, and it took three of them to peel Terry's hands from his antagonist's throat and pull him off...

Jimmy was a big city cop in the same state. Armed only with a little five-shot Smith & Wesson .38, he responded from off duty status to join the manhunt for a suspect who had shot and wounded two cops. Jimmy was searching a church basement when he jerked open a closet door and – BANG!

The suspect had been waiting inside. At a range measurable in inches, he shot Jimmy in the face with a .357

KEEPING GUN OUT OF UNAUTHORIZED HANDS is a priority for combat handgun owners. Magna-Trigger .357 is shown with author's booklet "GunProof Your Children," www.ayoob.com.

Magnum. The bullet entered just to the side of his nose, shattering the maxillo-facial structure, traveling under the brain and exiting just to the side of his spine and under the base of the skull. At the hammer-blow of the impact, the young officer toppled onto his back.

He told me a long time afterward, "Mas, you cannot imagine the pain. Picture a great big railroad spike. Heat it white hot. Now suppose someone hammers it through the front of your face and out the base of your skull and nails you to the floor with it.

"I wanted to die just so the pain would stop.

"And then I saw my daughters being told that I was dead."

It was as if something from outside his body had entered and re-animated him. Something unseen lifted him up off the floor. He reached down and picked up his fallen revolver and went after the man who shot him. Jimmy killed him where he stood. By now, the other cops who had heard the shots were there.

It was clear that Jimmy had sustained a perforating, large-caliber, close range gunshot wound to the head. They knew he could not possibly live, but they had to do everything they could. Rather than wait for an ambulance, they put him into a squad car and raced to the hospital.

Jimmy was calling for his daughters. A good supervisor knows his personnel and their families, and Jimmy had a good sergeant. It was day shift, and the sergeant rushed one patrol car to the high school and another to the middle school to pick up each of the girls.

By the time the kids reached the hospital, Jimmy was on a gurney outside the OR, about to undergo emergency surgery. In each of his bloodstained hands, he took one of theirs. The inside of his shattered head was so full of blood he sounded like a man talking underwater when he told his two daughters, "I'm gonna live! I'm gonna live for you!"

And he did.

It's as if inside each one of us there is a reserve battery for desperate moments, a last-ditch source of superhuman energy that is only tapped in the gravest extreme of crisis. And I have often wondered how many people couldn't use it because by the time that hidden battery kicked in, their body was already too broken to take advantage of it.

Remember the mother who was conditioned by her society to die rather than protect herself but is triggered to homicidal response by the Mother Wolf Instinct when someone attacks her cub. Most humans will fight harder to protect someone who depends upon them than they will to protect themselves.

Those of us responsible not only for training but for motivating individuals to fight for their lives, cannot lose sight of this. The next time you train your warriors, remind them what they're going to be fighting for.

Not for the next drink at the bar. Not for the next plaque on the wall.

Remind them that they're fighting to spare their parents the unnatural grief of burying a child. Fighting to return to the person with whom they swore a covenant to live out their life. Fighting to come back to every child they have brought into this unforgiving place, to be there for as long as they can be, to shepherd them through it. Because if they allow themselves to be killed, they will be separated from those loved ones as surely as if the loved ones had been murdered instead.

If they know from the beginning of the conflict that this is what they're fighting for, they'll be stronger, more determined, more likely to prevail. Let that reserve battery be triggered at the beginning of the fight, so they can fight from the beginning at maximum strength, and they will be more likely in the end to emerge from that fight unscathed.

❧

Another element of awareness and alertness is being *able to recognize* the given danger cues. "Body language" isn't junk science or Yuppie BS. It's an absolutely valid science. Being able to recognize pre-assaultive behavior cues can save your life. Being able to articulate and validate what you recognized can keep you out of prison or bankruptcy if your use of force to save your life is questioned in criminal or civil court. Since 1996, I've served as firearms editor for *Backwoods Home* magazine. Of all my articles that have appeared there over the years, the one that has generated the single largest number of requests to reprint for training purposes is this one:

BODY LANGUAGE AND THREAT RECOGNITION[2]

People have been hurt—sometimes by strangers, sometimes by people they knew and loved—when they failed to realize that the other person was experiencing a level of hostility that was about to boil over. Being able to recognize body language associated with imminent violent action can allow you to, in the best-case scenario, disengage and leave the scene. At worst, it can give you time to activate a plan of self-defense soon enough to effectively protect yourself and those for whose safety you are responsible.

DANGER SIGNALS

The eyes, it is said, are the windows to the soul. Often, the way in which a hostile person looks at you can be a predictor of what his plans are for you.

Cops, soldiers, and mental health professionals are all too familiar with "the thousand yard stare." This is the person who seems to be not so much looking at you as through you. He may be unresponsive or inappropriately responsive in other ways. What this should tell you is that in this moment he is in an alternate reality of his own, a place where you are probably not welcome. When you see this, start "creating distance" unless you in fact are a law enforcement officer, health professional, or someone else who has a responsibility for containing and restraining this person's actions.

The opposite of the thousand yard stare is the "target stare." This is the guy who narrows his eyes and glares directly at you. The narrowing of the eyelids does for our vision what shutting down the f/stop on your camera does for the lens: it enhances depth perception. It tells you that you have become a very intense focus of his attention. If the circumstances indicate that this individual is at all hostile, the target stare is not a good sign. If you're not a cop, psych nurse, etc., Mother Nature is telling you again to start creating distance between you and him.

There is also "target glance." Cops learned the hard way over the years that if a man casts a furtive glance in a certain direction, he may well be checking his avenues of escape: his quick look has just told the officers where he is likely to run. Is he staring at your chin? In a hostile situation, he's not admiring your Kirk Douglas chin cleft and he hasn't noticed a zit you missed this morning in the mirror. More likely, he's thinking about sucker punching you right "on the button." If his eyes go down to your crotch, he's probably not a gay guy scoping out your package…more likely, he's actively considering opening the fight with a kick to your crotch.

A brief aside to the shooters in the audience. You know how when you see a cop, you immediately look at his holster to see what sort of sidearm he's wearing? Have you noticed that every now and then when you do that, you get a dirty look from the officer, who may step back or otherwise change his physical orientation to you? The reason

BE WILLING TO TRY NEW TECHNIQUES. Police instructor Vince O'Neill demonstrates a technique developed by Paul Castle for firing one-handed with a shotgun if attacked while opening door. Forward hand has been pulled well back from muzzle.

is, he has been taught about pre-assaultive behavior cues, too, and he has learned to interpret a look at his holster as a "target glance" that may indicate the person is thinking about snatching his service pistol.

"FIGHT OR FLIGHT" INDICATORS

When the brain perceives that we are about to be in a strenuous physical conflict, a primitive mammalian survival reflex kicks in which prepares us to do battle or to flee. Quantified in the early 20th Century as "fight or flight response" by Dr. Walter Cannon at Harvard Medical School, this phenomenon may reveal itself to another person with subtle physical manifestations…if that other person is sufficiently alert and informed to recognize what they're looking at.

When we go into a high level of "body alarm reaction," the lizard that lives in the base of our brain and controls the machinery and the thermostats decides to kick up oxygenated blood supply. The heart begins to race and the lungs begin to take in more air. Watch for rapid breathing or panting in a person who has not performed any strenu-ous physical activity. You may even be able to see a pulse throbbing at the neck or the temple of some individuals.

Now, let's perform a process of elimination. There is no common danger that threatens those at the scene. You have done nothing to threaten him. Neither has anyone else. He has not been exerting himself. Yet, his blood vessels are pulsing violently and he is breathing heavily. By this process of elimination, we can determine where the fight or flight thing has come from: He has already decided that he is going to fight. (Or, if you are lucky, that he is going to run.)

The adrenal system instantly releases powerful chemicals in a fight or flight state, including epinephrine ("adrenaline"). One side effect of this is tremors, often violent ones, which will usually manifest themselves first in the non-dominant hand, almost immediately thereafter in the dominant hand, and then in the legs, particularly the knees. If you observe tremors in those locations in a situation that you perceive may turn hostile, go through that process of elimination again. Could the person be simply shivering in the cold? Do you have reason to believe he has Parkinson's disease or some other ailment of which trembling is symptomatic? If not, you know the diagnosis, and you know the first step of treatment—create distance.

NOT EVERYTHING IS RESOLVED with gunfire. At far left, role-player holds instructor Rick Devoid hostage with dummy gun, while author, far right and similarly equipped, engages him in verbal hostage negotiation as surrounding students look on. "If your only tool is a hammer," said Abraham Maslow, "every problem becomes a nail."

THE BODY LANGUAGE OF
FIGHT/FLIGHT

Facial expressions and body movements can give you early warning that the person you face has gone into fighting mode. All the way back to Dr. Cannon, certain cues have been recognized as classic.

The person is likely to "quarter," that is, step back with one leg, turning his hips to something approximating a 45-degree angle. In this posture, the body is best balanced to take or deliver impact in any direction. Fighters call it the "boxer's stance." Martial artists call it the "front stance." Shooters call it the "Weaver stance." Cops are taught to stand this way, prepared immediately to react and fight, in an "interview stance."

The hands will typically be up, between hips and face, usually level with some point on the torso. The fingers may be partially closed. (The hands clenched into fists, or opening and closing into fists repeatedly, is a particularly blatant sign that the "fight" side of "fight or flight" has been internally engaged.)

The knees may flex slightly. This is the true "combat crouch." The head is likely to be slightly forward of the shoulders, and the shoulders forward of the hips. Combat trainers call this posture "nose over toes." It's what they teach their students to go into intentionally when they prepare to fight to the finish. When someone does it instinctively, it has given you what we in police work call "a clue"...

Life experience has already taught you that emotionally aroused people may not realize that their facial expression is reflecting their internal emotions outward for all to see. This happens in hostile situations too. A snarl that brings the lips back from the teeth doesn't require a professional behaviorist to interpret for you: it clearly doesn't bode well. The human is a natural carnivore, and a grimace that exposes the canine teeth is a particularly overt indication of aggressive intent.

A seemingly opposite expression can mean the same thing. Tightly clenched jaws, which may even include grinding teeth, and tightly pursed lips, can also be signs of extreme anger.

Let's go back for a moment to fight or flight basics. The heart and lungs are sending oxygenated blood through the body as fast as they can. However, if no strenuous physical activity has yet taken place, the body is now over-oxygenating, and hyperventilation can set in. Generations

19

(1st of 6): HYPERVENTILATION AND TREMORS hit good guys and bad alike during fight or flight response. This sanchin exercise can help. Pressing hands hard against each other head-high while holding a deep breath...

(2nd of 6): ...ERIK PEPIN brings his tensely pressing arms downward, hissing the breath out slowly...

of medical professionals have advised hyperventilating patients to breathe into a paper bag. This causes them to inhale carbon dioxide they've just exhaled, and helps to quickly restore a normal O2/CO2 balance.

As it happens, people in actual fight or flight situations don't usually have access to paper bags. This includes both you and your potential opponent.

If you are the one hyperventilating—at a high risk scene or anywhere else—I and my fellow instructors will advise you to consciously perform what has been called "combat breathing," "stress breathing," or "crisis breathing." Martial artists call it "*sanchin* breathing." The breath is intentionally held, then slowly hissed out. It is the internalized version of the paper bag treatment. If you have been trained in the Lamaze Method of natural childbirth, you are familiar with a very similar version of stress breathing.

Sometimes, people do that automatically under stress without realizing it. If the person you are facing in a hos-

tile situation is breathing like this, wake up and smell the coffee. Remember when we did the math before. If there's nothing else to cause stress, it is reasonable to deduce that he is planning something stressful and strenuous. One particularly common manifestation is what my mom used to call, with perhaps more justification than she knew, "blowing off steam." This is the person whose cheeks work like a bellows as he seems to intentionally hiss out a long, hard exhalation of air. It may help reduce over-oxygenation in his blood, but guess what: if he's in an uncontrollable state of rage, that building head of steam isn't going to just "blow off." There's a good chance that it's going to "blow up" instead. And you know the response. Say it with me. "Create distance..."

Look for meaningless movements. The guy who bounces up and down on the balls of his feet. The "walk that goes nowhere," that is, purposeless back and forth pacing. And, as noted before, hands which clench and unclench. (Some-

(3rd of 6): …AND FINISHES with shoulders forward. This restores oxygen/carbon dioxide balance…

(4th of 6): …AND CAN ALSO be done with hard hand crush as shown. Wrists curled slightly inward increase hand strength, and this and previous isometric exercise burn off excess oxygen…

times, also, jaws that clench and unclench.) The body is subconsciously trying to burn off the excess oxygen, circulated through the bloodstream by the fight or flight response, to prevent hyperventilation. This doesn't mean the response is over with. The bottom line is, it means the fight or flight response is there.

Among Americans, nodding the head forward and back is a signal of "yes," and shaking the head from side to side is a cultural signal of "no." When you see your potential antagonist doing either of these things—*and no one has asked him a yes or no question*—you are experiencing another "create distance" moment. Whether he's thinking, "Yes, I knew they were going to come to take me away, and now I must attack them," or "No, I won't let them take me away this time," there's an excellent chance that what he is thinking does not bode well for you.

The folding of the arms can mean a lot of things in body language. Sometimes it just means, "I'm afraid and I'm drawing into my shell." Remember, though, that if they're showing they're afraid of you—whether or not it's a rational fear—it is the nature of mammals in general and humans in particular to lash out at what frightens them. If the folded arms are accompanied by a tensing of the muscles, and perhaps also by a glowering facial expression or any of the other possible assaultive behavior cues, you won't be far off if you read the statement as, "I am putting on my armor, because I am preparing to fight."

Look for changes in skin color. You already know that a Caucasian who suddenly becomes "red in the face" may be displaying what is culturally recognized as the color of anger. Be aware, however, that the opposite coloration effect can mean the same thing. When the body goes into "fight or flight," vasoconstriction occurs, redirecting blood flow away from the extremities and toward the internal viscera (to "fuel the furnace" for the strenuous activity that the primal brain anticipates) and to major muscle groups. This is

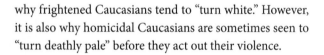

(5th of 6): ...IN THIS VARIATION OF sanchin, Erik Pepin is pushing instep out hard against upward pulling palm, still holding breath and slowly exhaling, to help reduce tremors in knees...

(6th of 6): ...AND A "GYM SHAKEOUT" of the hands after each such exercise seems to reduce tremors as well.

why frightened Caucasians tend to "turn white." However, it is also why homicidal Caucasians are sometimes seen to "turn deathly pale" before they act out their violence.

OTHER SIGNAGE

Street cops watch for subtle tattoos and other "subculture signals." In the gay community, a handkerchief prominently hanging out of one hip pocket or the other indicates whether you are a "top" or a "bottom." In some neighborhoods in Los Angeles, wearing red means you're with the Bloods, and wearing blue means you're with the Crips, and innocent people have found themselves dead or horribly injured for unknowingly wearing the wrong color in the wrong place.

A decade ago, I was an expert witness on the defense team for a police officer who was tried for murder after he shot and killed a man who attacked him, beat him, and tried to snatch his gun and slay him with it. A key factor

in winning his acquittal was that he was able to articulate that before he was attacked, he recognized his assailant's distinctive gang tattoos and correlated that knowledge with his remembered training, which had taught him that inner-city gang members often trained themselves how to disarm and murder police officers.

Teardrops tattooed on the face mean one to five years per teardrop of hard time served in prison, for example, depending on the given subculture and locale. The tattoo "AFFA" stands for "Angels Forever, Forever Angels," and marks either a genuine member or a wannabe member of the quintessential outlaw motorcycle club, Hell's Angels. A patch—whether motorcycle club patch, or police department shoulder patch—worn upside-down on a biker's vest signifies in the outlaw subculture that the wearer has taken it from a legitimate owner he has vanquished in combat. These things are good to know if you end up fighting someone who is "wearing the sign."

…BE ABLE TO DISTINGUISH between this "thousand yard stare"…

…AND THIS "TARGET STARE." Neither bode well for the person facing this man.

BECOME A FLUENT READER of body language. Quartered stance, tight or drawn back lips, clenching/unclenching hands are all signs of buildup to "fight or flight" …

Other symbols or "signage" can give you clues to where the other person is coming from. In the photos that (originally accompanied) this article, one of the role-players (was) wearing a cap with a logo that reads *Pilemos Estin Ergon.* That translates from the Greek as, roughly, "War Is Work." Could it give you a clue as to the personality of the wearer, when you face him in a hostile situation?

Let's keep this all in perspective. What we are talking about here is taking the above cues in context with a situation which is such that hostility can be anticipated by any reasonable and prudent person. Don't forget that the guy might be breathing heavily because he has recently exerted himself physically performing some perfectly innocent task. Always remember that the guy with the red face might simply have high blood pressure or a bad case of sunburn, or just be embarrassed, and that the person with the pale white face may come by that complexion naturally.

Let's also touch one more time on what your response should be to these "cues" we've been talking about. I cannot emphasize too strongly that "create distance" thing that has been repeated throughout this article. Any master martial artist, any role model military general, will tell you that the best battle is one you don't have to fight. The best course of action is always to avoid the conflict. The police officer, the psychiatric nurse, the professional security guard has a duty to stay at the scene and contain any violence that is threatened to those he is duty-bound to protect. For anyone else, the best thing to do is to abjure from the conflict, to back off and do everything possible to defuse the potential violence. The best fight is the one that never takes place. In many jurisdictions within the United States, the law expressly states that there is a "retreat requirement." This means that the private citizen who is assaulted is expected to retreat or at least attempt to retreat before using physical force in self-defense. There are only two exceptions. One is an attack by a stranger in one's own home; there, under what the English Common Law called the Castle Doctrine, retreat is not required. Attacked by an intruder in one's own home, one has the right to stand one's ground and use force immediately to repel the attack, but only equal force may be used. The other exception exists in every jurisdiction where the retreat requirement holds sway, and it says in essence, "Retreat is only demanded when it can be done with complete safety to oneself and others who are in danger."

Sometimes, the assault will come so quickly that you can't disengage, and you have no choice but to defend yourself. The law understands that. But even in that worst case scenario, being able to read the fast-developing and fast-breaking danger signals of the other person's behavior can sometimes be sufficient to buy you just enough time to react swiftly enough to defend yourself and your loved ones effectively. If things get cut that close—and they often do—the early warning of the danger signals the opponent put off can make the difference between survival and death for you and those you love. If he's going to serve up violent assault, you want to see it coming in time to return the volley more effectively than he served it, and win the match.

But if it's avoidable, recognition of pre-assaultive behavior cues may be your key to seeing it coming, in time to avoid it by breaking off contact entirely. The best advice on this doesn't come from me, or Jeff Cooper, or any of the other people who teach self-defense in violent situations. It comes from the humorous poet Ogden Nash. Nash wrote:

"When called by a panther…Don't anther."

TACTICS is second on the list of survival priorities, demonstrated by this police officer proning out behind barricade that replicates cover in a police pistol match. He seems to be focused more on marksmanship than cover.

PROPER USE OF TACTICS

Tactics are second only to awareness and preparedness in survival related priorities. It's not just enough to KNOW them; it's necessary to USE them. In studying officer deaths over the years, failure to use available cover has been one of the "deadly errors" that has been cited again and again. Another is approaching a known or obvious danger situation alone, when backup was readily available. Another was standing in the open when it was possible to either quickly gain cover, or at least make oneself a moving target. There are many others, of course, and we'll get to them in due time.

Tactics have to encompass things beyond who might get shot and who might not. Legal aspects have to be measured against tactics, and woven through the decision-making process as it is built long before an armed encounter begins. The reason is simple: it serves little to employ a tactic that wins the fight, but sends you to spend the rest of your allotted days on this planet rotting in a prison cell instead of a grave.

A useful case example is the shooting death of Jose Guerena in the spring of 2011 in Tucson, Arizona. Guerena was shot and killed by a SWAT team serving a search warrant on his home, when they made entry only to find him pointing an AR15 rifle in their direction. Many of those who criticized what happened that day did not understand details of warrant service that are mandated by law and therefore affected the manner in which the police made entry. Nor did they understand the powerful advantage Guerena held as the ensconced defender inside the house when the breaching team perceived him wielding the gun at them…an advantage that made it tactical suicide for them to hold their fire and shout "drop the gun" at that

TACTICS AND SKILL combine in shooting from behind cover. Officer in background seems to be doing so most effectively.

moment, as some critics insisted they should have done.

It appears from the evidence that Mr. Guerena was awakened by his wife and advised by her that there were armed men outside. He grabbed his loaded AR15 rifle and approached the front door. The entering SWAT cops saw a man pointing a gun at them – and, of course, opened fire. Some speculate that Mr. Guerena thought it was criminal home invaders, not police performing their lawful duties, at his door. If that was indeed the case, had he been wise enough to ensconce in the bedroom with his wife and little son, and immediately contacted 9-1-1, there is an excellent chance that this would have bought enough time for him to be notified by the 9-1-1 operator that he was dealing with law enforcement. There would very likely have been time for him to set down his weapon and avoid the confrontation that caused his death.

For an example of measuring tactics against the yardstick of legal requirements, let's look at a piece I wrote for my 2009 edition of the annual *Complete Book of Handguns*. The topic is how those two elements, tactics and perceived legality, relate to home defense.

HOME DEFENSE TACTICS[3]

Your home is your castle…but, in American jurisprudence, that doesn't really make you The King. Here's how *things really work, with nine documented cases to confirm the reality!*

American law substantially follows the English Common Law, one principle of which holds that "a man's home is his castle."

Some folks don't quite understand what that means.

In terms of using that classic tool of lethal force, the firearm, all it really means is that if you are attacked in your home by an outside intruder who has no right to be there, you are not required to retreat before defending yourself against reasonably perceived deadly force wielded by the intruder.

Let's examine that, term by term. *Attacked. In your home. By an intruder.* Who *has no right to be there.* Defending yourself against *reasonably perceived deadly force.*

As the old saying goes, the devil is in the details.

IN THE DETAILS…

Let's look at those details, in order. There's the *attacked* part. In an Eastern state, a dentist who didn't quite grasp the "home as castle" thing found a burglar in his home. He confronted the man at gunpoint. The burglar turned and ran out the door. As he ran, the homeowner shot him in the back…and was convicted of a wrongful homicide and sent to prison. Consider it **Case One.**

You can expect the judge and jury to see such a shooting as motivated by anger and revenge. Was it necessary to shoot the fleeing burglar? Therein will lie the fulcrum that determines whether the verdict see-saws toward guilt or innocence.

There's the *in your home* part. In **Case Two**, a man who lived in an apartment building had been frighteningly harassed by a man who lived next door. As the threats increased, he accepted the loan of an SKS rifle from his brother for protection. The day came when the next-door neighbor began yelling threats to the effect that he would beat the crap out of the man in the apartment, and started moving toward the door of the apartment building. The soon-to-be defendant grabbed his loaded SKS, left the apartment, and moved cautiously down the common hallway toward the main door of the building. He opened that door – and saw his large antagonist rushing at him. He opened fire, killing the man with a multiple 7.62X39 bullets.

The man who fired was charged with murder. The overzealous prosecutor asked the judge for an extra count of murder for every shot, since more than one of the multiple hits were determined to have been potentially fatal…and, incredibly, requested that a Castle Doctrine defense be disallowed since a man who rented an apartment wasn't a homeowner and didn't qualify! The wise judge, with a roll of the eyes, disallowed both motions by the prosecutor but allowed the murder trial to continue. Ultimately, the shooter was convicted of the lesser included offense of manslaughter and sent to prison.

In **Case Three**, a young husband and father whose home was located in a neighborhood that had suffered home invasions heard his wife scream in terror that people were breaking in. He grabbed his hunting gun, a Smith & Wesson .44 Magnum, and rushed downstairs. Perceiving movement at the front of the house, he flung open the front door. In the dim light, he saw a strangely dressed young man moving jerkily toward him, holding a metallic object the young homeowner couldn't identify. He aimed the .44 at him and screamed for him to freeze. The man continued to advance and finally, at close range, the homeowner fired from the open doorway and killed him.

The deceased turned out to be a Japanese exchange student, holding a small camera, and dressed like John Travolta in "Saturday Night Fever." His strange movements were apparently an attempt to mimic disco dancing, in keeping with his character: he had been en route to a pre-Halloween costume party and come to the wrong address.

In criminal court, the shooter was tried and acquitted… but in the civil lawsuit that followed, he was hammered. One strong theme that came out of juror comments after the verdicts in both Case Two and Case Three was that in neither case was the slain man actually inside the dwelling space. In both cases, the jurors' conclusion was that with the bad guy outside, the good guy who had ranged outward to engage the potential threat had been "looking for trouble" and was therefore culpable.

The lesson: Barricade inside! If the bad guy forces his way into the actual living space of your home, now your use of deadly force is much more clear-cut and much more solidly defensible.

There is the confronted *by an intruder* part. I own a classic old Colt that was once the service revolver of a city police officer who, in what was then that department's tradition, was presented his issue gun to keep as a souvenir after his honorable retirement. It became his bedside home defense gun that was in his hand when what I'll call **Case Four** went down.

The night came when the ex-cop was awakened bleary-eyed from sleep by noises in his kitchen. He reached over and touched his wife; she was there, asleep, and their kids were grown and flown. It must, he concluded, be an intruder! He grabbed the loaded Colt, cocking the hammer the way he had been taught with the bad old training of yesteryear, and made his way to the kitchen. There, he perceived a shadowy figure by the refrigerator. He pointed the gun at this individual, and with his other hand, flicked on the light switch…

…and realized that he was pointing his cocked revolver at his own elderly mother, who had just moved in with him, a fact that didn't register in his sleep-fogged brain when he was awakened by the suspicious sounds.

He didn't want the gun anymore. He gave it away. And he narrowly avoided a nightmarish tragedy. We all have to remember that not only might we have forgotten when roused from deep REM sleep that friends or relatives are in our house where they usually aren't, but we can easily forget that we've given keys to our home to relatives and close friends. Perhaps one of them has just suffered a horrible psychological trauma – let's say, a spouse who just screamed at them, "I hate you, get out!" They're not thinking straight, and as they drive around aimlessly, they

IF GUN IS unconventionally carried, user should practice drawing it from that location. In this case…

…IT'S A MODEL 3913 S&W 9mm in a car seat holster.

remember that your house is a friendly haven and they have a key…and it's three in the morning, and they don't want to wake you up…

Don't think that's far-fetched. One of my LFI-I civilian graduates called me not long after the class to thank me for saving a life in what I'll treat here as **Case Five**. "Before the class, I had figured I'd just shoot anyone I found in my house," he said. "But what I learned at LFI got me thinking. Anyway, last night I heard the 'bump in the night,' and grabbed my gun and my flashlight and went looking. I saw a human figure in my living room. I brought the gun up, but instead of just shooting him like I would have before, I turned on the flashlight…and it was my brother in law."

The brother in law was a college student due to visit in a couple of days. He had finished his exams early, and arrived in the wee hours of the morning. Finding the lights out, he had let himself in with his key and was preparing to go to sleep on the sofa. He had thought it would be

funny to surprise his sister and brother in law when they found him there in the morning … sigh.

The point is, you can't buy into the old cracker barrel BS (now, sadly, Internet BS) plan of "I'll kill anybody I find in my house!" It's a quick route to tragedy of huge proportion.

There's *the where the opponent has no right to be part*. It amazes me how many quickie CCW courses and self-defense classes overlook this when they talk about Castle Doctrine. Yes, the English Common Law from which our own derives says explicitly that your home is your castle, and attacked there, you need not retreat. However, we have to read the fine print! If you are attacked by *another person who lives in that house – which means it's their castle, too – you're back to square one!*

We see this come up a lot in domestic homicides. One thing the general public does not realize is that a significant percentage of "domestic homicides" between partners are in fact self-defense killings, in which the victim (usually, but not always, female) turns the tables and kills the homicidal abuser (usually, but not always, male).

A classic, and famous, example is **Case Six**, which occurred many years ago in a liberal New England state. The woman in question lived with her children and her boyfriend in a home owned by the latter. The male homeowner was abusive, and also known to her to be highly skilled in hand-to-hand combat. His abuse of her escalated until the day came when he said, "I want you and your (expletive deleted) kids out of here! If you're here when I come home tonight, I'll kill you!"

She appears to have been a second-generation victim of what the general public calls "battered woman syndrome" and psychologists call "learned helplessness." She did not call the authorities because she didn't think they could

COMBINING TACTICS AND SHOOTING SKILL, it's important to drill on shooting from behind cover, as mandated in this IDPA competition stage.

SAFETY TRUMPS MACHISMO. Instructor Peter Dayton is patted down before entering Simunitions™ exercise. If a functional weapon is found, culprit is expelled from the program.

help. She called a female relative who told her, in effect, "Honey, that's how men are, he'll get over it tonight." She returned to the house with her kids.

When the boyfriend came back from work, he was incensed with rage, and stated that he would carry out his threat. He attacked her. She broke free and raced to the recreation room with her kids. When he battered down the door, she took his loaded .22 rifle down from its rack and shot him dead.

The jury convicted her of manslaughter. An appellate court, in an unfortunately worded decision, said that she had failed in her duty to make a reasonable effort to retreat, and there was a phrase in the decision implying that she should have attempted to climb out a window. The governor of that state, an anti-gun liberal who later ran unsuccessfully as a Democratic nominee for President, was wise enough to commute her sentence. Later, a more conservative governor ushered in a state law that brought the state's Castle Doctrine back into line with the rest of a free America, at least in the home. The fact is, however, the conviction had some merit: she'd had ample opportunity to avoid what she should have known could be a killing

MAG INSTRUCTOR AND EX-SWAT cop Steve Denney sends a stream of .45 brass skyward while keeping the pistol on target with strong shooting stance and technique.

situation, and had failed to do so. Since her attacker not only lived in the same home but owned it, he was not the sort of unauthorized intruder that the ancient and well-established Castle Doctrine had targeted when authorizing deadly force in self-defense.

There's the *reasonably perceived deadly force* part. How many of us, when we were little kids playing softball, watched in horror as an errant baseball went through a neighbor's window...and then crawled inside to retrieve it? There are some who argue that the child doing so is fair game for a deadly force response by the homeowner. Come on, people, we don't even have to go any further with such a stupid concept here.

WRONG HARDWARE, BAD TACTICS

Having the best equipment to do a job is important. Knowing the best way to do the job is even more important. So it is with home defense. I want the most effective hardware...but I've learned that the best tactics are even more important.

Grabbing your gun and maybe your flashlight and going looking for the bad guy seems to be the intuitive thing to do...*but it's not the smart thing to do!* In **Case Seven**, a tough old lady out west determined that there was an intruder in her house. She called the police – doin' fine so far

– but then, she got her home defense handgun out of its hiding place and went looking for the bad guy herself.

She had made her way to the front door about the time the cops were pulling up outside. They had been dispatched to a possible home invasion, and what they were thinking was, "dangerous person with a gun, there now." They then saw the elderly lady silhouetted in the doorway, with a conspicuous gun in her hand.

They screamed, "Police! Drop the gun!" She turned toward the sound, and the gun turned with her. The figure in the doorway was now quickly turning toward them with a gun pointing in their direction.

What would *you* have done, in their shoes? Well, that's exactly what the cops did. They opened fire...and the lady died in her own doorway.

Once you have called the police to an emergency scene such as this, you have declared the arena to be theirs! If you then enter that arena with a gun in your hand, you contaminate the situation and set the stage for a tragic, mistaken identity shooting like this one!

29

TACTICS TRUMPS HARDWARE. LFI staff member Peter Dayton, left, and author, right, congratulate Gary Wistrand, center, on winning NTI. Gary, then head of training for NASA Security, was the first man to win one without being judged "killed" at least once.

Case Seven was not an isolated situation. **Case Eight**, in 2008, was somewhat similar. Homeowner both calls the cops and goes looking for the bad guy. While cops are en route, he *finds* the bad guy, and has to shoot him down in self-defense. Pretty clear-cut. Should have been clear sailing.

Until…

Cops arrive. They enter the home, guns drawn, shouting "Police!" The good guy turns toward the cops with gun in hand. Where the head goes, the body follows. The cops now reasonably perceive him to be swinging on them with a gun pointed in their direction.

They shoot. He falls. Another sad chapter is written in the history of Bad Tactics.

There are bad tactics, and there is bad selection of equipment. Some would say that the two overlap. I'll leave that judgment up to you.

Historically, conventional wisdom has said that a shotgun is the best home defense weapon, superior to a handgun because of its greater stopping power. If you don't think that hasn't come back to haunt armed citizens, you haven't read the details of the landmark 2008 US Supreme

BAD TACTICS can get you killed, as man who has silhouetted himself in doorway is about to learn the easy way, receiving a stream of Simunitions™ "bullets" during force on force drill.

Court's *Heller* decision. The gun-banning side brought that argument up repeatedly, saying people in Washington, DC didn't need to own the handguns that the city had unlawfully banned so many years ago, because even "gun experts" said that shotguns were better for home defense anyway. In his brilliantly written decision that overturned the DC gun ban, Supreme Court Justice Antonin Scalia made the point that using a handgun for home defense kept one hand free for tasks such as calling the police. Bravo, Justice Scalia: it is good to have one's beliefs validated

SEARCHING A HOUSE is extremely dangerous. These European officers practice for it with ballistic shields and team tactics.

by the Supreme Court itself, and I thank you for that, sir!

I've been saying the same thing for decades because it is simply the reality of a fast-moving, multi-tasking situation. A long gun, which needs two hands to effectively operate for its intended purpose, leaves no hand free to operate the critical communications devices Scalia spoke of, or to operate a separate illumination device, or to do any of several other things that might need to be done in a situation where you believe home security has been breached.

We talked earlier of going outside versus staying inside "the castle walls." But what do you do when there is a pounding on the door and you figure you can't call the cops just because someone is knocking?

In **Case Nine**, the good guy had a psycho next door neighbor who wanted to start a feud. On the day in question, he yelled across the fence that he would come and physically harm the good guy. Not having any training in how the criminal justice system works, the good guy didn't know enough to call the cops right then and there, report a case of criminal threatening, and establish himself as the victim complainant and the anti-social nut case next door as the suspect. He just went inside and hoped for the best...but, with the threats ringing in his ears, he also decided to load his 12 gauge pump shotgun "just in case."

Shortly thereafter, night having fallen, there came an ag-

gressive pounding at the door. Worried, the homeowner picked up his 12 gauge and brought it to the front door with him. As he opened the portal, his shotgun became visible. He saw a man running away from him, down the porch steps, and heard that man screaming "Gun, gun, gun!"

You guessed it. It was a cop. The whacked-out neighbor had called the police and told them that the good guy had threatened to harm *him*. When the responding officer came to the good guy's door, it opened...he saw the 12 gauge pump...and the situation went precipitously downhill.

Suffice to say that shortly thereafter, the good guy's home was ringed by squad cars and cops pointing long guns from behind engine blocks as a police supervisor said over a loudspeaker, "Sir! Put down your weapon, and come to the door with your hands empty and in plain sight..."

If that homeowner had simply loaded a pistol or a revolver, put it on his person out of sight but where he could reach it, and then opened the door, no gun would have been visible and his arrest for aggravated assault on a police officer, and the huge legal fees that came along with defending it, would never have happened.

What the long gun is good for is using it as artillery once the family has realized that the burglar alarm has gone off,

BALLISTIC SHIELDS (legal for citizens with clear records to own anywhere in the US) stop bullets and save lives. They're important equipment for those doing building searches.

A DOG CAN indeed be man's best friend during a search. Here's author with Katana, an Akita…and Steyr AUG .223 that runs well one-handed, another "best friend" in scary circumstances.

and they have wisely ensconced in a single place with good cover. Now, if the bad guys kick down the door to that last safe bedroom, it becomes logical, reasonable, and prudent to conclude that they are in deadly danger and the people kicking down the bedroom door need to be stopped. *This* is where the superior impact force and hit potential of the traditional home defense shotgun, or the "new paradigm" .223 home defense rifle, come into their own.

But if you're going to have to move – to shepherd kids into the safe room or answer the door or anything like that – you'll be better off with a handgun, in my opinion. That's why I consider the handgun to be *infantry*, the proper tool for a fast moving force that has to assess what's going on and react. It's why I consider the long gun *artillery*, not just because of its greater power but because it will be employed from a fixed location into an already-plotted quadrant of fire once the enemy invasion is obviously underway. It's not "handgun or long gun." It's, "have both,

and use each tool according to the task that must be accomplished."

A vitally important strategy element is that if you make the attacker come to you, you're in a better position both tactically and legally. From the jury's perspective, you didn't go looking for trouble, the trouble came looking for you. From the tactical perspective, the person who goes looking for the danger has to have a 360-degree view scan, something only a Human Fly could achieve alone. Conversely, the person who forces the assailant to come to him controls and "canalizes" the angle of possible attack and has vastly greater control of the situation. In other words, the person who remains static in the safe room becomes the sniper/hunter in the tree stand…and the person moving and looking for the other person becomes the quarry. Y'all can do what you want, but I'll be waiting for you in the tree stand.

ADDITIONAL ADVICE

Home protection dogs are a great thing to have. If you're worried about that bump in the night, send the canine to look for it. They'll hear things you can't hear, smell things you can't smell, and find people you can't find. However, once you've called the cops and they're on the way in, *call the dog back to you in the position where you have ensconced!* Your dog can't tell cops from home invaders. If he does the job he was trained for, he'll go for *any* stranger in the house…and the cops don't want to kill your dog after you called them to come there because you thought they were home invaders.

We have a responsibility to keep our lethal weapons accessible to *us*, but inaccessible to unauthorized hands. We have to realize that home defense goes far beyond the gun, involving "hardened target" concepts that include good locks, solid doors, state of the art alarm systems, and more.

It's more complicated than it looks at first glance.

But, really, so is every other aspect of human life.

CHOOSING THE LATEST, high-tech handgun is not the first priority of survival. S&W Model 10 .38, shown here in Border Patrol holster designed by Bill Jordan, was an American police standard in the 20th Century.

SKILL WITH SAFETY/RESCUE EQUIPMENT

Colonel Cooper nailed it once again when he famously said that owning a violin didn't make one a violinist, and owning even the finest defensive firearm didn't make one a gunfighter. You don't need to buy anyone's book to realize that a skilled hand with an 1899 vintage Smith & Wesson .38 Special revolver would be better backup in a shootout than someone with a several thousand dollar high-tech auto pistol who didn't know how to use it.

As we'll see, choice of gun and particularly ammunition can become a subject so contentious that it often takes on a quasi-religious zealotry. Yet even in that acrimonious debate, both sides seem to agree on one thing: when one assesses the nebulous topic of "stopping power," the most important factor in *stopping* is going to be the placement of the shot(s).

AUTHOR RECOMMENDS a high-hand grasp of handgun for better control. Grasp shown is "OK" for S&W .38 Special snub…

YOU DON'T NEED HAIR TRIGGER guns to shoot well. This qualification was shot with Glock 17 fitted with 8-lb pull NY-1 trigger system, and Cominolli manual safety to boot.

…BUT THIS HOLD will give distinctly better control of muzzle jump, and therefore faster hits.

Defensive use of firearms encompasses a broad skill-set. Reactive quick draw is obviously important to police and security personnel, who must be constantly ready to react to an unexpected, unprovoked lethal assault. However, for the law-abiding armed citizen, the ability to perform a fast, reflexive quick draw may be even more important. When an identifiable, uniformed police officer approaches a danger scene, citizen witnesses know enough to get out of the way because something dangerous is obviously going on to elicit this reaction from society's recognized protectors. However, the private citizen who lawfully carries a gun – or the off-duty or plainclothes cop who is not so readily identifiable as his uniformed counterpart – risks a mistaken identity tragedy or a panicky stampede if he draws a deadly weapon at the first whiff of danger. Therefore, the private CCW holder and the off-duty policeman alike may find it practical and expedient to wait longer to draw. This in turn narrows the window of reaction time,

and makes swift presentation of the firearm all the more important a life-saving skill.

There are lots of ways to shoot guns. Some, obviously, will work better under certain circumstances than others, and we'll get into that discussion in greater depth elsewhere. But once the gun is in the hand, there are certain simple basics that will serve any shooter well in a moment when pulse is racing, strength is out of control, coordination has gone down the tubes, and life comes down to "make a center hit or die, right now."

A while back, editor Dave Duffy at *Backwoods Home* magazine asked me to write an article-length tutorial on shooting a handgun accurately. I geared all the advice to shooting under pressure, and it came out like this:

HOW TO SHOOT A HANDGUN ACCURATELY[4]

"I want you to do an article on how to shoot a handgun

SAFETY IS THE OVERRIDING CONCERN with combat handguns. This one, a Smith & Wesson Model 66 .357 Magnum…

…HAS BEEN FITTED with MagnaTrigger by Rick Devoid (www.tarnhelm.com) and will only fire for someone wearing the special magnetic ring shown.

A VERY HARD GRASP is one of author's tenets for effective combat shooting with powerful "street guns." That is facilitated by high hold, curled down thumb on this S&W .357 Combat Magnum.

And few handguns have the inherent mechanical accuracy of a good rifle.

That said, though, you can make the most of your handgun's intrinsic accuracy by simply performing marksmanship basics correctly. If the gun is aimed at the target, and the trigger is pressed and the shot released without moving the gun, then the bullet will strike the mark. That simple. We need a few building blocks to construct this perfect shot, however. Let's build the structure brick by brick.

I teach my students a five-point "pre-flight check list" to go through before they fire the shot. As with any structure, you start from the bottom up. Those points are: 1) Strong stance. 2) High hand grasp. 3) Hard grip. 4) Front sight. 5) Smooth rearward roll of the trigger.

THE "POWER STANCE"

I've found that stance is the one thing I'm likely to have to correct first, even when teaching the experienced shooter. The edgeways stance of the duelist is necessary for skateboarding or surfing, but counter-productive to good shooting. If one heel is behind the other, the body does not have good lateral balance and will tend to sway sideways. (The miss will most commonly go toward the strong hand side.) If the feet are squared off parallel, in the old "police academy position" so often seen on TV, the body does not have good front to back balance, and the shots will tend to miss either high or low, most commonly the latter.

You want to be in a fighter's stance, a boxer's stance, what a karate practitioner would call a "front stance." The lower body needs a pyramidal base, a triangle with depth. If you are right handed and firing with your strong hand only,

accurately," Dave Duffy told me. "Make it 2,500 or 3,000 words."

Long ago, I would have answered, "Sure, and while I'm at it, how about a history of the world in, oh, 10,000 words or so?"

Today, with more than 45 years of handgunning behind me (yeah, I'm old, but I started early, too) I realize that you actually can cover this topic in a fairly short article. The reason is found in the classic statement of Ray Chapman, the first world champion of the combat pistol. "Shooting well is simple," Ray said, "it just isn't easy."

I'll buy that. It's true that the handgun is the most difficult of firearms to shoot well. There's less to hang on to. There's a shorter radius between the front and rear sight than with a rifle, meaning a greater unnoticed human error factor in aiming. You don't have that third locking point on the shoulder that you have with a long gun's butt stock.

WITH FLIGHT A POOR OPTION, student in foreground prepares to fight from the ground…

…OR STANDING ON THE ONE LEG he has to work with. Guns aren't called "equalizers" for nothing.

the pelvis wants to be at about a 45 degree angle vis-à-vis the target, with your left leg to the rear. If you are shooting two-handed and are right hand dominant, the hips still want that 45-degree angle but the left leg should now be forward and the right leg back. Now you're balanced forward and balanced back, balanced left and balanced right. It'll be easier to hold the gun on target.

In rapid fire, the shoulders want to be forward. This will get body weight in behind the gun and help control recoil. For very precise slow fire, some shooters like to cantilever the shoulders to the rear. This may make the gun seem to hang steadier with less effort, but it will cause the gun to jump up sharply upon recoil. This not only slows down your rate of sustained fire, but subconsciously, the more the muzzle jumped at the last shot, the more likely you are to jerk the trigger on the next one. Personally, I use the power stance with the shoulders at least slightly forward even in slow fire. Master shooters have a phrase that helps them remember this principle more easily: "Nose over toes."

HIGH HAND GRASP

With a double action revolver, you want the web of your hand all the way up to the rear edge of the backstrap, as shown in the accompanying photos. With a single action frontier-style revolver with the plow-handle shape grip, you still want a high hand grasp. On a semiautomatic pistol, you want the web of the hand so high that a ripple of flesh is seen to bunch up behind the backstrap of the grip at the top edge, where the grip safety would be on a 1911 style pistol.

The higher the hand, the lower the bore axis. This means much better control of muzzle jump and less movement of the pistol upon recoil. Since most handguns, particularly semiautomatics, are designed to be shot this way, it means that you will find it easier to press the trigger straight back as you make each shot. If your hand is too low on the "handle," a straight rearward pressure on the trigger will

INJURIES CAN HAPPEN in training. This student has broken a leg doing a Tueller Drill.

PLAQUES ARE NICE, but the skills honed and reinforced in competition are more important. Pistol is Kimber Gold Match .45.

COMPLETE COMBAT TRAINING demands weapon retention skills, and safety demands that they be learned with dummy guns. Left, S&W Centennial with Com-Tac dummy; right, Ruger Service-6 .357 with Lindell/Odin Press dummy copy.

tend to pull the muzzle down, placing the shot low.

A semi-auto is designed to operate as the slide moves against the abutment of a firmly held frame. A low grasp allows the muzzle to whipsaw upward from recoil as the mechanism is automatically cycling, diverting momentum from the slide through the frame. Now the slide can run out of momentum before it has completed its work. This is why holding a pistol too low can cause it to jam.

All these problems are cured with the high hand grasp.

HARD GRIP

In the debate about shooting techniques in the saloon after all the guns have been locked away, this issue will take up about three rounds of drinks. In the old days, the "quail grip" was taught. "Imagine yourself holding a live quail. Hold it just firmly enough that it can't fly away, but not firmly enough to hurt it."

We aren't talking about birdies. We're talking about guns. Specifically, we are talking about powerful defensive handguns and hard-kicking Magnums and large calibers used for outdoor sports such as hunting. The harder we hold them, the less they kick and jump. The less they kick and jump, the more efficiently we can shoot them.

This writer strongly recommends the "crush grip." How hard do you hold the handgun? As hard as you can. It was once advised to intensify your grip until tremors set in, and then back off until they stopped. In the real world, under stress, there's going to be some tremor anyway. Get used to it now. Hold the gun as tightly as you can and let it tremor.

The key is this: keep the sights straight in line. If the sights are in line, and the hand is quivering, the sights will quiver in the center of the target. When the shot breaks, the bullet will strike the center of the target. Once it has been center-punched, the target will neither know nor

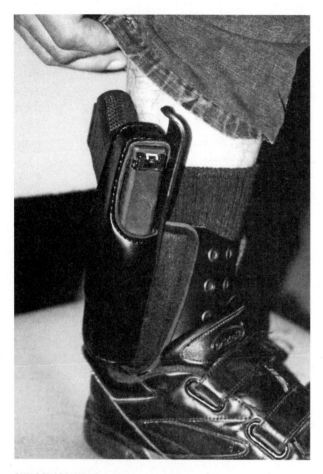

GUN CONCEALMENT options are better than they've ever been. Here's a baby Glock in a Gould & Goodrich boot holster.

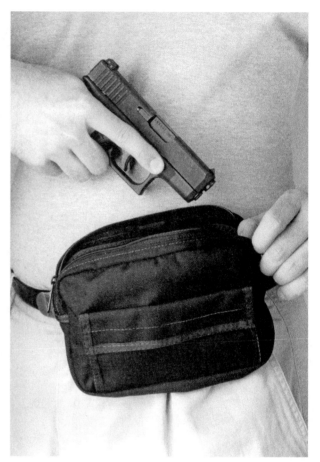

SAFETY IS PARAMOUNT. This shooter, drawing Glock from fanny pack, is sweeping own support hand with the muzzle.

care that the launcher was quivering before the projectile took flight.

Any marksmanship expert will tell you that consistency of grasp is a key to consistent accuracy. As stress levels change during shooting, which is really a multi-tasking exercise that gives you a lot to think about, the consistency of grasp can change too. If you think about it, there are only two ways to grasp the pistol with uniformity.

One is to hold it with virtually no pressure at all. This will give you poor control of recoil.

The other is to hold it as hard as you can, for each shot and every shot.

The hard hold has some other benefits. If you have accustomed yourself to always hold a pistol with maximum grip strength, you are much less likely to ever have it knocked or snatched from your hand. Moreover, you now have the ultimate cure for a handgunner's malady known as "milking."

"Milking," taken from the hand's movement when milking a cow's udder, occurs when the index finger closes on the trigger and the other fingers sympathetically close with it, changing the grasp and pulling the sights off target. Most commonly, this will pull the shot low and to the side of what you were aiming at. It is a function called "interlimb response." When one finger closes, the other fingers want to close with it.

Do this simple exercise. Relax your hand, and pretend to be holding a handgun. Now, move the index finger as if rapidly firing a handgun with a heavy trigger pull. You will see the other fingers reflexively contracting along with it. You have just seen and experienced milking in action.

Now do the same, but this time with all digits but the index finger closed as tightly as you can hold them. As you run the index finger, you'll feel the tendons trying to tighten the grasp of the other fingers, but you'll see that they actually can't. That's because the tight grip has already

EXOTIC WEAPONS are cool, but probably won't be with you when you're unexpectedly attacked in American society. The late Raoul Cantero, master instructor and multiple shooting incident survivor, is at right.

hyperflexed the fingers, and they can't tighten any more. The milking action has now been eliminated.

Thumb position is negotiable. Generations of shooters with the GI 1911 .45 learned to shoot with the thumb high, resting on the manual safety. Many competitive target shooters prefer to point the thumb straight at the target. This straight thumb position seems to align the skeleto-muscular structure of the hand in a way that allows the index finger its straightest rearward movement. With powerful guns, curling the thumb down to add grasping strength and enhance control is a valid technique. A lot of it depends on how the gun fits your hand. The controls may also be a factor. With a conventional double action auto that has a safety catch mounted on the slide (Beretta, S&W, and Ruger to name just a few), I like my thumb to be where it can not only push the lever into the "fire" position, but verify that the lever is in fact in the position it should be in.

Trigger finger contact? The old time marksmen liked the very tip of the finger on the trigger, on the theory that it offered more sensitivity. With a handgun that has a very light trigger pull, there may be some validity to that. Still

LEARN FROM PEOPLE who've won gunfights. Ed Mireles, left, the hero who ended the epic FBI firefight of 4/11/86, shares his experience with author.

others use the pad of the finger, which is basically the point at which you find the whorl of the fingerprint.

Personally, I've learned that contacting the trigger at the crease of the distal joint, the spot old time revolver masters called "the power crease," gives me much more leverage and therefore more control. This is particularly true on guns whose trigger pulls may be long and/or heavy: the double action handgun, the Glock, etc. A lot of this will depend on hand size and shape in relation to gun size and shape. There are many variables in the interface between human and machine.

HARD GRIP, finger on distal joint help control this light SIG P220-E .45 auto; curled down thumb won't over-ride the SIG's rear-mounted slide stop, nor bind the slide when wearing heavy gloves.

FRONT SIGHT

The conventional sight picture with conventional handgun sights is the one you see in the marksmanship manuals. The front sight is centered in the notch of the rear sight. The top of the front sight is level with the top of the rear sight, and there is an equal amount of light on either side.

Human vision being what it is, you can't focus on the sights and the target at the same time. Actually, you can't focus on both the front and the rear sight at the same time, either. Once the target has been identified as something you need to shoot, you no longer need your primary visual focus on it. Primary focus now goes to the aiming indicator, the front sight. Think of it as a fighter pilot would: "enemy craft sighted, lock missiles on target." The way we lock the handgun's missiles onto the target is by focusing on its front sight.

Failing to properly focus on the front sight is a widespread problem among shooters. Every good shooter with iron sights (as opposed to red-dot optics or telescopic sights) whom you know can probably remember when he or she experienced "the epiphany of the front sight." The

realization, "So that's what the coach meant when she said to watch the front sight!"

Watch the front sight hard. Apply your primary visual focus there. Look at it until you can see every little scratch in the machining on its surface. If it has a dot on it, focus on it until the dot looks like a soccer ball. Then you, too, will experience the epiphany of the front sight, and will see your shot groups tighten as if by magic.

SMOOTHLY ROLL THE TRIGGER

Remember the prime directive: once the gun is aimed at the target, the trigger must be pulled in a way that does not pull the muzzle off target before the shot is fired. This means that the trigger must come straight back.

You want a smooth, even, uninterrupted pull. You can say to yourself, "press the trigger." You can say to yourself, "sque-e-eze the trigger." I say to myself, "roll the trigger," because that connotes the smooth, consistent, uniform pressure I'm trying to apply. You don't want the shot to truly surprise you, of course, because that would be an unintentional discharge. Rather, you want the exact instant of the shot to surprise you, so you don't anticipate it and convulsively jerk the shot off target.

Experts agree that the best way to get the trigger pull down, once you know what it's supposed to be, is to practice it. Dry-fire, or "clicking" the empty gun, is the best

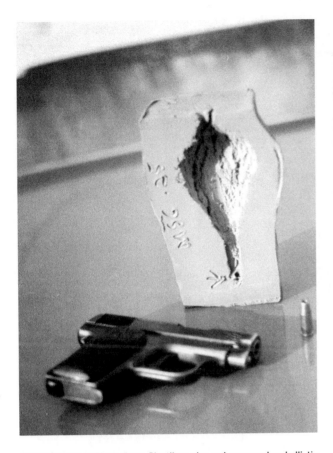

TISSUE STIMULANTS like Roma Plastilena clay and more modern ballistic gelatin must be taken in context with actual street shooting reports. MSC specialty round for .25 auto was "best of breed," but still not powerful enough in author's opinion.

practice. The position of the sights when the gun goes "click" will tell you whether the shot would have been on target or not. The more thousands of these repetitions you perform, the more the proper trigger pull will be hard-wired into your mind and body to the point where you can do it perfectly in an emergency without consciously thinking about the details.

The best way to learn it is with what I dubbed the "ex-emplar drill." Find an accomplished pistol shooter to assist you. Take a strong stance and firm grasp, and hold the gun on target. Let your index finger barely touch the trigger, and let that finger go limp. Ask the seasoned shooter to place his gun hand over yours, and his trigger finger over yours, and let his finger press yours straight back against the trigger. After several repetitions, you'll be feeling what he feels when he makes the perfect shot. This is the easiest way to learn what a good trigger pull feels like.

Now progress to the two of you pulling the trigger to-gether at the same pace. After some of that, you're ready

FANCY'S FINE, but function's more important. Master Instructor Clint Smith's personal Thunder Ranch Special .45 auto by Les Baer embodies both.

for the third stage. Now it's your finger pulling the trigger, his lightly touching yours to monitor its progress. Once you've got that down, let the coach sit back and watch as you "fly solo," making corrections as necessary.

SOME SUGGESTIONS

Observe all rules of safe shooting and safe gun han-dling, of course. Start with paper or cardboard targets in close, at three to seven yards. If your shot is off the mark by three inches at 25 yards, it might have been just the natural limits of the gun's accuracy. It might have been the ammo. It might even have been the wind. But if you're off by three inches at four yards, you'll know exactly what it is. The closer you are, the easier it is to correct whatever caused the bad hit on the target. Once you're hitting in tight groups at close range, move back incrementally. As the distance increases, so does the challenge.

The world champion was right when he said it was sim-ple, it just wasn't easy. The "not easy" part is taken care of in repetition. Fortunately, repetition means shooting, and shooting is fun.

Good luck. Stay safe. And enjoy.

⤳

OPTIMUM EQUIPMENT FOR PREDICTABLE THREAT

It's pretty obvious that if you're worried about being mugged in the elevator, a fourteen-pound .338 Lapua Magnum countersniper rifle will be altogether too un-wieldy to bring into action, and if you have to take the next "mad sniper" like Charles Whitman off a 330-foot vantage

"FRIENDS DON'T LET FRIENDS CARRY MOUSE GUNS." One of the "commandments" is to carry something more substantial than this FN .25 auto, which has just been used to shoot Roma Plastilena clay.

point such as the Texas Tower, a two-inch barrel .38 Special pocket gun won't give you your best chance of accomplishing that mission, either. Switch the guns, though, and your hand on the Airweight in your pocket might be just the ticket for dealing with the armed mugger in the elevator, and the .338 Lapua would have been admirably suited to cutting Whitman's rampage short, if only we could go back in time with one to do so.

The choice of equipment may be lowest in the priorities listed here, but it's still on the list for obvious reasons, and it's the one element of those priorities that we can most solidly lock in beforehand. Therefore, we'd be literally negligent to ignore and say to ourselves, "Eh, what the heck, a gun is a gun and a bullet is a bullet, and a gun where I can get to it reasonably soon is probably close enough."

A few years ago, gun-wise editor Shirley Steffen at Harris Publications asked me to put together a quick "Ten Commandments of Concealed Carry" for one of their annuals. It caught on and went viral. It follows here, and note that it encompasses not only the choice of the hardware, but the software practices necessary to make that hardware meaningful "when the day comes."

TEN COMMANDMENTS FOR CONCEALED CARRY[5]

I'm not Moses, let alone God, but the following ten bits of advice are written in stone nonetheless. Not by God, but by the vastly powerful mechanisms of logic, law, and reality.

Commandment I: If you choose to carry, always carry, as much as is possible.

Hollywood actors get to see the script beforehand, and nothing is fired at them but blanks. You don't have either luxury. Criminals attack people in times and places where they don't think the victims will be prepared for them. It's what they do. The only way to be prepared to ward off such predators is to always be prepared: i.e., to be routinely armed and constantly ready to respond to deadly threats against you and those who count on you for protection. It's not about convenience, it's literally about life and death.

Commandment II: Don't carry a gun if you aren't prepared to use it.

The gun is not a magic talisman that wards off evil. It is a special-purpose emergency rescue tool: no more, no less. History shows us that – for police, and for armed citizens alike – the mere drawing of the gun ends the great majority of criminal threats, with the offender either surrendering or running away. However, you must always remember that criminals constitute an armed subculture themselves,

42

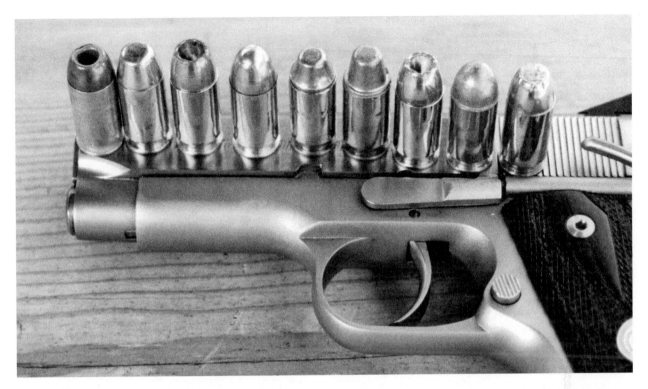

SOME OBSESS about what ammo to choose for defense, ignoring more important combat survival issues. Pistol is ParaOrdnance LDA .45.

living in an underworld awash with stolen, illegal weapons. They don't fear the gun: they fear the resolutely armed man or woman pointing that gun at them. And, being predators, they are expert judges of what is prey, and what is a creature more dangerous to them than they are to what they thought a moment ago was their prey.

Thus, the great irony: the person who is prepared to kill if they must to stop a murderous transgression by a human predator, is the person who is least likely to have to do so.

Commandment III: Don't let the gun make you reckless.

Lightweight pseudo-psychologists will tell you that "the trigger will pull the finger," and your possession of your gun will make you want to kill someone. Rubbish. The gun is no more an evil talisman that turns kindly Dr. Jekyll into evil Mr. Hyde, than it is a good talisman that drives off evil. Those of us who have spent decades immersed in the twin cultures of American law enforcement and the responsibly armed citizenry know that the truth is exactly the opposite. A good person doesn't see the gun as a supercharger for aggression, but as brakes that control that natural human emotion. The law itself holds the armed individual to "a higher standard of care," requiring that they do all that is possible to avoid using deadly force until it becomes

clearly necessary.

The armed citizen's firearm doesn't make him Superman, any more than a police officer's or soldier's body armor renders him bulletproof. The armor, and the need for the gun, remind the responsible person that they may be in dangerous situations that require great caution. The late, great big game hunter and gun writer Finn Aagard once wrote, "Yet my pistol is more than just security. Like an Orthodox Jewish yarmulke or a Christian cross, it is a symbol of who I am, what I believe, and the moral standards by which I live."

Commandment IV: Carry legally.

If you live someplace where there is no provision to carry a gun to protect yourself and your loved ones, don't let pusillanimous politicians turn you into a convicted felon. Move! It's a quality of life issue. Rhetorical theory that sounds like "I interpret the law this way, because I believe the law should be this way" – which ignores laws that aren't that way – can sacrifice your freedom, your status as a gun-owning free American, and your ability to provide for your family. If you live where a CCW permit is available, get the damn permit. If you don't, move to someplace that does. Yes, it IS that simple. And if you are traveling, check sources such as www.handgunlaw.us to make sure that you are legal to carry in the given jurisdiction. Don't let the legal system make you a felon for living up to your

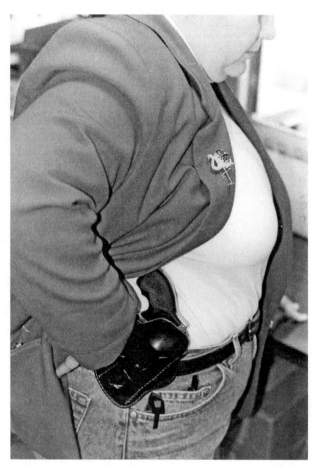

TODAY'S GUNs and holsters let you be armed virtually anywhere it's legal. Here, at the office, Kate Krueger is not visibly armed…

…BUT HER J-frame S&W is ready at hand.

responsibilities to protect yourself and those who count on you. If you carry, make sure you carry legally.

Commandment V: Know what you're doing.

The world of the gun is rife with urban legends. "If it was a clean shoot, you've got nothing to worry about." "It doesn't matter what gun or ammo you use, only that you were justified." "You can shoot any stranger you find in your house." "In my state, all you have to do is say it was self-defense, and you won't have to go to court."

It's all BS. Any time you hear such lines of thinking, you can be sure you're dealing with someone who has never been closer to the Justice System than the Internet or TV fiction. The fact is, there is a vast body of law and established caselaw which describes the relatively narrow parameters within which the use of deadly force against another human being is justifiable. Study deeply, and get all the training you can…not just in *how* to shoot, but in *when* to shoot.

Commandment VI: Concealed means concealed.

If your local license requires concealed carry, keep the

gun truly *concealed*. The revealing of a concealed handgun is seen in many quarters as a threat that can result in charges of Criminal Threatening, Brandishing, and more. A malevolent person who wants to falsely accuse you of threatening them with a gun will have their wrongful accusation bolstered if the police find you with a gun where they said it was. Yes, that happens. Some jurisdictions allow "open carry." This writer supports the right to open carry, in the proper time and place, but has found over the decades that there are relatively few ideal times or places where the practice won't unnecessarily and predictably frighten someone the carrier had no reason to scare.

Commandment VII: Maximize your firearms familiarity.

If you ever need that gun to protect innocent lives including your own, it's likely to happen very quickly, and the more competent you can be when acting reflexively, the better off you (and those who count on you for protection) will be. Practice with the gun, train with it, become so familiar with it that it seems like an extension of your

A 5-SHOT .38 like this S&W Model 640, if carried all the time, will protect you better than a higher capacity, more powerful pistol left at home in the safe.

hand. If and when the time comes that your survival is measured in split-seconds, you'll be glad you did. Practice safely clearing and holstering the gun as much as you practice shooting it, because you'll be handling that gun – loading it, unloading it, checking it, putting it on, putting it away – for the rest of your life. That puts you *constantly manipulating a loaded, lethal weapon in the presence of the people you bought that gun to protect: the people you most love!* Safety must be attended to layer after layer, and must become second nature.

Commandment VIII: Understand the fine points.

Don't just read the headlines or editorials, read the fine print. Actually *study* the laws of your jurisdiction. What's legal in one place, won't be legal in another. Cities may have prohibitions that states don't. Remember the principle, "ignorance of the law is no excuse."

Commandment IX: Carry an adequate firearm.

A Vespa motor scooter is a motor vehicle, but it's a poor excuse for a family car. A .22 or .25 is a firearm, but it's a poor excuse for a defensive weapon. Carry a gun loaded with ammunition that has a track record of quickly stopping lethal assaults. Hint: if your chosen caliber is not used by law enforcement or military personnel, it's probably not powerful enough for its intended purpose.

Commandment X: Use common sense.

Common sense – encompassing ethics and logic and law alike – must be your constant guide and companion when you carry a gun. Not idealism, not ideology, not rhetoric. When you carry a gun, you literally carry the power of life and death. It is a power that belongs only in the hands of responsible people who care about consequences, and who are respectful of life and limb and human safety...that of others, and not just their own.

✿

[1] ....

Chapter by Massad Ayoob in "Warriors: On Living with Courage, Discipline, and Honor", edited by Loren Christenson, Paladin Press, Boulder, CO 2004.

[2] ....

First appeared as "Body Language and Threat Recognition" by Massad Ayoob in *Backwoods Home* magazine, issue #87.

[3] ....

First appeared as "Handgun Home Defense Tactics" by Massad Ayoob in *Complete Book of Handguns 2009*, Harris Publications.

[4] ....

First appeared as "How to Shoot A Handgun Accurately" by Massad Ayoob in *Backwoods Home* magazine, issue #85.

[5] ....

First appeared as "Ten Commandments of Concealed Carry" by Massad Ayoob, Harris Publications, 2009.

CHAPTER TWO

LEARNING COMBAT SHOOTING

Combat shooting: Learning how to shoot under pressure when your skill with a gun may be the only thing that stands between you and Death. It's a serious topic.

The fact is, it's a life study. It encompasses kinesiology and physiology. It certainly encompasses psychology too. It encompasses knowing what you're fighting for. It encompasses preparedness to die for something more important than oneself. And it also requires a broad set of skills that ranges from threat recognition to unarmed combat ability, to skill with tools that are capable of overpowering forcible assault but unlikely to cause death, all the way up to Lethal Force: a degree of force, as defined by law, that is likely to cause death or great bodily harm, i.e., crippling injury.

One of the great myths of the discipline we call "combat shooting" is that the gunfight will begin with the first draw and end with the last shot. If you study it in depth, long before you've spent a lifetime in the pursuit of that knowledge you'll realize that the gunfight begins long before the participants face each other, and its terrible and powerful echoes may not finally go silent until you are on your deathbed.

But you will be ALIVE in those last moments on your deathbed. You will have filled your allotted years. You will be surrounded by those you love, and those who love you. You will have spent as much time on this earth as you can, doing good things for good people.

WEARING WELDER'S GOGGLES to simulate impaired vision and increase stress, participants in a National Tactical Invitational event in the early 1990s prepare to do a simulated building search.

And that is reason enough to study this discipline, a discipline that can keep you alive when, in an instant, some vicious predator chooses you at random as his choice for the victim he will murder tonight.

If you are attacked by someone who wants to kill you, you will be glad that you were skilled in these disciplines, and had developed the mental and emotional wherewithal to employ those skills when you were attacked. These skills and this knowledge will have literally saved your life. You will read in these pages about many good people – cops, military personnel, ordinary law-abiding armed citizens – who survived to live out their lives because they were able to beat their homicidal attackers at their own game and stay upright when the other guy went down for the permanent count.

If you are *never* attacked by someone who wants to kill you, rape you, or otherwise horribly hurt you, and you die old and fat and happy without ever having had to draw your gun, that's a wonderfully positive outcome. I'll be happy for you. Everyone who knows and loves you will be happy for you.

If you are like me, you will wind up in the middle. It is

WEARING PROTECTIVE GEAR and using Simunitions™ guns, a practitioner performs a building search in the famous Funhouse at Gunsite Training Center.

the space where most police officers, and most armed citizens who do need to resort to their firearms, end up. Your ability to get the gun out in time to ward off the attack will, in the statistics of the matter, probably shortstop the action right there. It has always been so for this writer…but let me be the first to tell you, I have been one of the lucky ones.

I've never been in a *gunfight*, which I would define as two or more people shooting at each other. (Get a whole bunch of people shooting at each other, and you have a *firefight*; I've had the good fortune to never have been in one of those, either.) What I *have* experienced is multiple *armed encounters*, I and someone else armed or reasonably perceived to be armed facing each other across the weapons. In every one of those, the other person ceased hostilities and either dropped their weapon and surrendered, or turned and fled.

In some of those cases I was an armed citizen. In some of those cases I was a law enforcement officer acting in the performance of my duties. In the end, it didn't really matter.

There was the time when two muggers jumped me in a city, and one pulled a knife. I pulled a gun. They both fled. Problem solved.

There was the time when I was a police officer making a traffic stop on the proverbial "dark and rainy night." The other guy pulled a rifle. I pulled a Colt .45 automatic. His advantage was that he got to start first. Mine was that I had apparently spent a helluva lot more time preparing for this moment than he had. Our movement paths crossed each other: he started first, but was slower and clumsier. I started second, but I was faster and surer. I knew in that

terrible slow-motion instant that his rifle could shoot through my pistol-rated body armor – it turned out to be a .30-30 Savage Model 340 rifle that he was trying to bolt a round into the chamber of as he pulled it out of the car – but I had already determined in that wordless thought that I was going to put him on the ground and take him with me. The safety was off on my Colt and I was starting to apply trigger pressure when he dropped the rifle and raised his hands, and it was over. I'm not sure if he ever understood how close he came to dying that night…but *I* damn sure know how close I came to it. We were absolutely on the razor's edge of life and death on that dark and rain-swept night.

I've never had to shoot anybody, and I'm damn glad to be able to say that. It's more than my father and my grandfather could say. They survived murder attempts because they had guns with which they could shoot back. Between the two of them, they left three men in the ground and went on to live long and good lives. My grandfather recovered from the pistol-whipping he received from the armed robber he had to shoot, and died in his 90s. He passed the fight-back-and-survive ethos on to my dad. My father had to shoot two men in self-defense when he was about the age I was when I was that young cop on the roadside that much-later night, pitting a .45 caliber pistol against a .30-

SIMULATED GUNFIGHTING is among the most useful training, done here "force on force" with Simunitions™ guns that shoot painful paintball-like pellets.

"STRONG HAND ONLY" shooting is often the fallback in real-world self-defense. You want it deeply ingrained.

30 rifle. In my father's shooting, one assailant put a revolver to his head and pulled the trigger. My father turned away as he felt the cold, hard muzzle, and when the shot went off the bullet missed his head but the muzzle blast destroyed his left eardrum and left him totally deaf in that ear for life. He returned fire and dropped his would-be murderer and his accomplice. The assailant who pulled the trigger died that night. His accomplice lasted a year or so.

My father passed that family history on to me, with suitable warnings about how to deal with life.

At the age of twelve, in the year 1960, I began working in the family jewelry store owned by my father. There were guns in there, and, of course, at home. My "how to shoot" education had begun at the age of four with a .22 rifle. My handgun work began at the age of nine. By twelve, I was working part time in a high-risk-of-armed-robbery retail enterprise carrying a cocked and locked Colt .45 auto behind my right hip. My father's customers included judges, lawyers, and the chief of police. They were kind enough to sit down and talk with an inquisitive youngster whose job description included the possibility of shooting grown-ups to death. I learned a helluva lot from them.

I read everything available in books and the early gun magazines of the time. It was all about how to shoot – and some of that was timelessly good – but none of it was about when to shoot, and even a pre-teen kid could figure out that this was at least equally important.

Life went on. It became clear that the family jewelry business was not my calling. To make a long story short, I wound up with 40 years as a gun writer, 37 years as a sworn police officer, and 39 years as a firearms/deadly force instructor, all overlapping, at the time I sat down to write this book. I started shooting in informal competition ("turkey shoot" matches with deer rifles, as incongruous as the turkey/deer juxtaposition may sound) at about age fourteen, and formal NRA pistol competition at nineteen. I'll be 63 when this book is published, so, do the math.

More to the point, as a writer I found myself in a particularly advantageous position to get access to people who had been in gunfights and were comfortable with their stories being told. For each of those stories, there were report packages that told the long and detailed stories of the investigations that followed the shootings. The documentation was even more comprehensive each time I went into a case where, as an expert witness, I had access to all the reports, autopsies, photos, sworn depositions of the witnesses and participants, et cetera.

Eventually, all of that detailed information builds up to the point where you can draw some conclusions as to what

YOU DON'T NEED EXOTIC equipment to learn from role-play. These practitioners are doing so with inexpensive toy "clicker guns."

happens in such events, and what works, and what doesn't.

Let's do a quick overview of some of the things those decades of study inside the disciplines involved have taught me, things that I want to share with other armed citizens and other cops who may unpredictably have to go to the same places as the people I learned from.

～

THE THINGS WE LEARN[1]

Once you get into the world of defensive use of force, you discover that things aren't the way they looked from the outside.

For most of America's history, gunfighting was taught strictly by and to police and military, and knowledge of deadly force law was just as tightly restricted to law schools and police academies. That left armed citizens only one course: to become self-taught, like kids in a schoolyard trying to figure out sex in the absence of structured sex education or parental explanation. In either case, the result can be pain and tragedy that come from preventable ignorance.

In the mid-1970s, that changed. Jeff Cooper founded the American Pistol Institute at Gunsite; Ray Chapman

A GUN THAT PROJECTS LASER BEAMS, engaging fast-breaking "shoot/ don't shoot" situations on the screen, fills in another piece of the deadly force decision-making puzzle.

and a handful of friends and investors created the Chapman Academy; and John Farnam developed the traveling school that became Defense Training International. Time has taken Jeff and Ray away from us, though Farnam still teaches nationwide, as a host of others do today. Including me: I founded the Lethal Force Institute in 1981, creating a curriculum that went more to the "when" than the "how" of it, and I spend more of my time doing that than anything else to this day. Now having left LFI, I teach through Massad Ayoob Group (http://massadayoobgroup.com).

TWO "S&W .38 Special Combat Masterpiece" revolvers. Top, a real one; below, an Odin Press dummy gun, important for safety when drilling on disarming and handgun retention.

Ken Hackathorn, another of the early pioneers, has estimated that there are thousands of people now teaching this stuff to private citizens, mostly part-time. There will be more when the current generation of combat troops return to civilian life after their service in "the sandbox."

I wish that such publicly accessible training had existed when I was starting to learn. We were stuck with books, with the anecdotal knowledge we could garner from debriefing whatever gunfight survivors we could, from talking to cops and lawyers and judges who'd been through all the aftermath elements of self-defense shootings. Each of us had to separately re-invent the wheel to find out what we needed to know. Today's situation is far, far better for the responsible armed citizen.

As time passed, I became a part-time, fully sworn officer responsible for training the entire police department in weapons and deadly force, a definite "brain cells front and center!" kind of moment. That led me on an odyssey to seek out the best such training in the U.S. and even abroad. Having also become a writer for gun magazines and police journals helped; it gave me entry into the law enforcement agencies who had done the best work and the

AUTHOR LEARNED MUCH, both in court and at the training center, from the FBI's legendary John Hall, right.

deepest study in terms of learning from past tragedies and keeping their members alive in gunfights. I got to go on stakeout with the NYPD Stakeout Squad, ride unarmed (thank God for hosting officers with backup guns!) on NYPD, and armed with my own guns on LAPD, each time in the heaviest-action precincts or districts. The situation allowed me to take the then-most-advanced officer survival training that the Federal Law Enforcement Training Center had to offer, and more like it elsewhere. Charlie Smith, late of FBI's instructor staff, created the first of the

IT WAS IN COURT CASES that author learned how unwise it is to remove or disable a safety device on a firearm. Tip of knife points to the commonly-removed magazine disconnector safety on Browning Hi-Power pistol.

MULTIPLE COURT CASES taught the author to avoid trigger pulls lighter than factory spec. Here master armorer Rick Devoid tests a handgun's pull weight with NRA approved testing device.

training schools sponsored by firearms manufacturers, the still-excellent Smith & Wesson Academy. SIG and HK followed. All became famous for high quality training.

By 1979, I had been tapped as an expert witness in court cases that would involve both criminal and civil trials, involving weapons and deadly force. *That* was an eye-opener! I discovered that the legal system we had all been promised in Civics 101 was sometimes more about drama than law, and that accusing prosecutors or plaintiffs' lawyers could make up the most outrageous BS and have it dignified in the courtroom as "their theory of the case," to be weighed by the jury as if it had the same credibility as the truth that was on the side of wrongfully-accused defendants who had used, or even only displayed, weapons in self-defense.

More than 30 years as an expert witness, well over that as an instructor, and now 37 years of carrying a badge and more years of carrying a gun have combined to help me learn a few things that weren't obvious when I started.

IT WON'T BE PRETTY

An entertainment media that glorifies violence has implied to generations of Americans that they'll shoot down the bad guys at high noon on Main Street and then just walk off into the sunset, triumphant. The reality is that it doesn't always work that way.

Very early on, it became apparent to me that people who'd had to kill in even the most righteous self-defense suffered for it. People look at you differently. Dr. Walter Gorski, the brilliant police psychologist who was probably the first to identify "post shooting trauma" as a separate and distinct subset of post traumatic stress disorder (PTSD), trained me circa 1980. Dr. Gorski coined the term "Mark of Cain" to explain the syndrome where people don't always treat you as the good cop, the good parent, or the good neighbor after you've killed another human being...they treat you as He Who Kills. Killing someone changes the way people see you, and it changes the way you see yourself.

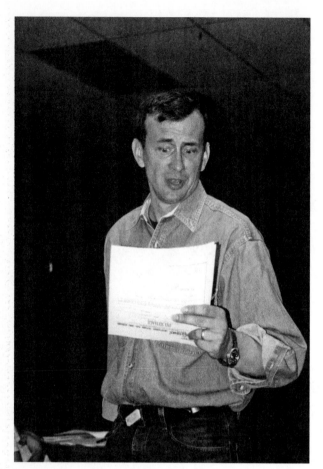

COL. DAVE GROSSMAN is a compelling speaker on survival topics. If you can't train with him in person, listen to his taped lecture "The Bullet-Proof Mind," and read his books On Combat and On Killing.

WITH VERN GEBERTH, the man who literally wrote the book on homicide investigation.

NO ONE CAN TEACH YOU more about a gun than the person who designed it. Dan Wesson, right, presents one of his guns to a much younger author, circa 1974.

You'll find your spouse listening to muttered comments in the market or the restaurant about you having "killed someone and gotten away with it." Your kids may come home from school crying after another child torments them with, "My daddy says your daddy's a murderer!"

A good friend of mine who has been forced to kill more than once, and never even had to go to court over the slayings, refers to this as "the cost of it." That cost runs deep and lasts your life long.

If you are not prepared for some of these sociological manifestations in the aftermath, they can tear you and your family apart. Divorce rates and other family estrangements run high after you've been forced to shoot in self-defense. "…in sickness and in health" does not include "oh, yeah, and when your spouse is demonized as a murderer by lawyers and newspapers, you're supposed to stick by him or her then, too."

And then, of course, there is the courtroom aftermath…

DAY IN COURT

Early in my career as an expert witness, I was called in for a case where a young officer shot and killed an even younger criminal who tried to pull a gun on him and his rookie partner while they were trying to arrest that person for illegal possession of a firearm. It was a classic case of justifiable homicide in the line of duty. However, the shooting was cross-racial; it triggered a violent race riot, and the city needed a scapegoat. The chief prosecutor of the jurisdiction – Janet Reno, who would later become US Attorney General under President Bill Clinton – charged him with manslaughter on the utterly trumped-up theory that he had recklessly and negligently cocked the hammer of his department issue service revolver, and accidentally discharged it in panic when the man turned with his hands raised in surrender.

Fortunately, Officer Luis Alvarez had two of the finest defense attorneys in America, Roy Black and Mark Seiden. After eight weeks of meticulously dismantling the state's BS case in court, they won an acquittal. (Which triggered another race riot, but that's another story.) You can read about it from the horse's mouth in Roy Black's autobiographical book, *Black's Law*.

An anomaly? Hardly. I take mostly defense cases, for the simple reason that the prosecution already has more ready and less expensive access to people in the same field as mine at their local police academies. I've discovered over the years that when a prosecutor hires an outside expert instead, it's usually because to make their case they need things to be said that no honest police instructor will say. There are exceptions – for instance, when they think the jury will perceive local cops testifying against a cop-killer as having an ax to grind – but those are uncommon.

I turn down more cases than I take. I won't sign onto a case unless I believe the defendant is on the side of the angels, after reviewing all available discovery materials (investigative reports, witness statements, sworn depositions, etc.). Yet, at any given time, I'm juggling about ten cases in progress, and I'm just one of many who work in the same field. That adds up to a helluva lot of wrongful prosecutions, and more unmeritorious lawsuits. (Quick translation: "unmeritorious" is the legal term for "BS.")

That tells you that there are a great many unjustly accused cops and armed citizens out there. FACT: There are more attorneys in the United States than police officers. FACT: Anybody pretty much can sue anybody for damn near anything. The quagmire of courtroom procedure requires countless hours of time from the attorney, which you have to pay for at a rate of three figures per hour. ($500 per hour is not an uncommon fee among the best attorneys.) Yeah, you can try to sue the estate of the violent criminal who forced you to shoot him, but that will probably be an expensive exercise in futility, because his "estate" probably doesn't add up to much more than a crack pipe and a cheap knife, and both of those are in evidence as property of the Court.

Most prosecutors I've dealt with over the decades are decent, honest men and women who understand that their job is to find justice, not to mindlessly pursue convictions. Unfortunately, a few of them are political creatures who are perfectly willing to destroy your life to pander to public opinion and gather votes for the next election. And

SUPPLEMENT YOUR TRAINING with reading. A gun magazine article convinced this officer to carry a .38 snub in an ankle holster for backup. Shot in the face from ambush (note scars on chin and jaw) and unable to reach his duty handgun, he drew this Colt Agent, shot down his assailant, and prevailed.

they are outnumbered by plaintiffs' lawyers who are far more concerned with money than with justice, and are totally prepared to smear you publicly and destroy your life with a false allegation if it might mean a big courtroom payday. One such attorney once told newspaper reporters that he considered the jury to be the tapestry upon which he would weave his alternate reality of the case. When put forth by a practicing attorney – an officer of the Court – that "alternate reality" is taken seriously, and you will have to fight it seriously…and expensively. I have seen people lose their homes, lose their businesses, and go bankrupt in the course of fighting to prove their innocence. Hollow victories aren't really victories.

WISHFUL THINKING VERSUS REALITY

The Sarah Bradys of the world will tell you, "You don't need a gun for self-defense. All that matters is that you not

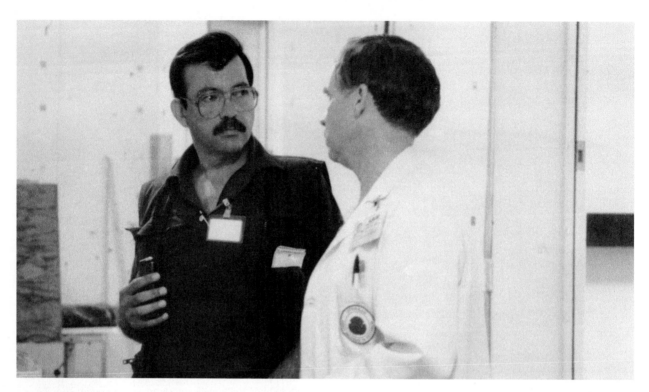

DR. MARTIN FACKLER, right, briefs the author on some of his wound ballistics research. Photo taken at Letterman Institute circa 1990.

go looking for trouble." You already know how false that is. Yet, amazingly, responsible people who've seen the logic of being armed and carry guns themselves will sometimes tell you, "You don't need to worry about the aftermath of a defensive shooting. All that matters is that it be a clean shoot." It's the same denial syndrome, just one level up in the game.

In Arizona, a hiker shot a violent man who attacked him at a trailhead. The lead investigator determined it to be self-defense, and so did the prosecutor's office…until influential, voting friends of the deceased presented a petition to the prosecutor to bring the shooter to trial. The prosecutor obediently did…and convicted the armed citizen of second-degree murder. The defendant went to prison, until a long and arduous appeal freed him. In Texas, a young cop shot and killed a man who was lunging at a brother officer with a knife. An obvious "clean shoot" … until Johnny Cochran labeled it racist police brutality, and orchestrated marches in the city's streets until charges of murder were filed. We won an acquittal on that one.

There are also those who say, "Those legal aftermath horror stories may happen in California or New York or New Jersey, but I live in gun-friendly Texas (or Arizona), so I'm

safe from that." Please re-read the paragraph above.

If you'll forgive a little triteness, "denial" is not a river in Egypt, and hope is not a strategy. Be aware that unmeritorious litigation may follow the most righteous self-defense shooting, criminal or civil or both, and be prepared for it. The wary hawk and eagle are far more effective warrior birds than the ostrich with its head in the sand.

HARDWARE

Over the decades I learned that a lot of the old, conventional wisdom was absolutely correct. For instance, "use the most powerful gun you can control," and Robert Ruark's famous book title exhortation, "Use Enough Gun." I saw case after case where .380s and less-than-optimal 9mm or .38 Special loadings left the guy on the other side of the gun up and running until he had been riddled with too many bullets to possibly survive, and the public got the impression that the dead man was a victim of malicious overkill. Trials usually resulted…if the shooter survived the murderous assault of the attacker who had to be shot that many times before he went down. In one case I did, the cop had to pump 17 rounds of 9mm into a suicidal/homicidal attacker before the man fell, literally at his feet, still holding the heavy metal pipe with which he'd attempted to bash three officers' brains out. Once finally cleared of wrongdoing, that officer finished his career carrying a 14-shot, .45 caliber Glock 21 on duty.

I learned that rounds which did great in testing protocols – the original 115 grain 9mm Silvertip in the Roma Plastilena clay of the time, the original 147 grain subsonic 9mm JHP in Fackler-formula gelatin – were mediocre man-stoppers at best in actual street gunfights. Winchester tweaked the Silvertip to where it worked better, and today all the makers have improved the subsonic 147 to where it will reliably open (with high tech bullet designs), but collective gunfighting history left me more comfortable with 124 and 127 and even 115 grain bullets that went much faster and damaged more tissue. Most of the police departments that adopted the early 147 grain 9mm loads either went to something hotter in the caliber, or – more often – approved or adopted more powerful pistols in .40 S&W, .357 SIG, or .45. As Santayana said, "Those who do not learn from history are doomed to repeat it."

I learned that all the "stopping power theories" – Momentum Theory, Temporary Wound Cavity Theory, Penetration Theory – had something to them, but that none was the whole solution to a very complicated puzzle that we'll probably never solve. I learned that each theory had some validity at its core, but no one factor was the "everything" its proponents said it was.

I learned this: *Everything is something; nothing is everything.*

I learned that only hits count. The men and women who took an instant to get their front sight on target made their hits. The Anchorage Police Department and the LAPD Special Investigations Section emphasized Jeff Cooper's concept of the flash sight picture in training, and were rewarded with hits in the 90% range in actual gunfights. Bill Allard of the NYPD Stakeout Squad, who killed more armed criminals in gunfights than even his more famous partner Jim Cirillo, used a hard marksman's sight picture for every shot he fired in action but one, and never missed the man he was shooting at. This was not a 20th Century discovery. In his 19th Century gunfights, Wyatt Earp later told his biographer Stuart Lake, he almost always raised his weapon to eye level, aligned the sights, and took care to squeeze rather than jerk his trigger.

I learned to tailor the tool to the task. In the 1970s, I was allowed to study the experience of the Illinois State Police, then the only large department issuing a semiautomatic service pistol, the S&W Model 39 9mm. I was able to identify thirteen troopers who had survived incidents in which they probably would have died had they been using

JOHN BIANCHI was a pioneer in holster design, and his security holsters saved many officers' lives.

revolvers. Two were firepower situations, where the armed attacker went down to the seventh or eighth pistol shot, and there would not have been time to reload after six. Two more survived in a single incident against a murderous two-gun outlaw biker, where sustained fire including fast reloading won the day, and it took more than a dozen gunshot wounds to end the fight. The other nine survived when the bad guys got their guns away from them, tried to shoot them with their own weapons, and couldn't. A few of those arose from the troopers pressing their magazine release buttons, dropping the magazine and activating the S&W disconnector so the chambered round could not be fired, as they felt the assailant winning the struggle. The rest were cases where the trooper carried on-safe, and the would-be cop-killer who gained control of his weapon couldn't find "the switch that turned on the gun" in time to carry out his murderous intentions.

Throughout the nation, I found other cases of the same

THE UNION CAN often tell you more than the chief about how certain guns and ammo are working out for cops on the street. Author debriefs John Dineen, right, then head of Chicago Lodge 7, fraternal order of police, mid-1970s. Chicago proved the efficacy of the lead .38 Special 158 grain +P load, which became known in the Midwest as "the Chicago Load."

pattern. I also found case after case where a second weapon saved the officer's life in such situations…and where a backup gun *might* have saved a murdered cop's life, if he'd only had one. I even found some armed citizens whose lives had been saved by a second weapon.

I learned to carry two guns.

I also saw cases where a good guy had to ram an auto pistol against a homicidal attacker's body and pull the trigger…and nothing happened. The auto's slide had been pushed out of battery and it couldn't fire. I learned to carry an auto and a revolver. If it turns out that St. Peter preferred Jeff Cooper *or* Bill Jordan, I figured I was covered.

AMMO ISSUES

Anti-gun types have attacked our ammo as well as our firearms since long before I came on the scene. It happens in the press, it happens in State Houses, and yes, it also happens in the courts. "Ladies and gentlemen of the jury, he established malice when he loaded his gun with hollow-nose dum-dum bullets, designed to rend and tear brutal wounds and cause horrible pain and suffering and

AUTHOR WITH BILL JORDAN, early 1974. Jordan's book *No Second Place Winner* remains a timeless study in gunfighting. Bill is holding S&W Model 57, chambered for .41 Magnum, a round he and Elmer Keith convinced S&W and Remington to bring out.

ensure the agonizing death of his victim!" It happens more routinely than you'd think in armed citizen shooting trials, though rarely in police shooting cases since hollow points became the law enforcement standard.

This argument is, no pun intended, easy to shoot down… if your lawyer knows how. We simply establish that you chose the same type of ammo as the police, for the same reasons. With hollow points, the bullets are less likely to over-penetrate the body of the dangerous felon and strike

THE GREAT RAY CHAPMAN shows the style that won him the world championship, here using an early Beretta 92. Chapman was an awesome instructor, and founder of the Chapman Academy.

down unseen innocent bystanders, and also less likely to ricochet and create unintended additional victims. More-over, since collective experience shows us the improved stopping effect of the HP (hollow point) ammo means the bad guy will have to be shot fewer times to neutralize his vi-olent activity, he is relatively less likely to die of his wounds. However, the argument in favor of hollow point ammo is useless if not effectively presented by the defense. Famed appellate lawyer Lisa Steele has seen defendants convicted with this argument when their trial lawyers failed to neu-tralize the poison. So have I. This apparently happened in the Arizona case mentioned above, contributing to what I for one believe was a wrongful conviction.

While it's a slam-dunk to defend your use of hollow point ammo, the use of handloads in a shooting presents much more serious problems to your defense team. Defensive shootings are often very close-range affairs in which gun-shot residue (GSR) from your muzzle is deposited on your attacker's body or clothing. This can become a critical evi-dentiary factor if the other side insists he was too far away from you to endanger you at the moment he was shot. The

distance testing is done with exemplar ammunition, that is, ammo identical to what was in your gun, but not the same exact cartridges. Don't count on the crime lab testing the remaining rounds from your weapon as taken into evidence at the shooting scene. If the fight was sufficiently intense, there may not be any rounds left in the gun that saved your life. Even if there are remaining cartridges in evidence, they may not be tested. The prosecutor can argue, "Your honor, firing those cartridges consumes them! It's destructive test-ing! The defense is asking the Court's permission to destroy the evidence! You cannot allow it!" Do you think that's a BS argument? So did I…until I saw a judge accept it, in a case where handloads were used in the death weapon, but the state crime lab tested with a much more powerful factory load, based on the headstamp on the reloaded casings. That gave a false indication of distance involved, and the defen-dant – whom I have strong reason to believe was innocent – was convicted of manslaughter.

You'd think the court would take the reloader's records into account and allow testing based on that. It doesn't happen. No one has yet been able to offer a case where the Court took the reloader's data or word for what was in the load. It's seen as self-serving "evidence" that can't be independently verified. Sort of like a rape suspect saying, "I couldn't have done it, because it says right here in my own diary that I was somewhere else that day."

LEARN FROM GUYS who've been there/done that. In early 1990s, WWII vet Jim Andrews shows how he was taught to shoot by the legendary British instructor, Major W. E. Fairbairn.

DR. VINCENT DIMAIO, JR., the brilliant forensic pathologist who wrote the classic text "Gunshot Wounds." He's shown going over evidence photos at a trial where he and author both spoke for defendant, who was acquitted of murder.

After seeing these things in court, I learned to avoid the use of handloads for defensive purposes.

A FINAL THOUGHT

Let me leave you with one final thought.

Remember that these things don't always end with the person who used lawful defensive force being put through legal and social hell in the aftermath. Most of the time, the system works and justice is done. Just as most of the time, we are not violently attacked with a level of force that warrants defensive gunfire. The fights we prepare for, on the street to start and in court later, are relatively rare occurrences. However, the degree of loss we face if we aren't ready to win those fights is so great that it warrants our preparation for them beforehand. It's true for the street, and just as true for court.

Most people who've had to do it will tell you that being forced to kill a person in self-defense in this society sucks.

But, they'll also tell you it beats hell out of being dead. It's sort of like taking radiation or chemotherapy after being diagnosed with cancer. The side effects will cause you to suffer, but it's better by far than dying of the disease.

In either case, there is a responsibility for those involved in the treatment protocol to warn the patients and prospective patients of those potential side effects.

Good luck. Stay safe.

〜

A MULTIDIMENSIONAL DISCIPLINE

The survival of violent encounters is a multidimensional discipline. No one is going to learn it all from one source.

Some courses of study seem to be outside the conventional wisdom, but you see their logic and relevance when you think about it. Body language, for example. When you use force on another human being, you have to explain

THERE IS MUCH TO LEARN from men like Walt Rauch, shown here competing at the IDPA Winter Championships at Smith & Wesson Academy.

yourself to the rest of society. "He looked like he was gonna hit me" sounds awfully nebulous to a jury, particularly when opposing counsel will probably have eliminated everyone with interest in or knowledge of the fighting arts during the jury selection process. "His eyes were narrowed as he looked at me with what I was taught to recognize as a target stare. His body was quartered to me in what I was taught to recognize as a combative stance. His hands were clenching and unclenching in what I was taught to recognize as a sign of rage that was about to explode. His head was forward of his shoulders, and his shoulders were forward of his hips, in what I was taught to recognize as an assaultive body posture and behavior cue." That sort of explanation will go much further toward making the jury understand the danger you faced when you took action with defensive physical force.

Any large bookstore should have several excellent volumes on body language. Read Gavin de Becker's book *The Gift of Fear*, which gives many examples that help the reader understand how our subconscious can read assaultive behavior cues. I would strongly recommend taking a course at a local community college or extension school

LT. COL. JEFF COOPER, USMC-ret., right, was a giant in the world of combat shooting, pioneering many techniques and principles that are taught as standard today.

on this topic. It would not hurt at all to have someone in your community available to testify as a material witness to the fact that he or she taught you to recognize certain behaviors and correlate them with indicia of impending physical attack. One of the best traveling lecturers on this topic is Tania Penderakis. Her website can be found at www.AthenaTraining.net.

Study the work of those who have investigated how human thought and action processes work when under life-threatening attack. Lt. Col. David Grossman, a psycholo-

KEN HACKATHORN was one of the modern pioneers of combat shooting. Here, with a Performance Center pistol, he shoots a stage at the Winter National Championships of IDPA.

gist, specializes in this topic. Read his books *On Killing* and *On Combat*. If you can, take one of his classes; the man is a compelling and inspirational speaker. If you can't, at least avail yourself of his recorded lecture, "The Bullet-Proof Mind."

Study what happens when bullets meet human bodies. This body of knowledge teaches essential lessons of what it takes to incapacitate another human who is intent on maiming or murdering you or other innocent, intended victims. "Gunshot Wounds" by Dr. Vincent DiMaio, Jr., is must reading. Another excellent written resource is "Medico-Legal Death Investigation" by Drs. Werner Spitz and Russell Fisher. I've had the privilege of meeting Dr. DiMaio and Dr. Spitz, and working on cases with them where we all served as expert witnesses for the defense of police officers accused of wrongful killings. (And we won those trials.) Many years ago, I spoke with Dr. DiMaio's father, Dr. Vincent DiMaio, Sr. who had been chief medical examiner for the city of New York when he advised the members of the NYPD Stakeout Squad how fast a pelvic break could drop a violent offender with handgun bullets, and exactly where to aim for the most effective brain shot.

AT THE NOMINEES' TABLE, Ray Chapman, left, and author, right, congratulate Bill Blankenship, center, as he is announced Outstanding American Handgunner of the Year. Six national championships made Blankenship a storehouse of shooting info.

Members of the Squad told me that Dr. DiMaio, Sr.'s advice worked out wonderfully for them. I learned a huge amount from Dr. Joseph Davis, the legendary chief medical examiner of Dade County, Florida during the years when Miami was the murder capital of the nation. Dr. Davis, by the way, was also a gun enthusiast on his own time, and a strong supporter of gun owners' civil rights. His work on murder victims had taught him the importance of intended victims being able to protect themselves. I also

WITH DEAN GRENNELL, right. Few people knew more about handgun ammunition than Dean.

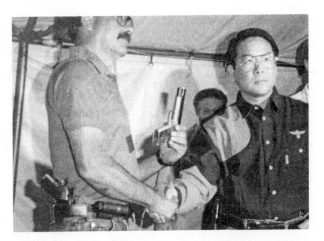

AUTHOR RECEIVES NATIONAL TACTICAL ADVOCATE AWARD from Richard Jee, then the owner of Gunsite, 1995. Gunsite, today run by Buz Mills, has long been a leader in combat shooting training.

had the pleasure of taking the week-long Medical-Legal Death Investigation course for forensic pathologists and homicide detectives hosted by Dr. Davis, his distinguished staff, and such voices of experience as Lt. Dave Rivers, the legendary detective who earned fame during his years on Metro-Dade Homicide.

I took basic and advanced officer involved shooting (OIS) investigation schools when they were offered at Ordnance Expo in Los Angeles in the '80s, with some of the program conducted at the LAPD Academy and with the OIS courses taught by the legendary Lt. Ray Higby and his staff. Higby was the founder of the LAPD OIS investigation team, which set a national standard for this sort of work.

Over the years, I had the privilege of both teaching and studying at the International Homicide Investigation Seminars. These conclaves share collective experience in recognizing and correcting the many kinds of misunderstandings that can arise in the aftermath of self-defense shootings.

Consider, for example, the person who swears he fired at the knife-armed assailant as the thug was coming at him, but forensic evidence shows the bullets entered the body behind lateral midline. I did my first such case in the mid-1980s, *Florida v. Mary Menucci Hopkin* in Dade County. When her long-abusing common-law husband lunged at her with obvious homicidal intent, she raised a .22 revolver and pulled the trigger three times. One entered the front of the chest, one hit behind lateral midline, and one square in the back. She was certain that as soon as he turned away, she had stopped firing. The State's Attorney's office in Dade County under Janet Reno thought otherwise, and charged her with murder in the second degree. Thanks to the able direct examination by her brilliant defense attorney Mark Seiden, I was able to show the action/reaction paradigm that had been at work in this instance.

The human body can make a quarter turn in a quarter second, and a 180 degree turn in half a second. Reaction to unanticipated stimulus takes much longer. As she fired the first shot into him, the attacker spun instantly and reflexively away from the danger, and perhaps also from the pain of the bullet, though the little .22 bullet itself certainly didn't spin him around. However, Mary was firing as fast as she could pull the trigger. With a double action revolver like hers, the typical person can fire four shots per second. Meanwhile, the shooter's brain has to go through the OODA loop defined by the great mid-20th Century trainer of fighter pilots, Col. John Boyd. One must **O**bserve the sudden and unexpected change of events, in this case, the breaking off of the attack. One must **O**rient,

YOU CAN LEARN MUCH from hero cops and gifted trainers. Legendary supercop Bob Lindsey was both, seen here charging through a live fire scenario at Chapman Academy with his service revolver at the time, a 6" S&W Model 19.

cognitively recognizing that the terrifying assault may be over and the use of deadly force may no longer be necessary in self-defense. One must **D**ecide what to do, which in this case would have been the decision to stop shooting. Finally, one must **A**ct, which in this case occurred when Mary stopped pulling the trigger and ceased fire.

Unfortunately for her attacker, by the time it was humanly possible for Mary to go through the four steps of OODA reaction, he had already turned his back into the stream of fire he had forced her to launch. This accounted for him being "shot in the back" twice in legitimate self-defense. The jury understood, and they acquitted Mary Hopkin. That scenario has played out in many courts over the many years since. More excellent reading on this, and many other phenomena that are not within the knowledge of the general public which constitutes the jury pool, can be found at the website of the Force Science Institute in Mankato, Minnesota, founded by Professor Bill Lewinksi. If you ever have a chance to take one of Bill's lectures or courses, do so; the man is a treasure of the training community.

Mark Seiden defended Mary Hopkin splendidly. It was neither the first nor the last time I worked with Mark and

THE EARLIER YOU START, the more you can learn. Author, in early 1970s, "kneels at the feet of the masters": standing from left, Bill O'Brian, Steve van Meter, and Wally Tompkins. The S&W Academy instructors didn't rib him too much about his Ruger .357.

his colleague, famed defense lawyer Roy Black, in murder or manslaughter cases. Mark and I later served for a couple of years as co-vice chairs of the forensic evidence committee of the National Association of Criminal Defense Lawyers. Mark figures prominently in Roy's book *Black's Law,* in which Roy discusses four of the cases he was most proud of in his distinguished career. Two of those cases are of interest to anyone who keeps or carries a defensive firearm. One was a police officer charged with manslaugh-

KEEP YOUR LEARNING up to date, because rapidly advancing disciplines are involved. This is Vince O'Neill of the Oklahoma state law enforcement academy, a pioneer in applying neuro-linguistic learning principles to combat survival training.

FEW KNEW MORE about the hardware side of shooting than Bill Ruger, Sr. Here he and the author discuss improvements to the SP101 revolver.

LEARN FROM THE PEOPLE who are responsible for training cops to shoot. John Cerar, then supervisor of the NYPD Firearms Training Unit, briefs a class of other police instructors on his department's shooting statistics and learning experiences.

NOT ALL GREAT MASTERS teach nationally. The late Bill Groce, here testing one of the first S&W .45 autos, was a brilliant instructor and innovator who never left the Ohio Peace Officer Training Academy. We had to go to him…and it was worth it.

ter after his shooting of a man pulling a gun on him and his partner triggered a riot. The other was a private citizen who was charged with murder and facing a death jury after a failed suicide intervention. We won acquittals in both cases, and each of those complicated trials brought out learning points that aren't usually taught in either law school or concealed carry classes.

There are things that can be learned from people who've fired in self-defense. Some went through the ordeal of trial and some did not, but all found themselves treated differently after the incident. I've been able to reach them as a writer, and some have come to me afterward to talk because they knew of what I teach. There are probably such people near you. Invite them to give a talk at your gun club. They have knowledge that can benefit others who might go through what they went through…knowledge that will help the next good person down the road survive both the physical attack and the many elements of the aftermath.

There are other relevant subject matter areas to consider. I've learned a lot from my old friend Walt Rauch. His career took him from the U.S. Secret Service to the Philadelphia Warrant Squad to private investigations. He has a huge number of articles in print, and much insight can be found in his book *Real World Survival! What Has Worked for Me.* Walt's years gave him much insight into predators, the sort of creature he calls "otherhuman," and he has a great deal of wise advice to offer. Like many others who've

LEARN FROM YOUR PREDECESSORS. Jan Stevenson, left, was handgun editor for GUNS magazine before author took the position in the 1970s; here, in 1979, they've just finished shooting Pistol '79 in England.

made a life study of this discipline, Walt shoots "combat matches" as a self-test of skill, and made many important contributions to the disciplines of IPSC and IDPA. Brother Rauch was also one of the founders of the National Tactical Invitational competition/training event.

The serious student of this topic wants to read *Cooper on Handguns and Principles of Personal Defense* by Col. Jeff Cooper. Many of the late Colonel's videotapes are still available, and of particular benefit is his classic lecture on mindset of self-defense and the color code concept of alertness to danger and preparedness to respond. Bill Jordan's classic *No Second Place Winner* may be somewhat dated in terms of the hardware, but his commentary on the mentality of gunfighting is absolutely timeless. I for one learned a great deal from both men, and found Jordan in particular to be a mentor.

There are top instructors living at this writing who will be remembered as the Coopers and Jordans of their generation. Louis Awerbuck, Jeff Chudwin, John Farnam, Ken Hackathorn, Marty and Gila Hayes, Bill Rogers, Pat Rogers, Scott Reitz, Dave Spaulding, Chuck Taylor, and Larry Vickers, and many more come to mind. There are many

LEARN FROM THE PAST masters while you can, as author is doing here with Col. Rex Applegate in the early 1990s.

other instructors who also have a great deal to offer. We are in the golden age of firearms training not only for the professionally armed, but for private citizens as well.

You can compile a substantial little library from the books and articles written by the people above and others. You never know which tidbit of their knowledge it's going to be that might save your life down the road.

Senior instructors for various law enforcement agencies can be great sources of research. The ones for the large departments get input on lots of shootings, and the ones

THE EARLIER YOU START building skills, the better. This is author's older daughter at age 10, firing a machinegun for the first time, ably assisted with the R4 by Phil Honeyborne in South Africa. Photo by Cameron Hopkins.

at the state and regional academies also have a large data base. How is a certain type of ammunition working out in the field? These guys can tell you. How is a given technique correlating with their field experience? That's useful information. I met and learned from many such people during the nineteen years I spent as chair of the firearms committee of the American Society of Law Enforcement Trainers, and almost a decade now on the advisory board of the International Law Enforcement Educators and Trainers Association, and time spent both teaching and learning at the conferences of the International Association of Law Enforcement Firearms Instructors.

Over the years, I discovered another unexpected source of info from law enforcement: the union representatives. They functioned outside "the official word and policy of the agency," and if the guns and ammo they were being issued didn't work well, they'd damn sure let you know about it. When the New York City Police Department's official word was that the 158 grain round nose lead .38 Special ammo they issued, and the six-shot revolvers they mandated for duty, were all just fine, the PBA (Patrolman's Benevolent Association) would be able to show you mul-

LEARN FROM THE SUFFERING of others. Mark Branham, accused of murder after a self-defense shooting, goes over a fine point of law with his expert witness. The ordeal ended with acquittal.

tiple cases where that feeble ammo had failed to stop attackers expeditiously, and cases where six shots weren't enough and an outgunned cop got hurt or killed. They raised hell about it, eventually winning speedloaders in 1986, semiautomatic 9mm pistols in 1993, and at last, hollow point ammunition in 1999.

A similar situation existed on LAPD. Except for the SWAT team, which had 1911 .45 pistols and 230 grain hardball, street cops and detectives were mandated to carry high speed round nose lead bullets in .38 Special re-

TEACHING COMPLETES THE CIRCLE OF LEARNING. Here, third level Lethal Force Institute students teach a basic handgun course to youngsters.

volvers. LAPPL, the Los Angeles Police Protective League, stood up and made an occupational safety issue of it. Eventually, the department issued both semiautomatics and hollow point ammunition.

By contrast, Chicago cops were issued lead +P semi-wadcutter hollow point .38 Special early on, and their representative organization (Fraternal Order of Police Lodge #7) told me the ammo had made a huge positive difference. They didn't feel a need to agitate for anything more powerful for their revolvers, only for semiautomatics to achieve more firepower. You can learn a lot from the unions; they speak for the people on the street.

Share your skills when the opportunity develops, it will make you a better practitioner yourself. Teaching is instructive in both directions. At the American Society of Law Enforcement Trainers, our motto was *qui docet, discet.* From the Latin, it means "who teaches, learns." When you deliver hands-on training in particular, you quickly learn which techniques are the most intuitive and the fastest to pick up, and which are so complicated that only the most dedicated student will be able to master them. Teaching forces you to delve deeper into the source of each concept or technique, and to deeper research its validity and applicability. When

you learn to diagnose technique failures in others, you better grasp how to perform those techniques yourself. Teaching sharpens the instructor's own skills as a practitioner, as double-stamping sharpens the imprimatur on a coin.

Take training in hand to hand combat. Most people, and certainly most cops, are far more likely to be in a struggle where they have to physically restrain and subdue an individual than in a situation where they have to shoot someone. Any cop can tell you that bad guys study on their own, even in prison, on how to disarm policemen and murder them with their own guns, a skill they can turn on any armed citizen they engage. It's important to know handgun retention, the art and science of defeating

SHARING KNOWLEDGE with like-minded people from other cultures can be instructive. Here, remote camera catches author and multiple gunfight winner Fernando Arcaya teaching behind the firing line at Magnum Galleria, Caracas, Venezuela, 1985.

an attempt to disarm you. In tandem with that you need to learn handgun disarming, partly because it's a safety net if the bad guy does get your weapon away from you…partly because, in close, it's often faster to get your hand on his gun, deflect it, and flow into a disarm than it is for you to draw and fire your own…and partly, because you may be someplace where the bad guy has a gun and you don't.

Intermediate force tools are important. Whether you choose pepper spray or a "civilian TASER" (check local laws on both) or a Kubotan™ keychain, get training with it and stay proficient with it. You need something for that broad area between verbal crisis intervention and defensive gunfire.

Don't tell me "I want a gun so I don't have to get into martial arts!" The use of the defensive firearm most certainly is a martial art. Eighteen months before writing this, I tested for Shodan (first degree black belt) in Hojutsu, the ancient martial art of firearms that was resurrected in modern times by Soke Jeff Hall. One requirement for the test was to write an essay on the topic. Mine went like this:

THE MARTIAL ART OF COMBAT SHOOTING[2,*]

Col. Jeff Cooper may not have been the first to call defensive shooting a martial art, but he did much to popularize the thought. The comparisons go far deeper than the obvious reading of each as "arts of war."

Each requires *kime*, or focus, if one is to excel in their practice. Not just focus at the instant of the shot or the strike, but a focus long beforehand that encompasses learning and self-application. A deeply focused sense of self-analysis: *Can I destroy another human being's body, and perhaps end his life, if I must? If I am badly hurt, have I inculcated the strong mental program to Finish the Fight, as Soke Hall puts it with eloquent simplicity?* A commitment that profoundly changes the practitioner's lifestyle in ways that go far beyond the time schedule.

Each requires the practitioner to absorb impact, deliver impact, and maintain balance. The shooter must recover from the recoil of a powerful weapon and use his body mechanics reflexively to bring the weapon back on target or to the next mark for an instant follow-up shot. The *kara-te*, the empty hand, must deliver its blow with full power but without overextending and thus compromising the balance of the body, and maintaining the ability to flow into the follow-up punch that ends the encounter and brings peace.

...AND HERE, with Odin Press dummy gun and live "attacker," author tries it the other way around.

LEARN EVERY TECHNIQUE in all its dimensions. Here, an NYPD instructor demonstrates with real revolver on paper target the department's recommended hip-shooting procedure...

The empty-hand combatant learns *ukemi-waza* to break his fall, and is practiced and comfortable fighting from any position on the ground. The same should be true of the defensive firearms practitioner. Each knows that force goes in both directions in a fight, and that any moment the practitioner may suddenly find himself prone or supine or even twisted upside down, but will still have a duty to continue the conflict and prevail. The fighter on the street who breaks free of his opponent's strangle hold, reverses it, and renders the opponent unconscious has much in common with the Missouri State Trooper who, struggling with a would-be cop-killer who had grabbed at his service weapon in the front seat of the patrol car, finished the fight by firing upside-down – suspended by the seatbelt after the cruiser went out of control and overturned – and killed his assailant.

The empty hand and the gun hand alike must be directed by a mind that fully comprehends the ramification of the force the hand has become skillful at wielding. The power to kill or maim in an instant does not belong in the hands of those who hurt for pleasure. The ancient and honored principles of *bushido* must guide the hand of the unarmed priest *and* the katana-wielding hand of the *Samurai*.

The confidence and self-worth instilled by accomplishment

70

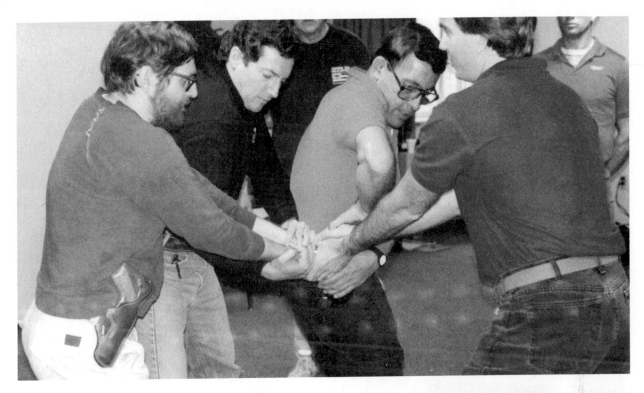

LEARNING WEAPON retention is critical. Here, author lets three men grab the gun in his holster, and using a technique learned from legendary master Jim Lindell…

in both sides of the arts can become its own *raison d'etre*. How many of our brethren have become successful tournament fighters in limited contact *kumite* or champions in the various combat shooting sports, only to lose sight of the original rationale for sharpening their skills in competition? The purpose of competing is to temper the already forged living blade, and hone it ever sharper, not to turn the practitioner into the human counterpart of a fighting saber that eventually morphs into a blunted *epee*, a symbol of skill in something that has lost its roots and devolved into practical uselessness.

In the mirror worlds of the *gi* and the gun, it is understood that power and responsibility must always be in a commensurate balance. Power without responsibility begets brutality and oppression, while responsibility without power is an exercise in futility. Morality and ethics must accompany the power on either side, and perhaps the ethics more than the morality. Morals (root word: mores) are fungible: the accepted customs of a given society at a given time. Ethics (root word: ethos) are benchmark values that have remained constant stars to steer by since the dawn of the civilized human experience. The murder of the innocent might be acceptable within the moral code of the *Yakuza*, but the ethics of the *Samurai* would forbid it. A strong ethi-

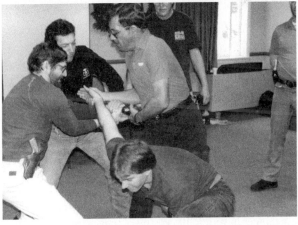

…SECURES THE GUN and pivots into the attack, peeling all three off the weapon.

cal base is fundamental in both the traditional martial arts, and the modern evolution of firearms combatives.

Is combat shooting a martial art? Without question, the answer is yes. There are too many stark and obvious parallels for it not to be so.

Respectfully submitted to Soke Hall,
Massad Ayoob
01/09/2010

BEING ABLE TO SHOOT while moving is a critical skill.

Jeff Hall's resurrection of Hojutsu opened a timely chapter in the book of defensive firearms training options for today's world. Here's how I explained it in the pages of *Black Belt* magazine.

HOJUTSU: THE MARTIAL ART OF THE GUN[3]

The kata is underway. You block the invisible punch, and counter with a reverse punch and a front snap kick. Sensing danger to your flank, you pivot to face the threat as you draw your pistol from the holster on your obi and...

What? *What?? What?!?!?*

Welcome to Hojutsu, the martial art of the handgun. Born in the 1530s when the Portuguese first brought gunpowder to Japan, Hojutsu (literally, "fire art," and loosely and more efficiently translated, "the art of firearms") flourished for a time, and ultimately fell dormant. Resurrected and modernized in the early 2000s in the United States by Jeff Hall, it has been quantified as the first modern small arms shooting system in the mold of traditional martial arts.

Hall, recognized as the Soke of the system by the United States Martial Arts Hall of Fame, the Universal Martial Arts Hall of Fame, and the World Sokeship Council, is

CROSS-TRAIN between armed and unarmed skill-sets. Robert Bussey, master instructor in Togakure-ryu ninjitsu, left, thanks author for sharing armed combat skills with his students.

a traditional martial artist with roots that go back to the early '80s. A fourth degree black belt in Shudo-Kan karate, he also holds Sandan rank in Hakka-ryu jiu-jitsu and Okinawan Kobu-do. Hall has studied under some of the great masters including Tak Kubota, Kiyoshi Yamazaki, Dr. Charles Scott, and the late Professor Wally Jay.

It was Master Yamazaki, he says, who gave him the epiphany that convinced him to revitalize the long-lost martial art.

(1st of 3): YOU'LL NEED HAND-TO-HAND SKILLS for moments when you don't have (or can't use) a gun. Here, a downward attack is blocked…

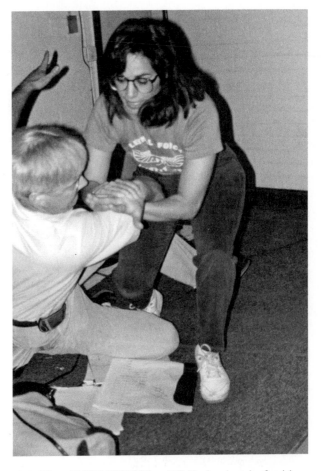

(2nd of 3): …BY THE LEGENDARY world kickboxing champion Graciela Casillas, who flows into a takedown…

THE LIGHT BULB TURNS ON

On that inspirational day in the early 2000s, Yamazaki told his class that the key elements of effective karate were stance, balance, focus, execution of technique, and follow-through. Hall – who had been a police firearms instructor nearly as long as he had been a karateka – realized that those exact same five principles were the core elements of effective shooting. Hall had long dreamed of a martial art that would combine shooting with bushido, and at that moment, he resolved to create one.

For Jeff Hall, the concept was more than academic. At that time, he was approaching retirement from a distinguished, decades-long career with the Alaska State Troopers. Those troopers cover huge areas of rural Alaska alone and without backup, and Hall realized early on that when the going got rough, he needed more than his strapping six-foot-four frame to come out intact. His martial arts training allowed him to win fights that were often stacked

against him, not just with skill but with the confidence and determination he had learned in the dojo. For much of his career Hall was a member of the SWAT team, and over the years he won more than one gunfight. He came to understand the importance of infusing the discipline and the self-confidence of the dojo into men who carried, and sometimes used, guns as a tool of their trade. Teaching police around the country, Hall's most famous lecture was one he called "Finish the Fight," and it drew as much from his martial arts background as it did from his extensive and deep law enforcement experience.

FINDING THE MIX

Wearing your gi with a holster on your obi is a strange experience. (For one thing, the gun rides higher than it would on a trouser belt or police uniform belt.) But, mostly, it's a jarring incongruity.

Hall feels that it shouldn't be.

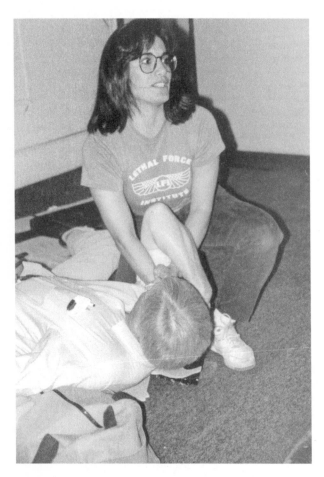

(3rd of 3): …AND FINISHES in a restraining armlock, all while maintaining eye contact with the LFI class she's teaching.

Kobu-do has the bo and the sai, the tonfa and the kama and of course the nunchaku. Iaido, Kendo, and other traditional arts encompass the sword. Arnis and its mother art Kali focus heavily on the knife and the stick. Kyudo, the martial art of archery, is far from dead.

While some purists feel only ancient weapons have a place in the dojo, many practitioners have adapted to modern ways. Decades ago, Dr. Maung Ghee ignited controversy when he included the pistol and the .30 caliber carbine into his teaching of Burmese Bando. Many famed martial artists who've graced the covers of *Black Belt* have integrated firearms into their personal defensive skills – some conspicuously, like Chuck Norris and Steven Segal, and some quietly, like Bill Wallace and Graciela Casillas.

Soke Hall's approach is to teach the empty hand and the gun hand together, in the same spirit of discipline and bushido.

THE CURRICULUM

Being a martial art of shooting, Hojutsu's focus is about nine-tenths on firearms, says Hall. The remainder is split between empty hand fighting and traditional, more primitive weapons: the knife and the stick. One can progress through Shodan with just the pistol, but beyond that first degree of the black belt, the Hojutsu student must broaden into the rifle and the shotgun. And lest it be said that tradition is neglected in the ryu of Soke Hall, advanced dans are required to shoot Shodan-level scores with the slower, old-fashioned revolver instead of the modern semiautomatic pistol, while their speed and accuracy with the latter type of handgun is expected to advance proportionally with each promotion test. Nidan and higher belt ranks are awarded only to those Hall or his shihans have seen teach, and whom they've deemed to be sufficient in both dedication and teaching ability to impart the spirit of Hojutsu.

For purposes of this article the writer took a Hojutsu seminar hosted at the Las Vegas Metropolitan Police Range and heavily attended by working law enforcement officers, with a few civilians thrown in. About a quarter of the time was spent in the makeshift dojo at a local community center. The gi, while not mandated, was strongly urged as the dress code of the day, and we bowed as we entered and left there, a practice not required on the firing range. On both the range and the mat, however, we were expected to address the instructors with the traditional titles of respect, in this case taking our training from Soke Hall, Shihan Rod Kuratomi, and Sensei Karl Knowles.

Kata work was unique to the art, encompassing not only the traditional blocks and parries, punches and kicks, and takedowns, but also gun-related movements. Many of these focused on countering disarming attempts, and the armed portion of the kata included drawing and holstering with clean and positive technique. Movement with the drawn gun was emphasized over static stand-and-shoot patterns, with firing on the move resembling a stepping pattern from White Crane kung fu, and non-shooting movement incorporating a relatively recent development in the world of the gun, Position Sul. In this "hold," the handgun is tucked close to the body, its muzzle down and to the side, as the practitioner moves. It was designed to keep police and military raiders in stack formations from covering one another with muzzles of loaded guns as they made entry into target premises, and Hall, an old SWAT hand, has incorporated it into his rejuvenated and updated style of Hojutsu.

LEARN FROM YOUR PEERS by co-teaching. Mike Izumi, right, author of "In Self-Defense," team-teaches a Lethal Force Institute class with author.

LEARN FROM THOSE with large research bases. Then-Captain John Cerar, right, shows author one of the first 600 Glock 19s to be issued experimentally to NYPD officers, early 1990s.

The majority of the seminar was spent on the firing range. All the work was done with pistols (it was a Shodan-level seminar), and distances ranged from close contact to 50 yards. Half a football field away from the target, you could almost hear Yamazaki and Hall alike reminding you, "Focus!"

Like most great martial arts instructors, Jeff Hall is a compendium of the masters who formed him, and you can see it in some of his techniques and principles as surely as you can see a father's genes in the features of his son's face. One of Hall's mentors in firearms training was the late Col. Jeff Cooper, whom Dennis Martin of Britain's *International Fighting Arts* magazine once called "the Funakoshi of combat shooting." Cooper's famous "Four Rules of Firearms Safety" (every firearm is always loaded; never point the gun at anything you are not prepared to destroy; keep your finger out of the trigger guard until you are on target [intending to fire]; and always be certain of your target and what is behind it") suffuse Hojutsu gun handling. Cooper's influence is also seen in the core two-handed firing platform: the Weaver Stance that Cooper made famous, which is essentially an isometric push-pull executed with front stance foot placement.

VERN GEBERTH, the legendary NYPD homicide investigator, explains a fine point to the author.

THE MELDING

Watching advanced Hojutsu practitioners is pleasing to those who already possess combined background in both empty-hand arts and firearms. The flow from the punch to the draw appears seamless, rapid, and fluid. After decades of teaching police officers to flow up and down law enforcement's "force continuum," Hall felt a need for the same principle in other training theaters, and he appears to have succeeded brilliantly in combining the two worlds in Hojutsu.

IF YOU'RE GOING TO FACE people with knives, learn what skilled knife fighters can do. Master martial artist Paul Vunak, right, shows author how to defeat a lunging stab. Fortunately, the knives are made of wood.

Hall has found that martial artists learn the gun faster than shooters learn the empty hand side of the system. He believes it comes from better-developed learning ability with psychomotor skills, and also an ingrained willingness to follow the teacher's instructions. The heir apparent and second in command of Hall's Hojutsu-Ryu, Soke-dai Rod Kuratomi, is a classic example. Kuratomi holds the same position under Soke Takayuki Kubota in Gosoku-Ryu karate, and before studying the gun with Soke Hall, Kuratomi had won the International Grand Champion title in both sparring and weapons at the IKA's World Cup Tournament in 2000. Today, Kuratomi flows seamlessly between hand-to-hand kata and deadly accurate, high-speed live fire with a Glock .40, delivering champion-level performance with one foot in each world.

An example Hall likes to use is the day he took Master Yamazaki to the range to fire a pistol for the first time. "He had never fired a pistol before, but at the end of his first ten minutes, he was shooting one-inch groups with a (.45 caliber) 1911 Colt. I think that was my first inkling of how easy it is to turn a dedicated martial artist into a shooter."

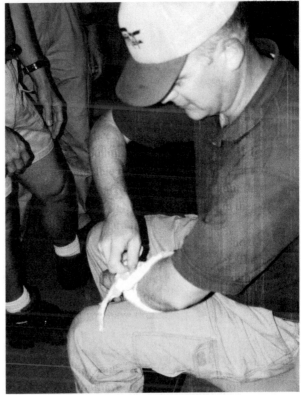

IF YOU KNOW HOW TO WORK the accelerator, know how to work the brakes. This practitioner is learning self-treatment of gunshot injury in case there's no one there to help him.

TWO-TIME GUNFIGHT WINNER and advanced martial artist Jeff Hall resurrected Hojutsu, the lost Japanese martial art of the firearm. His 1911 .45 was done by Nighthawk.

Soke Jeffrey Hall has resurrected and modernized Hojutsu as surely as Jim Arvanitis did the same with ancient Greek Pankration, perhaps the first mixed martial art. The best sources of information and training are Soke Hall's website and Soke-dai Kuratomi's, which can be found at www.hojutsu.com and www.martialartofthegun.com respectively.

*Glossary of martial arts terms:
Bo: Long staff
Bushido: Code of honorable warriors
Gi: Classic karate/judo uniform
IKA: International Karate Federation
Kama: Short sickle
Kata: Practice movements similar to shadow boxing
Katana: Long sword, colloquially, "Samurai sword"
Kime: (pronounced key-MAY) Focus
Kobu-do: An Okinawan martial art focusing on weaponcraft
Kumite: (KOO-mih-tay) Sparring, may be light to full power contact
Nidan: Second degree black belt
Nunchaku: Two short sticks chained or corded together, can be used as flail or "nutcracker"

SOKE JEFF HALL explains how the empty hand and the gun combine in Hojutsu.

HOLSTERED DUMMY GUN hanging from obi of his gi looks incongruous as karate champ Rod Kuratomi instructs a Hojutsu class, but soon students will exchange it all for range wear, duty belts, and live guns and ammo to stamp the other side of the coin.

Obi: Belt worn with gi, its color usually connoting rank
Sai: Short trident, outer prongs shorter than center prong, normally wielded in pairs
Sandan: Third degree black belt
Sensei: (SEN-say) Instructor
Shihan: Master instructor
Shodan: First degree black belt
Soke: Founder/grandmaster of a fighting system
Soke-Dai: Second in command and designated heir to Soke
Tonfa: Short stick with side handle, usually wielded in pairs
Ukemi: The art of the controlled fall, or break-falling

↪

Reading is good. Watching the many movies in the many media now available is good, too. But none of it supplants hands-on training, under the eye of a watchful, competent instructor who can quickly diagnose and correct things you're doing imperfectly. Training is the fast track to competence, and there are more good trainers in combat shooting and its related disciplines available today than there have ever been.

Combat shooting is, in its essence, preparation for life-and-death encounters. All other things being equal, the better-equipped practitioners prevail in the real-world crucible.

In the next segment, we'll look at three men whose lives prove that fact beyond doubt.

[1] Awaiting publication at Publishers Development Corporation.

[2] First written for *shodan* essay requirement for Soke Jeff Hall, subsequently reprinted in 2012 *American Cop Annual*, special edition.

[3] First appeared as "HoJutsu: the Martial Art of the Gun," by Massad Ayoob, *Black Belt* magazine, December 2010 issue.

↪

STATUE OF WYATT EARP in Tombstone, compiled from many descriptions and images of Earp, all describing him as heavier and broader-chested than he described himself, or appeared in the one photo of him in shirtsleeves during that period. Was body armor helping to fill out those clothes?

THREE GUNFIGHTERS

To George Santayana we owe the famous quote that those who do not learn from history are doomed to repeat it. It is said that experience is the collected aggregate of our mistakes. Otto von Bismarck said that wisdom was found in learning from the collected mistakes of others.

Put that all together, and it makes huge sense to learn as much as we can from those who have gone before us. We want to focus on those who were conspicuously successful at the endeavor we ourselves wish to succeed in, should we ever have to undertake it. We want to analyze what they did correctly, and be alert for things that worked for them, in their time and place, but may not work for us in our time and place.

All of us have the opportunity to study the combatants of the past, and some of the present. A goodly number of autobiographical books have been written by American warriors returning from the conflicts in Iraq and Afghanistan, and a substantial body of literature exists written by their predecessors in every American war going back to the Revolution. The guns and the uniforms and the battlefields may change, but the core lessons of human beings in lethal conflict are timeless.

In many respects, the much more scarce reminiscences of police officers who've been in gunfights are even more useful, if only because they took place on the same sort of turf where the armed citizen can expect to engage the same foe: the violent criminal in America.

Due to limited space, three such are presented here. I chose men from three markedly different, but overlapping, time periods. One thing you discover in studying this discipline is that the guns they used, the clothing they wore, and the vehicles that brought them to the fight may evolve and change over time, but the principles of good men fighting bad men to the death are absolutely timeless.

19TH CENTURY: WYATT EARP[1]

During the inquest into the shootout at the O. K. Corral, Wyatt Earp testified as to the opening moments thus:

"When I saw Billy Clanton and Frank McLaury draw their pistols, I drew my pistol. Billy Clanton leveled his pistol at me, but I did not aim at him. I knew that Frank McLaury had the reputation of being a good shot and a dangerous man, and I aimed at Frank McLaury."

Earp testified that Clanton shot at him, and he at Frank McLaury, almost simultaneously. Clanton missed, Earp did not.

"The fight," Earp then testified in a classic example of understatement, "then became general."

Wyatt Earp had followed a key principle of gunfighting with multiple opponents. You don't aim necessarily at the nearest opponent, or necessarily at the one with the deadliest weapon. You direct your fire first at the one most likely to kill you in your present position.

Earp's telling first shot that folded Frank McLaury over kept the man most likely to kill any of the Earps from doing so. Young Clanton, whom Earp had suspected would break under pressure, did. Though only five to six feet away from Earp, he fired at Wyatt two or three times – and missed.

Earp's end score was the best of the fight. He was the only person on his side of the gun duel to go unwounded. He deliberately shot Frank McLaury, may well have shot Billy Clanton, and some insist he also shot Tom McLaury, already mortally wounded by Doc Holliday's shotgun blast.

His marksmanship under stress, like his coolness under fire, was exemplary. It may have been as high as a 100 percent hit potential.

In his book *Gunfighters*, Col. Charles Askins, Jr. – a man of no small gunfighting experience himself, and one who did his homework – concluded, "(Wyatt Earp) had fired two shots and both had found their mark. He had killed Frank McLowrey (sic) and had his lead in Billy Clanton. Extreme range of the fight was 20 feet, a proximity which might have induced some gun-swingers to hurry. Not Earp. In commenting on the battle many years afterward he said, 'I don't make fast draws. I pull my gun deliberately, aim carefully, and don't jerk on the trigger.'" [a]

What is even more interesting is that the O.K. Corral incident was Wyatt Earp's first gunfight, and he was by no means the world's most seasoned lawman. He had some six years of law enforcement experience, some of it full-time in Dodge City and Wichita, Kansas, and was a part-time cop and full-time coach guard for Wells Fargo at the time of the Tombstone gun battle.

It was his first gunfight, but not his first shooting. In July of 1878, a cowboy raced past Assistant Marshal Earp and Officer Jim Masterson, Bat Masterson's brother, and fired three shots from a Colt .45 that narrowly missed the marshal. As he rode off, Earp, Masterson, and possibly others opened fire.

Though no one could be sure, Earp was credited with the shot that struck the fleeing George Hoy in the arm and caused him to fall from his horse. The arm wound became gangrenous and, despite amputation, Hoy died just under a month after the shooting.

Even if it was Earp's bullet that caused Hoy's death, however, this "fleeing felon" shooting was by nowhere near as harrowing as a gunfight, let alone the experience of three men trying to kill you, your brothers, and your friend.

A study of Earp's life shows that, 100 years before the term "officer survival" became a buzzword, Wyatt Earp was practicing its tenets. Consider the following examples.

STUDYING PREDECESSORS

In his memoirs, Bat Masterson said people wondered why Earp hung around with a psychopath like Doc Holliday, whom Masterson and most others in their circle personally despised.

Part of it was put down to the story of Holliday saving Wyatt's life by risking his own, grabbing two revolvers and facing down multiple men who had Earp at gun point in a Dodge City incident in 1878. However, reading between the lines, one sees another reason for Earp to have opened a relationship with Holliday.

He knew that the tubercular dentist was a seasoned killer, and that one day, in all probability, he would have to kill men in gunfights himself. There were things Holliday could share that would teach him to survive.

LEARNING FROM THE BENCH

There was precedent in Earp's background for this. Earp was born in 1848; he would have been 23 in 1871 when, in Kansas City, he began to gather the advice and the oral histories of those who had gone before.

He told his biographer, Stuart Lake:

"The spot favored by the men best known in frontier life was a bench in front of the police station where Tom Speers, then marshal of Kansas City, held forth each afternoon. Because these hunters, freighters, and cattlemen knew so much of the country and the life which held my

IN THE 1880S, Wyatt Earp carried two handguns, and both rifle and shotgun in saddle scabbards. Here in the 1990s, police were emulating him with standard gear. Left, Capt. Ayoob with Benelli auto 12 gauge; right, Chief Russ Lary with Ruger Mini-14, one of each in every patrol car. Each carries issue .45 auto and concealed backup gun.

interest at the time, I spent most of the summer on or near Tom Speers' bench.

"I made acquaintances that I was to renew later, all over the West, on the buffalo range, in cowtowns, mining camps, and along the trails between, some as far away as the Alaskan gold fields in '97 and '98.

"I met Wild Bill Hickok in Kansas City in 1871. Jack Gallagher, the celebrated scout, was there; and I remember Jack Martin, Billy Dixon, Jim Hanrahan, Tom O'Keefe, Cheyenne Jack, Billy Ogg, Bermuda Carlisle, Old Man Keeler, Kirk Jordan, and Andy Johnson. The names may not mean much to another century, but in my younger days each was a noted man. Much that they accomplished has been ignored by the records of their time, but every one made history…

"I was a fair hand with pistol, rifle, or shotgun, but I learned more about gunfighting from Tom Speers' cronies during the summer of '71 than I had dreamed was in the book. Those old-timers took their gunplay seriously, which was natural under the conditions in which they lived.

"Shooting, to them, was considerably more than aim-

ing at a mark and pulling a trigger. Models of weapons, methods of wearing them, means of getting them into action and of operating them, all to the one end of combining high speed with absolute accuracy, contributed to the frontiersman's shooting skill.

"The sought-after degree of proficiency was that which could turn to most effective account the split-second between life and death. Hours upon hours of practice, and wide experience in actualities supported their arguments over style." [b]

For the last 25 years, police survival instructors have brought in gunfight survivors to lecture to their young officers. They have studied videotaped analyses of such disastrous gun battles as the Newhall Massacre of four California Highway Patrol officers in 1970, or the Miami shootout of 1986 in which seven FBI agents were shot, two fatally. Earp, clearly, had been ahead of his time.

PHYSICAL CONDITIONING

Today's officers learn cardiovascular fitness and physical conditioning, with emphasis on endurance. Hard physical labor when he was growing up apparently took the place of exercise studios in developing these characteristics in Earp.

Those who knew him described him as whipcord-tough, extremely skillful as a boxer, and believed to have won every fistfight he ever engaged in. This included one memorable 15-minute exchange with a larger, stronger man whom Earp left helpless on his knees with a face like mincemeat and a dislodged eyeball.

SECOND GUNS

Most officer survival instructors today encourage the carrying of a backup handgun. Earp was ahead of the curve on that as well. Again, from Stuart Lake, Earp is quoted:

"That two-gun business is another matter that can stand some truth before the last of the old-time gunfighters has gone on. They wore two guns, most of the sixgun-toters did, and when the time came for action, they went after them with both hands. But they didn't shoot them that way.

"Primarily, two guns made the threat of something in reserve; they were useful as a display of force when a lone man stacked up against a crowd. Some men could shoot equally well with either hand, and in a gunplay might alternate their fire; others exhausted the loads from the gun in the right hand, or left, as the case might be, then shifted the reserve weapon to the natural shooting hand if that was necessary and possible.

"Such a move – the border-shift – could be made faster than the eye could follow a topnotch gun-thrower, but if the man was as good as that, the shift seldom would be required."

Earp also noted, "Jack Gallagher's advice summed up what others had to say, to wear weapons in the handiest position – in my case as far as pistols were concerned, in open holsters, one on each hip if I was carrying two, hung rather low as my arms were long, and with the muzzles a little forward on my thighs.

"Some men wore their guns belted high on the waist, a few, butts forward, army style, for a cross-draw; others carried one gun directly in front of the stomach, either inside or outside the waistband, and another gun in a holster slung below the left armpit; still others wore two of these shoulder holsters. Style was a matter of individual preference." [c]

COMBAT MARKSMANSHIP

Speaking of principles of surviving a shooting, Earp told his biographer, "The most important lesson I learned from those proficient gun-fighters (starting in 1871) was that the winner of a gunplay usually was the man who took his time. The second was that, if I hoped to live long on the frontier, I would shun flashy trick-shooting – grandstand play – as I would poison.

"Later, as a peace officer, I was to fight some desperate battles against notorious gunmen of the Old West, and wonder has been expressed that I came through them all unscathed…Luck was with me in my gunfights, of course – so were the lessons learned in Market Square during the summer of '71." [d]

In studying the different accounts of the O.K. Corral shooting, it becomes apparent that Earp coolly and carefully extended his revolver to arm's length, aligned the sights, and carefully squeezed the trigger. He was not alone in taking this approach to shooting when his life was on the line. Bat Masterson, his contemporary and friend, felt the same way.

Historians argue about how many men Masterson killed. One says perhaps none at all. Others put the number at three, and Earp credited Masterson with four. However, others put the number in the 20s, which is actually quite possible if one counts Indians Masterson shot at during the Battle of Adobe Walls.

Masterson's biographer Robert K. DeArment has this to say: "As much as he may have enjoyed impressing young (observers) with his hip-shooting ability, however, it is clear from Bat's own words that he considered the sights on a weapon of great importance in an encounter with an armed adversary.

"In the series of articles on western gunfighters he wrote in 1907, he cited a pistol fray involving Charlie Harrison and Jim Levy, celebrated gamblers and gunmen who faced each other across a Cheyenne street and settled a personal difficulty with hot lead.

"Levy downed his opponent, wrote Bat, because 'He looked through the sights of his pistol, which is a very essential thing to do when shooting at an adversary who is returning your fire.' Another well known western sport and pistolero, Johnny Sherman, once emptied his revolver at a man in a St. Louis hotel room '…without as much as puncturing his clothes.' Sherman, said Bat, '…forgot that there was a set of sights on his pistol." [e]

TAKE YOUR TIME, FAST

Earp clarified what he was talking about. "When I say that I learned to take my time in a gunfight, I do not wish to be misunderstood, for the time to be taken was only that split-fraction of a second that means the difference between deadly accuracy with a sixgun and a miss.

"It is hard to make this clear to a man who has never been in a gunfight. Perhaps I can best describe such time-taking as going into action with the greatest speed of which a man's muscles are capable, but mentally unflustered by an urge to hurry or the need for complicated and nervous muscular actions which trick-shooting involves. Mentally deliberate, but muscularly faster than thought, is what I mean."

Great minds think in like directions. In his classic 1966 text on police gunfighting, Bill Jordan would comment, "At the time I knew (Captain John Hughes of the Texas Rangers) I was a young man just starting in law enforcement, while he was quite elderly and long retired from active service. Like most old timers, he was reluctant to talk of personal experiences but occasionally passed out advice well worth heeding.

"One such gem that I have always remembered and will pass on was, 'If you get in a gunfight, don't let yourself feel rushed. Take your time, fast.'" [f]

NO POINT SHOOTING

Concluded Earp, "In all my life as a frontier peace officer, I did not know a really proficient gun-fighter who had anything but contempt for the gun-fanner, or the man who literally shot from the hip. In later years I read a great deal about this type of gunplay, supposedly employed by men noted for skill with a .45.

"From personal experience and from numerous sixgun battles which I witnessed, I can only support the opinion advanced by the men who gave me my most valuable instruction in fast and accurate shooting, which was that the gun-fanner and the hip-shooter stood small chance to live against a man who, as old Jack Gallagher always put it, took his time and pulled the trigger once." [g]

Today's instructors say, "Remember the basics! Keep It Simple, Stupid!" Getting a little déjà vu?

Today, the Modern Technique pioneered by Jeff Cooper that takes an instant to visually verify a flash sight picture before the trigger is smoothly but quickly compressed, has re-proven the wisdom of what Gallagher taught Earp, and what Earp and Masterson taught us.

On the LAPD, both handgun hit potentials under stress and police survival ratios in gunfights have soared since this sort of training was instituted in the 1980s, replacing "point-shooting."

ESCALATION OF FORCE

One goes from physical presence to verbal crisis intervention, to the application of bare hands, the use of "inter-mediate weapons," and finally, as a last resort, lethal force. Earp practiced these principles more than a century ago.

Those who followed his career noted that he made wise use of his reputation to the point where men who might have fought another marshal would become quiescent in his very presence. Those who met him remember him being scrupulously fair and, for the most part, hearing each side of the story when two men squabbled, and letting the man he was about to arrest have his say.

All of this follows the principles taught and proven today of command presence and verbal crisis intervention skills.

Though a bit quick to use his hands by today's standards, Earp used his open hand or his fists in situations where some of his contemporaries would have manufactured an excuse to shoot the suspect. There were no pepper sprays at the time, and except for the occasional cane, no impact weapons analogous to the PR-24 or the telescoping police baton of modern times.

Earp and his older brother frequently struck men with their guns, a practice decidedly frowned upon today. But in fairness, at least a few of these incidents probably ended an encounter with a concussion instead of a fatal gunshot wound that would probably have had to be inflicted if things had taken their natural course otherwise.

It is significant that at the end of the O.K. Corral fight, Wyatt Earp and his brothers did not finish off the dying Billy Clanton, who was sprawled by a building with a Colt .44 in his left hand that he was trying to balance on his knee and fire at them.

Earp made it clear to Lake that they felt Clanton was done for at that point and of no further danger. The most compassionate of today's police are trained to shoot a man in such a scenario as Billy Clanton presented at the end, and the Earps are fortunate that he didn't get his "second wind."

(Doc Holliday, however, was not cut from the same cloth. One historian has him pulling his trigger on Clanton at the end of the fight, and the hammer of his nickeled Colt falling with audible clicks. Holliday had run his revolver dry).

Judge Wells Spicer noted in exonerating the Earp faction for the shooting that if the triple homicide had been maliciously motivated, Ike Clanton would surely have been the first to die, since the Earps hated him most of all as their prime enemy among the cowboy faction. Earp not only didn't kill the older Clanton, he shoved him aside when he grabbed Wyatt's arm, and Earp told Clanton, "Go

BAT MASTERSON, LEFT, AND WYATT EARP, RIGHT. In this rare picture of Earp without vest and one or more coats, he appears thinner than described by those who "saw him on the street." More indication that he might have worn early body armor beneath his silk vest and frock coat or overcoat.

to fighting or get away."

Earp testified, "I never fired at Ike Clanton, even after the shooting commenced, because I thought he was unarmed. I believed then, and believe now, from the acts I have stated and the threats I have related and the other threats communicated to me by other persons as having been made by Tom McLaury, Frank McLaury, and Ike Clanton, that these men last named had formed a conspiracy to murder my brothers, Morgan and Virgil, Doc Holliday and myself. I believe I would have been legally and morally justified in shooting any of them on sight, but I did not do so, nor attempt to do so." [h]

BODY ARMOR

Earp sustained no gunshot wounds in the O.K. Corral affair, though Billy Clanton and others shot at him multiple times from as close as five feet away. He was also unscathed in his shotgun duel with the highly skilled gunfighter Curly Bill Brocius, a known cop killer whom Earp slew at Iron Springs.

Richard Davis of Second Chance, the inventor of modern, concealable soft body armor, is a student of his product's history and finds tantalizing the rumor spread by Earp's enemies that he wore a bulletproof vest. Military labs are today working with "super-silkworms" with a view toward getting them to produce body armor, since certain kinds of silk can, in enough layers, indeed stop bullets.

Did Earp, Davis wonders, somehow discover this ahead of everyone else, and have a vest made of layer after exhaustively piled layer of tightly woven silk, perhaps combined with something else?

This would account for frequent depictions of Earp wearing such a garment. Of course, silk vests were in fashion at the time.

Other observations support the possibility. Wyatt Earp himself and those who knew him intimately described him as standing just over six feet tall and weighing somewhere between 145 and 150 pounds for most of his life. This is a man who would look almost gauntly slender, as Earp indeed does in a photograph of him with the shorter, stockier Bat Masterson where both are in shirtsleeves.

However, most casual observers of Wyatt Earp seem to have described him as a big, strapping man who gave the appearance of weighing perhaps 180 pounds. This is exactly the effect that one would expect if a tall, thin man was wearing an armored vest – especially a thick, primitive one – under his clothing.

It would also account for him being so often impeccably dressed, complete with a dark, frock coat of heavy fabric – the sort of garment that would hide the outlined edges of such a vest.

Earp himself took the accusation seriously enough to deny it. He told his biographer Lake, "Certain outlaws and their friends have said I wore a steel vest under my shirt. There have been times when I'd have welcomed such a garment, but I never saw one in my life outside of a museum, and I very much doubt that any other frontiersman has, either." [i]

Of course, if Earp did wear a "bullet-proof vest," one wonders if he'd have discussed it. A keenly intelligent and intensely practical man, Earp even in his old age might not have wanted to give away his secrets to potential enemies.

In the early days of current soft body armor, Richard Davis and others tried to keep the concealed vests a "secret weapon," but the media let the cat out of the bag. Earp would have been justified in keeping quiet; as soon as the trumped up NBC White Paper on cop-killer bullets was aired, reminding the TV-watching public that cops might have bullet resistant torsos, we started getting the cases of murdered officers deliberately shot in the head and elsewhere to bypass the armor.

We'll never know, but the possibility exists that Wyatt Earp was the first American law enforcement officer to have worn a ballistic vest concealed under his shirt – and indeed, might have been the first such "save."

SURVIVAL LONG GUNS

The contemporary rule is, "If you know you're going to get into a gunfight, bring a rifle or a shotgun." Earp always did, and his not carrying one on Oct. 26, 1881, is further proof that he didn't intend for the Clanton/McLaury confrontation to escalate to a gun battle.

The shotgun was his favorite weapon, and throughout his law enforcement career he kept short double-barrels stashed in the saloons and gambling halls he frequented, and other strategic locations, often with a shell belt of buckshot rounds.

Today's police firearms instructors are increasingly pushing for carbines – in rifle or pistol calibers – to augment the riot shotguns in their patrol cars. Again, Earp was a step ahead.

He observed, "When mounted on a horse and 'armed to the teeth,' as the saying goes, a man's rifle was slung in a boot just ahead of his right stirrup, his shotgun carried on the left by a thong looped over the saddle-horn.

"With the adoption of breech-loading weapons, a rider equipped with two pistols, rifle, and shotgun customarily had one of the belts to which his pistol holsters were attached filled with pistol ammunition, the other with rifle cartridges, while a heavier, wider belt filled with shotgun shells was looped around the saddle-horn underneath the thong which held that weapon. He was a riding arsenal, but there might well be times when he would need the munitions." [j]

It is quite likely that Wyatt Earp was so equipped when he led the hunt for the men he felt had murdered his brother Morgan, personally killing three of them, two with shotgun blasts and one with his .45 revolver.

CUSTOM COMBAT GUNS

Today's police handgun masters may not carry tricked out guns (though more than one well-known and well-respected police survival instructor wears a pistol with a compact recoil compensator, Bo-Mar sights, and other combat amenities), but almost all have revolvers with slicked up actions and auto pistols with "carry melts" (rounded edges) and "reliability tunes" (all critical internal parts polished, including optimum trigger pull).

Earp is known at one point to have acquired a pair of revolvers second-hand when his employer would have paid for new ones, because he wanted guns that were well broken in, with smooth actions.

He told his biographer, "Cocking and firing mechanisms on new revolvers were almost invariably altered by their purchasers in the interests of smoother, effortless handling, usually by filing the dog which controlled the hammer." He seems to be talking about filing the sear down for a lighter, easier trigger pull.

Speaking of custom guns, did Earp really use the Buntline Special, a Single Action Army .45 with 12-inch barrel supposedly made on special order for him? Earp told Lake that it did indeed happen, and that the long tom revolver was his favorite and was frequently used, including the day he shot down Florentine "Indian Charlie" Cruz, a man he suspected of murdering his brother.

He said that Masterson had cut (his own Buntline Special's barrel) short, but other gunfighters (who received them) kept theirs at one-foot length. Earp didn't feel it slowed him down, and he carried one of his 7 ½-inch single actions on his left hip for backup.

Earp historian Alford Turner says it didn't happen, and that the Colt factory could show no records of such a spe-

cial order. However, Colt authority James E. Serven implies that the guns might indeed have been made up – they just wouldn't have been Buntline's brainchild.

"Revolvers of standard barrel length were sometimes used with the detachable stock (as allegedly came with the Buntline Specials)," wrote Serven, "as well as those with the longer barrels, up to 16 inches in length. Colt advertised that the cost of these special long barrels was $1 per inch over the standard 7 ½-inch maximum." [k]

LAWMAN AS HUNTER

The old NYPD Stakeout Squad preferred hunters for their dangerous job, primarily because such men had a proven ability to sit and observe a danger scene with a gun in their hand for long periods of time without their mind wandering or their alertness fading.

Their ability to hit moving, live targets at unmeasured distances didn't hurt, either, nor did the fact that they'd already proven that they could fire bullets into living flesh.

Earp had been a professional buffalo hunter in the Indian Nations during his early 20s. Though he sometimes used the traditional buffalo rifle, he preferred the shotgun.

He explained, "My system for hunting buffalo was to work my way on foot nearer to the herds than the rifle-users liked to locate. The shorter range of my shotgun made this necessary, but I could fire the piece as rapidly as I wished without harming it. I planned to get within 50 yards of the buffalo before I started shooting, and at that range pick off selected animals. I would shoot until I had downed all the skinner and I could handle that day." [l]

Not abusing his guns seems an incongruous concern for a man who frequently used his revolver as a club, but Earp was keenly aware that the man who held the record for the most buffalo kills from a single stand had ruined his expensive Sharps rifle. He didn't see that as a problem with a slug-loaded shotgun at 50 yards, or closer. He claimed to have made a very good living at it while it lasted.

Earp's friends and contemporaries Bat Masterson and Bill Tilghman were also successful buffalo hunters, whose skills learned in that environment served them well later when they shot for survival.

From Charlie Askins to Jim Cirillo to Dave Wheeler and many others, champion shooters of the 20th century have traditionally fared dramatically better in gunfights than their less-skilled brother officers.

Wyatt Earp's experience seems to be a precursor of this survival reality, too. Though he never sailed for England to test his revolver skills against Walter Winans at Bisley, Earp apparently shot in the informal matches that were frequently held at the edges of the cowtowns, and seems to have done well.

UNTOUCHABLE FACTOR

There is one vital component of police survival that can only be found within. The best instructors can inspire it, but they can never directly transfer it. This is the ability to unswervingly face danger in the line of duty, ignore and suppress absolute terror, and prevail.

Writing in 1907 of the Western gunfighters he had known, Bat Masterson, quoted here by Don Chaput, had this to say about his old friend: "Wyatt Earp is one of the few men I personally knew in the West in the early days, whom I regarded as absolutely destitute of physical fear.

"I have often remarked, and I am not alone in my conclusion, that what goes for courage in a man is generally the fear of what others will think of him – in other words, personal bravery is largely made of self-respect, egotism, and an apprehension of the opinions of others.

"Wyatt Earp's daring and apparent recklessness in time of danger is wholly characteristic; personal fear doesn't enter into the equation, and when everything is said and done, I believe he values his own opinion of himself more than that of others, and it is his own good report that he seeks to preserve." [m]

Wyatt Earp, dead these many years, is back in the limelight today. I picture a young probationary rookie coming home from a tough day on the job and relaxing in front of the home screen with a tape of Tombstone or Kevin Kostner's Wyatt Earp.

Certainly, there were dark sides to the man that veteran cops will recognize from the workplace. I wouldn't want the hypothetical young officer to steal the lady of a brother cop, nor dump his previous significant other so cruelly that she committed suicide, nor pistol-whip suspects who were aggressive with him, nor hang out with psychopathic killers like Doc Holliday. History shows us that Earp did all these things.

At the same time, there were strong things in Wyatt Earp, things that make him by and large a damn good role model for anyone, in any time, who undertakes the difficult and thankless job of going armed in harm's way to preserve the public safety.

Footnotes

[a] Askins, Charles, *Gunfighters,* Washington: NRA Publications, 1981, P. 3.

[b] Lake, Stuart, *Wyatt Earp: Frontier Marshal*, Cambridge: Riverside Press, 1931, pp. 33 and 37.

[c] Ibid., pp. 40-41, and 38.

[d] Ibid., pp.37-38.

[e] DeArment, Robert, *Bat Masterson: the Man and the Legend,* Norman and London: University of Oklahoma Press, 1979, P. 78.

[f] Jordan, Bill, *No Second Place Winner,* 1965, Police Bookshelf, pp. 106-7

[g] Lake, op. cit., p. 39.

[h] Turner, Alford E., editor, *The O.K. Corral Inquest,* College Station, TX: Creative Publishing Company, 1981.

[i] Lake, op. cit., p. 38.

[j] Ibid., p. 38

[k] Serven, James E., *Colt Firearms From 1836,* Santa Ana: Foundation Press, 1967, p. 221.

[l] Lake, op. cit., p.53.

[m] Caput, Don, *The Earp Papers: In a Brother's Image,* Encampment, WY, Allied Writers of America, pp.205-207.

❧

The gunfights of Col. Charles Askins, Jr. took place primarily in the second quarter of the last century, spilling over into the 1950s. He remained on the scene for decades thereafter as one of the leading authorities on firearms and gunfighting. Earp was alive in Askins' younger days, and while there's no evidence that Charlie ever sought him out to pick his brain, we know that Askins studied his exploits and those of the other Western handgun artists who painted in hot lead. Indeed, in his later years, Askins would write a book about Earp and others of Earp's period, titled *Gunfighters*. I knew Askins, visited him at his home in Texas, and chatted with him when we'd meet at the annual gun industry trade shows, first the one for sporting goods wholesalers, and later the SHOT (Shooting, Hunting, and Outdoor Trade) Show.

There was, and still is, much to learn from him.

SECOND QUARTER 20TH CENTURY: CHARLES ASKINS, JR.[2]

The death of Col. Charles Askins, Jr. closed a hell-for-leather life that lasted nine decades. He was a national pistol champion, one of the first winners of the Outstanding American Handgunner of the Year Award, and a big game hunter with an impressive collection of trophies from all

CHARLIE ASKINS studied the Old West gunfighters in his younger days, and wrote about them later in his life.

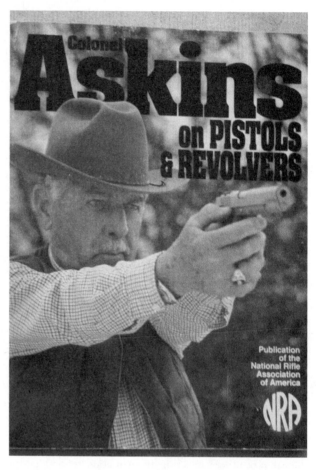

COL. ASKINS as he appeared later in life, posing with a customized 1911 for the cover of one of his many books. He had shot 2- and 4-legged creatures with 1911s, and won a National Championship with one. He left us a rich legacy of gunfight survival knowledge.

over the world. He aggressively sought out maximum action in his careers, first as a lawman and then as a soldier.

He was also a stone cold killer. For those of us who knew him, there was just no gentler way to put it.

Charlie's contemporary, Bill Jordan, once said that killing your first man is the hardest and after that it gets easier, but for a certain kind of man, it can get too easy. Some thought old Bill was talking about Charlie. Not without reason did Askins title his autobiography *Unrepentant Sinner*.

Any future history of 20th century gunfighters will have to devote a substantial chapter to Col. Askins. The son of a prominent hunter and gunwriter, Junior followed in Senior's footprints and left some marks deeper than his dad.

Charles Askins, Jr. killed dozens of men, both in war and on the streets. When asked for an official body count, the Colonel replied, "Twenty-seven, not counting (blacks) and Mexicans."

Askins was bright, thoughtful, and without fear, but he had a darker side. The man's prejudices spoke for themselves. Charlie once confessed to a friend that he thought he was a psychopathic killer, and that he hunted animals so avidly because he wasn't allowed to hunt men anymore.

He was sometimes too willing to kill. A reading of *Unrepentant Sinner* shows confessions to murder and manslaughter. Yet among the many Askins gunfights, there were also acts of heroism, shootouts against the odds that he won with his coolness under fire and his deadly marksmanship.

He spent a lot of his life teaching assorted Good Guys to win firefights, and when the Final Ledger is tallied, one hopes that is taken into account on the credit side.

Let's examine some of the life-saving lessons Askins left behind.

Askins learned early that a rifle or shotgun always beats a sidearm when trouble is in the offing. His favorites includ-

CLOSEUP OF THE COVER of the book Gun Fighters by Col. Charles Askins, Jr. That's Charlie (a southpaw) in the drawing, taken from a famous photo of Askins. Note that the revolver is a Colt New Service with cutaway trigger guard and King sight rib, a motif Askins favored, and that the holster is a Berns-Martin breakfront. His contemporary Bill Jordan later spoke of how fast Askins was with that combination.

ed the lever action Savage Model 99 in caliber .250/3000. For close work, he was partial to the Remington Model 11, a clone of the Browning 12 gauge Automatic-5, with an extended magazine. Night sights not yet being available, he tied a white bandage around the muzzle to index the weapon in the dark.

Askins put the speed of fire to good use. He wrote of one shootout in East El Paso, where he employed a Winchester .351 semiautomatic carbine:

"One night at the foot of Piedras Street, which runs slapbang into Cordoba Island, a team of (Border) Patrol officers watched a gang of smugglers scramble out of the willows in the river bottom and pile their load of liquor into an old Hudson sedan.

"Then the cargadores turned and raced nimbly for the protection of the Mex side of the line. Three cholos piled into the old car and commenced to drive away. The BP vehicle pulled up beside the runner's vehicle and, with guns drawn, we motioned the driver to halt.

"The Hudson came to a stop just as I set foot on the

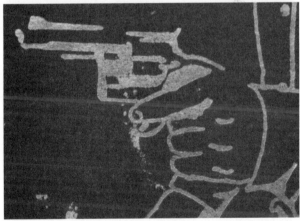

ground. The officer who was in the rear seat also alighted. The driver of the gov't vehicle threw the door open on the left side and hit the ground. He stepped down just as a gunman sitting beside the driver of the old Hudson swung a Model 94 carbine behind the driver's head and let go at the Patrol officer in front.

"He was struck in the head by the .38/55 bullet and fell dead. The bullet broke up in his skull and a major fragment exited and by a strange coincidence struck the patrolman alighting from the back seat in the head. It did not kill him, but knocked him unconscious.

"Thus in the space of two heartbeats and with only a single round, the contrabandista had knocked out two patrolmen and had only myself to contend with.

"I ran round behind the smuggler's car and opened fire. I shot the gunman through the eye, the bullet exiting through his temple. I kept right on firing and shot the driver through the kidneys. He later died. A third smuggler in the back seat cautiously poked a sixshooter up over the back seat and got shot through the hand for his pains.

"By this time I was busy reloading. The gunman, despite the fact that he had a bullet through his right eye which had passed out through his temple, managed to pull the driver from beneath the wheel and with him out of the way, got in the driver's seat and drove the old sedan for a couple of blocks down the street where he crashed it into a tree.

"The Border Patrol in those days, as I have said, had no radio communication. I cranked up the old patrol car, after loading the dead and wounded, and got to a telephone and called Patrol headquarters. Before the night was done the trio, the dead and wounded, were all rounded up. It had been a big evening. I did not feel much regrets over the loss of the patrolman. I had never liked him much anyway. The second lad, who picked up a jacket fragment, was not seriously hurt." [n]

BLUE WHISTLERS

On another night, Askins used the Remington autoloading shotgun, loaded with the 00 buckshot he called "blue whistlers." He recounted:

"They came out of the shadows and, as it was brightest moonlight, I could see every manjack had a long gun in his hands. We let them get up to within nine paces of us and I fired the first shot.

"I had the old Remington with its 9-shot magazine and I knocked down the first two rannies in as many shots. I then switched my attention to the other three who did not like the heat. They ran back into Mexico, a distance of about 60 yards, and opened fire.

"An interesting facet of this little exchange was that the lobo in the lead had an old Smith & Wesson .44 Russian. Despite the fact that he had a load of my 00 buckshot through his middle and one of the boys had hit him spang on the breastbone with a .351 slug, he dropped to his knees behind a cottonwood sapling and kept right on firing.

"The .44 Russian is a single-action and this bravo had to thumb the hammer back for each shot. He got off three rounds before a second charge of my buckshot ended his career.

"Quite as interesting, really, was the second gunman who had a Westley Richards 10 gauge loaded with Win-

chester High Speed #5 shot. We had killed him before he could touch off either barrel. A most happy circumstance since the distance between both parties was only nine steps. I have the Westley Richards today, a memento of lively times long past." [o]

Today, (an attorney such as) Johnnie Cochran would be hired by the families of the deceased to sue Charlie and the whole Border Patrol for opening fire on the heavily armed gang without warning. Yet doing as they did undoubtedly saved multiple Patrolmen from being killed or maimed. As the saying goes, "Things were different then."

WEAPON RETENTION

Weapon retention is the art and science of retaining control of your firearm when the criminal tries to disarm you and turn your firearm against you. Plan A is to execute a technique and peel the offender off the gun. If that can't be achieved, Plan B is to shoot him.

There wasn't much in the way of gun retention techniques in Charlie's time, and Plan B was his Plan A. He made it work more than once. He recounted the following in (the) *American Handgunner* Annual in 1988:

"I got to my feet and made a run at this coyote and just as I reached him, I tripped and fell down. This bastardo, as quick as a cat, grabbed my gun, which I had drawn, and standing over me commenced to tussle enthusiastically to get it away.

"I had no illusions as to what he'd do if he succeeded. He had thoughtfully wrapped his hands around the cylinder and while I had my finger on the trigger I could not fire the weapon because he would not permit the cylinder to turn.

"Very energetically I rolled up on my shoulders and kicked this sonofabitch in the belly. It broke him loose from my pistol. He wasted no time. He ran for the river which was only 30 steps away. I saw him very clearly against all the lights of Juarez and I let him run until he was in the Old Rio Grande up to his knees.

"I held the gold bead front sight in the white-outlined rear notch and put the gold right in his back just at the belt line. On the shot he pitched forward as though spanked with a baseball bat.

"Three days later the BP Chief told me, 'They dragged a dead Mex out of the river of the Socorro Headgates yesterday. The U.S. Consul in Juarez told me.' I didn't say anything. I wasn't any too proud of the fact that I had stumbled and the wetback had almost killed me with my own

Well-known Border Patrol officer, crack shot, and contemporary gunfighter Colonel Charles Askins carried this modified .38 Colt in many skirmishes on the Mexican border. An escaped convict and a German sniper in World War II were downed with gun. Askins's weapon of choice on the border was a specially modified revolver that shot two men during WWII.

IN LARRY WILSON'S EXCELLENT BOOK The Peacemakers (Chartwell Books, 2004), we find this photo of Charlie Askins' personalized New Service .38, with which he shot at least two men during WWII. Charlie donated it to his good friend John Bianchi for John's museum.

gun. (A customized Colt New Service .44-40)."

The colonel continued, in the same issue of the magazine:

"One chill evening, it was January 1931, we jumped out a big gang of smugglers in the Standpipes district. We halted them on the levee and I ran up to the bunch and some bravo reached out and caught the old Remington by the muzzle and gave it a hell of a jerk. He aimed to catch me by surprise and get my gun, which you may be sure he'd have reversed in a twinkling and given me a dose of those big 00 pellets.

"He jerked on the muzzle and I jerked on the forestock and the pistol grip. As I gave the gun a hell of a tug, I pulled the trigger. The charge of buckshot got this coyote right through the left eye. The force lifted him completely off his feet and pitched him some four to five feet off the levee. The back of his head was quite a mess.

"I reckon I was just too impetuous in those days, for it wasn't three months later until we ran up on another gang of freebooters, this time near the Nichols Packing Plant. I got too close to the leader and he grabbed my gun muzzle and tried to whip it out of my hands. He jerked in his direction and I jerked in mine – and I pulled the trigger.

"The nine big slugs took him right above the knee. The City-County Hospital took his leg off the next morning. The worthless scoundrel had syphilis and the last I heard the amputation would not heal. I reckon it sorta put an end to his river hopping." [P]

Charlie's actions in the two shotgun grabs would almost certainly be ruled justifiable even today. The shooting of the fleeing man who had grabbed his Colt revolver unsuccessfully, however, would probably be seen as excessive force in light of the Supreme Court's mid-(19)80s Garner decision.

Askins had no patience with suspects who grabbed police guns. One of his partners was pistol-whipped almost to death by a hobo who had disarmed him of his Colt 1917 .45 revolver. The patrolman had already sustained multiple skull fractures and brain damage from the clubbed revolver when Askins stopped the assault.

At a distance of 10 paces, he killed the assailant with three shots in the chest, double-action, from his pet .44-40 New Service 4-inch with D.W. King sights, the weapon the previously mentioned suspect tried to take from him near Juarez.

ASKINS' TECHNIQUES

When he was actively in the field, Askins seems to have almost always fired the sidearm one-handed. In his later years he would enthusiastically recommend two-hand positions for defense, but he was not an early advocate of the concept.

It would appear that in most of his shootings, Askins aimed rather than pointed. He practiced a good deal, drawing and firing from the point-shooter's crouch position, but practiced more with a sight picture at arm's length for the matches.

He wrote that during one 10-year period, he logged 334,000 practice shots. Though in some articles late in his career he had good things to say about point-shooting, I can find mention of only two such incidents in his personal reminiscences of gunfights.

One was a mistaken identity shooting in which he exchanged shots in an alley with a rifle-armed U.S. Customs agent. The distance was 10 yards. The man with the rifle fired twice and missed both times. Askins also fired twice; one shot missed, and one struck the other man's rifle stock.

He point-fired (in that instance) because he had to; his gun that night was a Colt New Service .45 sixgun, its barrel chopped to two inches with no front sight.

He would write later, "To say that I took a ribbing was an understatement compared to the comments over firing two shots at another feller at 30 feet, down a narrow alley, and missing him. It was a disgrace which took a long time to live down!" [q]

Charlie later mentioned that he had point-shot without a specific sight picture when he shot the man who was pistol-whipping his brother officer. Reading Askins' own account, he seems mildly surprised that he hit him shooting like that.

He wrote, "Each time one of the big flat-nosed 240 grain slugs hit him, it brought forth a little puff of dust. This 'bo had been riding the freight for several days and his clothing was full of dust. I cannot begin to tell you how happy it made me to see those bullets raise that dust! It made my day, believe me!" [r]

ASKINS' GUNS

A southpaw, Askins liked ambidextrous autoloaders and lever actions for long guns – the Savage Model 99, the .351 Winchester and the 12 ga. Remington. The latter, he said, was cut to 22-inch barrel length for him by J.D. Buchanan, who also affixed a full length extended magazine that held eight shells, bringing total capacity to nine rounds.

For a time when it first came out, Askins carried a 4-inch Smith & Wesson .357 Magnum in a Berns-Martin breakfront holster, although I can find no mention in his work of him ever using it in a gunfight. Virtually all his

shootings with handguns found him using one or another Colt; not until the very end of his man-killing days would he shoot a human with a Smith & Wesson.

Askins began his law enforcement career as a forest ranger, using a stock GI 1911 .45 auto swapped from his lifelong best friend George Parker. "It was stamped 'U.S. Property' and had been purloined from the ordnance stores at Fort Huachuca," Charlie later admitted. He wore it in a Sam Myres holster. This was also his first sidearm when he joined the Border Patrol, but he quickly switched to a Colt New Service .44-40 with 4-inch barrel.

The large-frame Colt double action was always an Askins favorite. The sawed-off snubnose version he had acquired for plainclothes wear quickly fell out of his favor when, sans sights, he fortunately missed the two shots he fired in the mistaken identity incident.

The same big gun in its long-barreled .38 Special target format, the Shooting Master, was Askins' choice in the centerfire class of bullseye pistol, the discipline in which he captured 534 medals, 117 trophies, and the National Championship of the United States. When he became chief firearms instructor for the Border Patrol, he again showed his preference, though his choice of caliber was surprising. He wrote:

"As the Great Depression eased somewhat, the Border Patrol at my insistence purchased new revolvers for the entire service. I had small love for the Smith & Wesson, a dislike which I share to this day, and so I elected the Colt New Service in .38 Spl. caliber. The revolver had a 4-inch barrel, fixed sight, and a square butt.

"There were 642 revolvers purchased, at a cost to the U.S. Gov't of $19 each. I had the entire shipment sent to me in El Paso. I shot each revolver and sighted it in. The sights were all the fixed type, the front sight was a great upstanding chunk of metal and the rear sight was a rectangular notch cut into the top strap. I made a tool to bend the front sight either right or left to bring the gun to zero, I filed down the front sight if the gun shot low and filled (sic) the rear notch if it shot high." [s]

In the .22 events, Askins shot a Colt Woodsman auto with a lead weight under the barrel. In the .45 category, his choice was a Colt Government tuned by the same "Buck" Buchanan who had tuned his shotgun and was now working for the legendary Frank Pachmayr.

In the national individual championship, an externally-stock GI .45 was required, and Askins used one that Buchanan and Pachmayr had internally accurized and fitted with a 4 lb. trigger.

This was one of the guns he took with him to the European Theater in World War II. He swapped between it and his personal New Service .38, that one fitted with a King sight rib and a cutaway trigger guard. He shot men with both guns.

He used 230 gr. Ball in the .45 and Winchester's slow 200 gr. Super Police roundnose lead in the .38. Askins believed that an accurate handgun with a smooth action, sighted to point-of-aim, made the most sense as a defensive sidearm.

LAST DEAD MAN

Based on his autobiography, the last man he killed was in 1957. Charlie was a U.S. military advisor in Vietnam. While hunting in the jungle one day, he ran across a Viet Minh soldier. Askins was carrying a Savage .358 lever action rifle (with which he had blown away a couple of other Viet Minh who interrupted his hunting on another occasion) but chose to draw his new Smith & Wesson Model 29 and fire it left hand only.

"I let the ambusher have the first 240 gr. slug right through the ribs on the left side. It was probably the first man ever killed with the .44 (Magnum) because it was quite new in those days," Askins observed casually. He finished the man with a second shot to the throat. [t]

In his later life – I got to know him in the early 1970s – he told me he generally carried one or another single-action .45 auto. At one time Charlie was quite partial to the small, lightweight Star PD.

FINAL LESSONS

I knew Charlie Askins as a man who was fun to drink with, but a man you wouldn't want to get drunk with. He was an adoring husband and father, a lover of horses and a sucker for stray dogs. When his many fans wrote him, he answered them promptly and (usually) politely. Perhaps it was a natural compensation for the part of him that went beyond survival euphoria in the pleasure he took after killing a man.

I've heard people comment, "Whatever else you say about Askins, he sure didn't suffer from that 'post shooting trauma' stuff." I beg to differ.

One of the virtually inescapable things in the aftermath of killing is what Dr. Walter Gorski defined as "Mark of Cain syndrome." This is the sense that having killed people has changed the way that others look at you, and the way you look at yourself.

There is no doubt that this was true of Charles Askins.

The men he had killed, and the gunfights he survived, defined him in a very real way. Not just to others, but to himself. You didn't have to know him and talk to him to see it. It was inescapably visible in the body of his written work.

There were facets of Charlie that I wouldn't want in a cop. There was racism. There was a killer instinct, too strong, strong enough to sometimes slip its leash. Some of his shootings, if they'd been adjudicated, could have earned him "life without parole."

Yet Charlie was also the man who first organized firearms training in the Border Patrol, laying a foundation that sees that agency today as one of the world's leaders in law enforcement gunfight survival.

His tenacity, his courage, his coolness and above all his skill at arms are qualities we can all strive to emulate, though few of us will manifest them to the degree that he did.

Let that be the legacy of Col. Charles Askins, Jr. May he rest in peace.

Footnotes
[n] Charles Askins, *Unrepentant Sinner,* San Antonio: Tejano Publications, 1985, 58-59.
[o] Ibid. 59-60.
[p] Charles Askins, "Ride the River With Colonel Askins," *American Handgunner* Annual 1988: 52-55.
[q] Askins, *Unrepentant* 81.
[r] Askins, "Ride the River," 51.
[s] *Unrepentant* 75-76.
[t] *Unrepentant* 245.

⤺

Charlie Askins had a lot of fans. I was (and remain) one of them. After the comments above came out in *American Handgunner* magazine, some folks thought I was unduly harsh on Charlie. I respectfully disagree. Charlie saw himself as a man-killer, and was proud of the gunfights he had survived. I knew him, and I think he would have liked the article.

Another man I knew was Jim Cirillo, whose gunfights took place in the 1960s and '70s. Charlie and Jim knew each other and got along well. Both pistol champions, they well understood how skill and confidence developed on the range carried over into actual gunfights. Both set trends in both the competition world and the world of combative handgun training.

JIM CIRILLO WAS A DYNAMIC SPEAKER and a most impressive teacher. He spent the second half of his career teaching both cops and armed citizens to survive gunfights as he had.

THIRD QUARTER 20TH CENTURY: THE LESSONS OF JIM CIRILLO[3]

Situation: A master shooter applies his skills to a high-risk felony squad…and learns that there is more to gunfighting than shooting.

Lessons: One of the last of the modern master gunfighters, Jim Cirillo left us a rich legacy of wise advice.

On July 13, 2007 – Friday the 13th, oddly enough – I received a phone call from Jim Cirillo, Jr. He told me his father had been killed in a traffic accident the night before. As I set the phone down, I was flooded with the memories of a man I had known for some 35 years. Gun enthusiasts and trainers knew him as the epitome of the modern police gunfighter.

He was one of the most misunderstood men I've ever known. Too many never got past the trigger finger to see the heart and the mind of Jim Cirillo. A cop on NYPD for a decade before he had to kill a man, six or so tumultuous, bullet shattered years on the famed Stakeout Unit (SOU) defined him in the public eye. It was easy to forget that after he retired from The City, his next career as an in-

JIM CIRILLO shares some pointers with the author.

structor – first with US Customs, then at the Federal Law Enforcement Training Center, and at last in the private sector after he "retired" – saw him save even more lives than those future deaths he prevented when he shot down vicious armed robbers who gave him no choice.

Jim wrote an excellent book still available from Paladin Press, *Guns, Bullets, and Gunfights*. If you're serious about armed self-defense, it belongs in your library as surely as *Cooper on Handguns* and *No Second Place Winner*. The direct quotes that follow, unless otherwise noted, come from that important book.

CIRILLO, A PASSIONATE DEFENDER of the Second Amendment, lectures at Andy Stanford's historic Snubby Summit in Titusville FL, 2005.

Jim could have written another, perhaps in several volumes, on his own experiences in this vein. I can't cover all Jim's incidents in the 3000 words I'm allotted here. I'll cover three of them. If the choice of those particular incidents surprises you, it probably indicates that you didn't know Jim Cirillo.

THE DAIRY STORE

Cirillo's first gunfight was his most famous. It occurred just two hours into his very first stakeout with the new unit. Three armed robbers hit a New York City dairy store. They positioned themselves in such a way that Cirillo's partner, armed with a buckshot-loaded shotgun, could not fire for fear of hitting customers. Only Cirillo had an acceptable shooting angle. He told the story in his book:

"I was never so terrified in my whole life. They never told me in the academy that the targets were going to jump and move all over the place. There wasn't one three-by-two-foot target to shoot at like on the police range. One gunman only gave me a six inch circle of his moving head to shot at. The other two jumped behind the cashier and only exposed about nine inches of their bodies on each side of her.

During those hectic microseconds when I popped up from concealment, my protective crotch piece fell off my bullet-resistant vest. I prayed that none of the gunmen would hit me in what I considered a most vital area.

"When the metal nylon-covered crotch piece fell to the floor with a resounding clunk, all three turned toward the sound and pointed their handguns in my direction. The next thing I knew, I heard shots. I felt my Model 10 Smith & Wesson bucking in my hands, and I was asking myself mentally, 'Who the hell is shooting my gun?'

"When the smoke cleared, I did not see one gunman anywhere. I cursed myself for the fear that overcame me and was terribly embarrassed by what I thought was a

FROM LEFT: Walt Rauch, Jim Cirillo, and Mas Ayoob at the Snubby Summit in 2005.

total loss of control and accuracy. When the cashier told me that one robber was still there, I quickly drew my second revolver, but she stated, 'Don't worry. He isn't going anywhere.' As I jumped down from the manager's booth where I was positioned, I was partially relieved that at least I had stopped one of the robbers."

He had done better than he knew. The robber who wasn't going anywhere was mortally wounded by a bullet through the brain. Jim had hit him three times in the head with 110 grain Super Vel semi-jacketed hollow point .38 Special. Two of the bullets had skidded off his skull, leaving him up and running. The third had ended his deadly threat.

The other two thugs had escaped, one half-carrying the other. Both were arrested that day when they attempted to seek treatment for gunshot wounds. Cirillo had hurt each of them badly enough to make them desperately flee the fight.

Sergeant Joe Volpato, acting commander of the Stakeout Unit when I visited there in the early 1970s, told me that reconstruction showed that Cirillo had fired six rounds, and shot all three armed felons, in three seconds.

Jim told me that at the beginning of the fight, he was so scared his tongue was stuck to the roof of his mouth, but when his .38 came up and he saw a sight picture, a strange

JIM CIRILLO SHOWS ONE OF HIS FANS the fine points of fitting a revolver. Despite his star-level reputation, he was a friendly, self-effacing man with an earthy sense of humor.

calm seemed to descend upon him, as if something was telling him that he was in his world, on his turf, now. Automatic pilot took over as his finger rolled the trigger, the way it did in PPC matches, of which he had already won so many. Jim experienced a phenomenon known as psychological splitting, a sense that there were two of him. There was a passive, Conscious Jim, who focused on the front sights and watched the blurred figures he was aiming at react to the shots, as Conscious Jim thought to

A four-inch heavy barrel S&W Model 10 .38 Special like this one was Cirillo's primary handgun in his gunfights. This one has S&W finger groove grips; Cirillo made his own to fit his hands.

himself, "Who the hell is shooting my gun?" And there was the active, Subconscious Jim, who was tracking the moving targets and smoothly stroking the double action S&W's trigger.

Cirillo would later write, "I could not comprehend how I was able to take out three gunmen when I was so consumed with fear prior to the gunfight. I dared not speak of the strange phenomenon where I felt that someone else was shooting my revolver. Later, I understood that this miraculous reaction, which most probably saved my life, came from the subconscious…It was now evident to me that the subconscious can take over during moments of great stress. When it does take over, it is infallible – it can only achieve perfection. The shots that I made in that first gunfight were so precise and so quick that I have never been able to duplicate the feat at a range on paper targets."

To fully understand why Jim's performance that day, some forty years ago, has become so widely recognized as a genuine "feat of arms," one has to remember the distances involved. Jim fired those shots at 60 to 75 feet – up to 25 yards – from the perpetrators, in a crowded market, shooting two of the perps out from behind a human shield.

AUTHOR MET CIRILLO circa 1972 and became friends with him. Perhaps modeling on Cirillo's belief that handgun hunting was useful for self-defense, he nailed this Corsican ram at 76 yards at Y-O Ranch, firing double action with Hal Swiggett's six-inch Moran Custom Colt Python and the then-new 125 grain Remington .357 Magnum hollow point.

THE KID

You won't find this one in Jim's book, because he titled that *Guns, Bullets, and Gunfights*, and this story would have been off topic. I wish he had written another book and called it *The Job*. I suspect this incident would have been one of the first chapters.

I once asked Jim which of all his encounters he was

most proud of. It turned out to be an incident where he and his partner looked through the one-way glass at the stakeout scene and saw a young man who obviously had a hidden gun. They were poised to open fire as soon as he made a hostile move, but something told Cirillo that things weren't as they seemed. Telling the partner to cover him, Jim took off his armor and his heavy duty belt with its two .38s and five reloads of ammunition, stuffed one of his Model 10s into his belt to supplement the Colt Cobra he always carried in a pocket, and put on a windbreaker to cover his uniform. Then he slipped out of hiding and out into the store.

Cirillo made his way to the suspect, realizing as he approached that the guy was even younger than he looked through the milky one-way glass. He jumped the suspect, disarmed him, and put him on the floor. By the time the suspect was handcuffed, he and his partner realized that their gunman was a young teenager with a starter pistol.

A supervisor put in for Cirillo to receive a medal for his courage above and beyond the call of duty. It was overruled by higher brass. They had decided that taking off the armor he was supposed to constantly wear on stakeout had violated unit regulations, and thus, could not possibly be rewarded. The NYPD is a department with a lot of heart, but in any organization of more than 30,000 people, it is possible for the heart to be choked by regulations.

THE HOTEL LOBBY

People who didn't know Jim and signed up for one of his classes often expected him to do nothing but brag about his own exploits. Anyone who thought that, didn't know the man. Few American cops have ever earned more "been there, done that" creds in gunfighting, but Jim learned early that no two shootings were likely to be the same, and he was more likely to draw learning points from the many other gunfights he had studied than from his own. One he frequently cited was one in which he participated, but in which his own life was saved by his partner, one of his best friends.

A tip had been routed to the SOU that there would be a robbery at a hotel airport. The commander assigned his two most accomplished marksmen. If memory serves, the site was the Air Host Inn. With Cirillo was his most frequent stakeout partner, Bill Allard. Bill was as good a bulls-eye shooter as Jim was a PPC competitor, though he was no slouch at either game. Allard shot whenever he could as a military reserve at Camp Perry (where he would one

day win a national champion title), and one year there had purchased a beautiful Colt National Match .45 auto. It was his favorite handgun, and as designated firearms instructor for the SOU, he had a loophole that allowed him to carry it "experimentally" on duty even at a time when official regs restricted officers to .38 Special revolvers. While the department mandated issue, non-expanding 158 grain standard pressure lead .38 ammo at the time, the penalties for carrying something else were not as strict as they would be later, and both Cirillo and Allard were fully prepared to endure a slap on the wrist if their non-approved ammo ended a gunfight more quickly. On this particular stakeout, that .45 auto was Allard's primary weapon, and in its chamber – backed up by a magazine of hollow points – was a handload he and Jim had worked out, featuring a cup-point bullet with full wadcutter profile.

Let Jim tell the story: "I had confronted what was supposed to be two juveniles who had previously held up a certain hotel, always with their hands in their pockets. Bill and I had set up a plan with the desk clerk where he would use a code word when speaking to this juvenile team. When we heard the coded word, one of us would go out a side door and cut off their escape.

"Sure enough, the clerk panicked and gave us the code word, only this time it was with a different armed team. As I slipped out the side door, what a surprise I received – both individuals were armed with autos! They both pivoted at my movement. The first gunman swung his weapon in my direction, but I dared not fire with a lobby guest directly in the line of fire. The gunmen then swung their weapons back and forth between me and the clerk. I yelled for them to drop their weapons. I knew the first character was doped up and wasn't going to let anyone get in the way of his next dose. As he swung his weapon back on me, I prayed that his shot would miss my unprotected neck and head.

"It seemed like an eternity before I saw the billowing dust and gun smoke pour out from behind the hotel desk and then heard the shot from Bill's .45. The first gunman reared up from a crouch, walked backward on his heels for about four steps, then fell backward. He was dead before he hit the hotel floor. The second gunman dropped his weapon and ran for the exit. Neither Bill nor I fired for fear of hitting pedestrians outside the hotel entrance.

"At the postmortem examination, we saw that the .45 wadcutter had entered the gunman's sternum, clipped the pericardium sac, and come to rest along the left side of the spine. It had expanded to more than an inch in diameter.

CIRILLO CREDITED MUCH of his gunfight survival to his combat match shooting experience. Here he engages through a low window circa 1999 at the Winter National IDPA Championships at Smith & Wesson Academy.

Had Bill used a standard .45 bullet, I probably would not be writing this…"

Jim so frequently used this incident as a case study in class because it was high in learning points and low in machismo. It pointed up the need to rely on your partner, and the fact that no one person can always manage things alone. Just as movement of innocents in the dairy store had prevented his partner from firing but permitted Jim to shoot because of his slightly elevated position in the manager's booth, the Air Host Inn situation left Cirillo unable to shoot because of the unexpected movement of a hotel guest into his field of fire.

OTHER LESSONS

Cirillo emphasized tactics as much as he did marksmanship. Studying the SOU in the early '70s, I accompanied Stakeout sergeants Tom Derby and Augie Luciente as they scoped out establishments that were candidates for SOU protection. Angles of fire, angles of view, paths of access and egress were all carefully examined. Sometimes, the unit would literally restructure their potential battleground. Installation of one-way mirrors was one of their

JIM CIRILLO, the legendary NYPD Stakeout Unit gunfighter.

favorite strategies. Jim always pointed out to his students the importance of predicting what could happen, and controlling the scene as much as possible before the gunfire erupted, and reminded them that the same principles applied to armed home protection.

He understood that the term "gunfight" is a misnomer. The guns don't fight, the involved human beings do. Cirillo observed that the best gunfighters on the unit were competitive shooters accustomed to shooting accurately under pressure, and hunters, the latter less because they had taken some degree of life than because they had conditioned themselves to watch an area for certain things with unrelenting focus, without being distracted.

Those who came to know Cirillo were often surprised that he was far from the steely-eyed killer they expected to meet based on his reputation. Jim was an ebullient, outgoing man, always smiling and always joking. Facing death had taught him to love life. He was very much a family man, a loving dad to son Jim, Jr. and daughter Margie, and was devastated by the untimely death of his wife and soulmate Mildred. For the last nine years of his life, he found happiness again with partner Violet Martinez. Hunting or fishing, dinner out or just good conversation with friends, Jim was a man who had learned to appreciate – and do something useful with – every minute.

He coped better than many with the fact that he'd repeatedly had to kill men. He had strong religious faith, and that seemed to help him a lot. So did his strong love of family. Jim wrote, "The family man…was even more superior, for he took fewer chances. He wanted to go home. He wasn't about to let some beast of prey hurt him. He gave us safety and deliberation."

Not all of his colleagues coped so well as he. The SOU had a high incidence of cardiovascular problems, ulcers, PTSD, and other stress-related problems. One member's heart stopped at age 36.

Even Cirillo couldn't escape "post shooting trauma" entirely. One element of that is what police psychologist Walter Gorski described as "Mark of Cain syndrome," the situation of being seen by others primarily as a killer instead of the good person you are. Jim learned that despite strong recommendation for promotion by the superiors who knew him, it had been turned down farther up the NYPD food chain by a commissioner who had said, "If we promote Cirillo, it would be telling all the young cops who come on the job that we promote cops who kill."

THREE MEN, COMPARED

The comparisons between Wyatt Earp, Charlie Askins, and Jim Cirillo are striking. All three were hunters, for one thing. Earp did it professionally; Askins did it throughout his life, recreationally (and in a sense professionally, since his written legacy is rich with tales of hunts around the world); and Cirillo was an avid hunter who used handguns almost exclusively.

Each man shot in competition. Earp appears to have done so casually, in the format of informal matches, but organized competition with handguns was embryonic in his time. Askins was a national champion and won many state and regional championships. Cirillo had won the state championships of New York and New Jersey at the time of his first gun battle.

All of them made it clear they'd rather be holding a rifle or a shotgun than a handgun when trouble started, but religiously carried sidearms throughout their lives for the moments when trouble came on them by surprise and the portable pistol would be all they had. Earp used one or another single action Colt .45 at the O.K. Corral and to kill Florentino Cruz, but used a shotgun to kill Frank Stilwell in the train station shooting and Curly Bill Brocius in the gun battle at Iron Springs. After Earp's death, his widow supposedly told a researcher that Wyatt had used a rifle to kill Johnny Ringo, a shooting for which he never personally took credit. Charlie Askins killed his various opponents with double action revolver and with semiautomatic pistol, with assorted rifles and the .351 Winchester carbine, and with shotguns. Jim Cirillo shot all his opponents with either a Smith & Wesson Model 10 .38 Special revolver, or a 14-inch-barrel Ithaca Model 37 12 gauge pump gun. He never mentioned shooting anyone with a rifle, but noted that the .30 caliber M1 Carbine with 110 grain expanding bullets had worked remarkably well for some other members of the Stakeout Squad.

All of them understood the rationale of the backup gun. You see Earp's explanation here earlier, in his words to his biographer Stuart Lake. Charlie Askins didn't mention it often, but in a mid-century article on hideout guns in one of the Gun Digest publications he mentioned that he often carried a short-barrel .38 revolver concealed as a backup weapon. While on the Stakeout Squad, where each officer was required to carry two handguns in addition to the issue long gun, Jim Cirillo wore a four-inch heavy barrel

Model 10 as the primary duty sidearm on his right hip, a second Model 10 with tapered four-inch barrel as his secondary (worn butt-forward on his left hip, accessible to either hand), and his ever-present two-inch barrel Colt Cobra .38 with hammer shroud in a pocket. He told me that on some particularly high risk jobs, he would have a fourth handgun, a totally-forbidden-by-the-department Walther PPK .380 auto, tucked behind his waistband in case he was surprised from behind at gunpoint, patted down, and disarmed of everything else.

All three of these men had custom guns that became their trademarks to one degree or another. For Earp, of course, it was the Buntline Special. I've discussed this with Western historian Lee Silva, who is convinced that Earp did indeed own a long-barrel Colt (more likely ten-inch than twelve in barrel length), and according to Lake, Earp used it to kill Florentino Cruz, one of the men he held responsible for the murder of his brother Morgan. Many years before Colt brought out their distinctive Python with ventilated rib barrel, Charlie Askins had a King vented barrel rib complete with adjustable sights on a Colt New Service .38 Special he shot men with, in the European Theater during World War II. Among gun enthusiasts, Charlie earned fame for coming up with the idea of a gun that would absolutely dominate the Centerfire class at the National Bullseye Championships, a game then dominated by thumb-cocked .38 Special revolvers. It was a .22 Colt Woodsman target autoloader, converted to work with a centerfire small caliber French Velo Dog, a low-power, light-recoil cartridge then technically legal for the game. He got so many accusations of cheating that he never actually used the modified pistol there, and the National Rifle Association was so shaken by the whole "Askins Affair" that it changed the rules to make .32 caliber the smallest that could be used in the Centerfire matches. Jim Cirillo is believed to have been the first man to use a "PPC gun" in PPC shooting, getting his friend Austin Behlert to put a massive one-inch diameter barrel on a Model 10 frame. The trend he began would change the game, with that type of custom revolver dominating utterly for decades. And all, of course, made sure to carry guns with particularly smooth actions for "serious business," with Askins and Cirillo employing the best gunsmiths to achieve the smoothest trigger pulls, and Cirillo often doing his own action work.

All were very strong family men. Earp's loyalty to his brothers is legendary, and the ambushes that killed Mor-

gan Earp and permanently crippled older brother Virgil led Wyatt on the famed Vengeance Ride that left a trail of deserving corpses. Earp's first wife died young, and his second long-term common law relationship ended badly, but he was totally devoted to Josephine Sarah "Sadie" Marcus from a time beginning before the O.K. Corral incident to the day of his death so many decades later. Throughout Askins' writing we can see his utter devotion to his father. You have to dig harder to find his long, devoted marriage to his wife, though his love for his sons shone through in much of his writing. Cirillo, too, was deeply dedicated to family. Jim wrote that the men who felt that way were more likely survivors; they knew what they were surviving for, and therefore, fought harder and took fewer foolish chances.

There is much to be learned from men such as these.

[1] First appeared as "Wyatt Earp: the First Practitioner of Officer Survival" by Massad Ayoob, *American Handgunner* magazine, March/April 1995.

[2] First appeared as "The Gunfights of Col. Charles Askins," in the "Ayoob Files" series in *American Handgunner* magazine, November/December 1999.

[3] First appeared as "The Lessons of Jim Cirillo," in the "Ayoob Files" series in *American Handgunner* magazine, January/February 2008.

IN COMPETITION, you can run with the big dogs, and learn from them. This is world champ Dave Sevigny, with his trademark Glock.

104

CHAPTER FOUR

COMPETITION AS TRAINING

E *"Every bit of information that may be picked up on the range will prove useful in war. True, it will not always – nor often – be possible to assume the exact, orthodox positions used in competitions and there is the matter of adjusting oneself – mentally and physically – to the stress and strain of battle but, just the same, all those fundamental principles will have an important, even if sub-conscious influence, tending to increase the rifleman's effectiveness."*

--From Herbert W. McBride's introduction to his classic book, A Rifleman Went to War

Earlier in this book, we saw that one thing Wyatt Earp, Charlie Askins, and Jim Cirillo had in common was that they competed in the pistol matches of their time. All seemed to feel that this experience stood them well when they had to "compete" against men who were pointing their guns at them instead of at the same bank of targets as they were.

Early in my career I had the good fortune to know and be mentored by Lt. Frank McGee, the legendary NYPD firearms trainer. Frank was the one who turned the department's firearms training unit into the Firearms and Tactics Unit (FTU). He incorporated practical shooting stances instead of target shooting into the marksmanship side of it. He was the first on NYPD to use role-play training. He emphasized such tactical elements as the use of cover, arraying automobiles, mailboxes, and telephone poles on the ranges of the training facility at Rodman's Neck in the Bronx to get the cops accustomed to putting something between them and the incoming fire that at least some of them would inevitably face.

TOP THREE SHOOTERS in Master Stock division at Second Chance national shoot, early 1990s. From left: 1st place Ken Tapp, with Springfield Armory .45 auto; 2nd place Mas Ayoob, with four-inch S&W 625 .45 ACP tuned by Al Greco; 3rd place Mike Shovel, with 8 3/8-inch Model 25, also tuned by Greco. All shot for Team CorBon and used +P .45 ACP ammo.

Frank's unit was responsible for gathering the information for SOP-9. Inaugurated circa 1970, Standard Operating Procedure Number Nine was an in-depth debriefing of every MOS (Member Of the Service) involved in any sort of discharge of a weapon outside the training ranges. The debriefing included such questions as, "Did you use your sights? Did you fire double action or single if you used a revolver? What was your shooting position at each point in the fight? Did you hold the gun with one hand or two?" The responses would be correlated with facts learned from the investigation, such as how many shots were fired vis-à-vis how many hits, at what distance, and similar things.

It occurred to members of the Firearms and Tactics Unit that it would be useful to cross-reference the hit percentage in actual gunfights of each member of the department, with what that member's score was in regular qualification at the main NYPD range at Rodman's Neck and the satellite indoor ranges around the city. Quite apart from the obvious benevolent interest in officer safety – if the more highly skilled shooters were more likely to survive, the city might budget more money to train more officers

COMPETING WITH THE GUN you actually carry is the most relevant "competition as component of training" experience. This one is a Colt Lightweight Commander .45, tuned for duty by Bill Laughridge at Cylinder & Slide.

to that skill level – the FTU also stood to benefit from a positive correlation. If their training in marksmanship skill was saving more lives, they would get much positive reinforcement.

Alas, Lt. McGee told me, there was no correlation to be found. Not the expected positive correlation of high scores equaling high field performance, but no negative correlation either that might have indicated good shooting skills were somehow deleterious to survival-oriented perfor-

AT 100 METERS, these half-size steel ram silhouettes in NRA Hunter Pistol are challenging targets for a combat handgun, and great confidence builders for the practitioner.

mance. With this in mind, the FTU simply redoubled its emphasis on tactics and mindset, which unquestionably did improve gunfight outcomes and save officers' lives.

In the years since, other instructors around the country came to the same conclusion. However, while never officially studied by a police department to my knowledge, there is another comparison that results in a different conclusion. Those who shoot in competition seem to have a remarkably high hit potential and survival ratio in actual gunfights.

ONE-HANDED SHOOTING at seven yards is part of some police combat matches, and a valuable survival skill.

HISTORICAL PRECEDENT

This seems to have been pointed out by soldiers before it was pointed out by cops. In his book *A Rifleman Went to War*, H. W. McBride wrote extensively of his experiences in the trenches and on the battlefields of WWI. He had been a competitive rifle shooter before signing up so he could fight in The Great War. Once on the battlefield he killed soldier after enemy soldier, one bullet at a time, with the unerring marksmanship he had learned on competitive rifle ranges in North America.

After WWII, Lt. Col. John George wrote *Shots Fired In Anger*, subtitled *A Rifleman's View of the War in the Pacific,*

1942-1945. He had begun his adulthood as a skilled competitive rifle shooter. He felt that skill would serve him well in the jungles of the Pacific Theater. It did. His outstanding book shows multiple cases where he used essentially the same techniques, and the same coolness under stress, in combat that he used on shooting ranges. The result was a very significant number of enemy dead…and an American fighting man who returned home both victorious and unscathed after extensive mortal combat.

Fast forward to the Vietnam conflict. The most famous

AT AN NH POLICE ASSOCIATION STATE SHOOT, these officers use their issue weapons from the 15-yard line...

...THEN GO TO LOW ready to await the next rapid fire command.

rifleman to emerge from it was Carlos Hathcock, memorialized in the biography *Marine Sniper* by Charles Henderson. Hathcock was credited with 93 confirmed kills of enemy personnel, some at extraordinary distances and under extraordinary circumstances. Perhaps the most storied was the incident in which he faced another master sniper. The man was aiming at him as Hathcock put a bullet through the enemy's telescopic sight from front to back, into his eye, and thence into his brain, killing him barely in time to save his own life.

Hathcock had been a member of the U.S. Marine Corps rifle team, the crème de la crème of American military marksmanship, and had won the Wimbledon Cup, which is essentially the United States Championship of long range shooting with high powered rifles, before ever seeing an enemy combatant in his gunsights. It is apparent that the 93 confirmed kills were merely the tip of the iceberg, due to the strict reporting requirements of the

USMC Scout Snipers, and that his actual body count was well into three digits. It is clear that the coolness, the focus, and the mastery of his weapon under pressure that he learned on the rifle ranges of Quantico and Camp Perry translated extremely well to the jungles and rice paddies of Southeast Asia.

Over the years, police learned the same lesson when they bothered to look for it. One of the most legendary police gunfighters was Delf "Jelly" Bryce, who first earned his reputation as a street cop in Oklahoma and was subsequently recruited – purely for his gunfighting prowess, it is said – by J. Edgar Hoover in the formative years of the FBI. A master gunfighter, Bryce earned his first badge by winning a pistol match in front of a very impressed chief of police.

In another section of this book, we note that Wyatt Earp, Charles Askins, and Jim Cirillo all shot competition and did very well at it prior to the gunfights that made them famous. Earp did not discuss it much with his biographer, Stuart Lake. However, it's abundantly clear in Askins' writing that he was as proud of his match shooting awards as he was of his victories in gun battles, and the correlation between the two was just as abundantly clear without saying. In his book *Guns, Bullets, and Gunfights*, Cirillo came out of the match-shooting closet and flatly stated that the competitive shooters had the highest hit ratios – and the most dramatic win records – of all the thirty-plus members of the NYPD Stakeout Squad.

Competence develops confidence; confidence, in turn, leaves one cool enough under pressure to exercise competence. Decades of studying and teaching this full time have convinced me that the two are inextricably intertwined. There is no centrifuge into which we can throw those two elements, spin them, and determine that the formula is X% competence and Y% confidence. It suffices to know that they feed off each other and become more than the sum of their parts. If one had to make a diagram of the two factors interrelating, it would probably look like a circle, or perhaps a yin/yang symbol.

Cirillo and Askins were not by any means the only police champions who became gunfight survivors after honing their skill and confidence. Ohio police officer Kerry Hile had won multiple consecutive national championships in PPC, or "police combat shooting," before he was invited to join the SWAT team. He accepted the invitation. He had never been in a shooting before. The night came when the SWAT team was arrayed in plainclothes on stakeout for a

OFFICERS COMPETE on intermediate distance stage in a New Hampshire Police Association state shoot.

particularly dangerous suspect. When cops moved in, the man came up with a gun and opened fire. Multiple other officers shot at the gunman without effect. Hile, some 35 yards away, coolly raised his service handgun and rolled off four fast, smooth shots. The gunman collapsed, killed by four center hits from Hile's gun. The superb marksmanship and coolness under life-threatening stress that Kerry Hile had learned on the ranges in the pressure of top-level championship matches had saved his life and the lives of his brother officers.

It takes a bit of digging beneath the surface to see the difference between a soldier or peace officer who passes a qualification test, and one who shoots in competition, as it relates to preparing either gun-wielder for maximum performance under life-threatening stress. The soldier or Marine would certainly like to win an expert medal to pin on his chest after qualification, but knows that if he doesn't earn the higher honor, merely passing the test at minimum qualification level will suffice to keep his job and career. There is motivation, but not huge motivation.

That military man or policeman also knows that even if he fails to qualify, he'll get another chance. In between the last failure and the next try, there will also be remedial

AT GRASSROOTS LEVEL, police combat matches are more challenging than old PPC formats. Here, the officers have to sprint from start line, reach firing line, and engage targets in a short time-frame.

training, perhaps one-on-one coaching, and perhaps even another attempt in the future if the next one fails, too.

The competitive shooter is different. He is acutely aware that he will get no do-over. He knows, in the immortal words of the great International Practical Shooting Confederation champion Tom Campbell, "practice ain't race day." The match is a do-or-die performance on demand experience. He's not there to finish in the middle of the pack, he's there to win, and that raises both the stakes and the blood pressure.

The competitive shooter puts his or her ego and reputation on the line. It becomes intensely personal. Being a denizen of the "middle of the pack" is not going to be good enough. Often, that intense "this is it!" element tricks the lizard that lives in the base of our brain into thinking it's a real fight or flight situation, and the body actually goes into body alarm reaction. Any of us who have shot a lot of matches can tell you we've both seen those manifestations in others and felt them in ourselves.

The heart pounds. The proverbial butterflies in the stomach flutter. We look down and see that our hands, and per-haps even our knees, are trembling. We suddenly experience dyspnea, or air hunger, as if we're beginning to suffocate. We experience dry mouth. The fingers and lips may tingle. The shooter's face may be seen to go suddenly very pallid.

All of these things are manifestations of body alarm reaction, the highest form of which is the true fight or flight response. The tremors are a direct side effect of epinephrine dump, as the body's endocrine system goes into action to strengthen us for the great effort it instinctively senses may be about to come. Vasoconstriction occurs; blood flow is redirected into the major muscle groups and the internal viscera, again to "fuel the furnace." This means that blood flow is taken away from the extremities. That's why fingers and lips go numb, and why Caucasians under either match pressure or genuine danger are so frequently observed to go deathly pale. Blood flow away from the fingers seems to be the real reason we become clumsy under stress, not the epinephrine-generated tremors. It is what makes crime victims and gunfighters alike feel so terribly clumsy, and why a person in this condition feels as if "they're all thumbs" as they handle what used to be a gun so familiar to them that it felt like a natural extension of their hand.

THESE OFFICERS engage first around the side of barricade…

…AND THEN over the top under tight time limits. They're required to use the handguns they carry on duty.

SHOOTING TEAM COMPETITION adds a psychological factor: others are counting on you to perform. Team Triton at Second Chance match, 1998. From left: Mas Ayoob, Justine Ayoob, Mark Morris.

A TRUE SERVICE GUN can be competitive in IDPA competition. This shooter has just shot a perfect score on IDPA Classifier with duty Glock 22, fitted with NY-1 trigger and 5.5-pound connector, with total trigger pull weight of about eight pounds for each shot.

it goes unchecked, it will cause us to pass out.

We are used to framing these experiences within the context of the circumstances that trigger them. If it happens in ordinary life without a particular "trigger moment," it is generally diagnosed as an anxiety attack. The soldier or cop experiencing it in the course of human conflict comes to call it "pucker factor." The hunter calls it "buck fever," experienced when a trophy male deer is spotted within shooting range. And the competitor calls it "match nerves."

It's all different terminology for the same effect.

There is a definite element of "stress inoculation" in match shooting. It gets you accustomed to trembling hands, shaky knees, and all the rest, with a gun in your hand.

And … *it makes shooting under pressure the norm, instead of a terrifying "this is it" experience.*

No one is ever going to say that shooting a match is scarier than shooting for your life, least of all this writer. The fact remains that some who have survived gunfights have found it so.

One was Dave Wheeler, who retired from a distinguished

The air hunger comes from another element of body alarm reaction. Anticipating a need for explosive, sustained physical exertion, the human body begins to pump blood and suck in oxygen at an accelerated rate. However, no muscular exertion is yet "burning off" that surplus of oxygen racing through the bloodstream, and hyperventilation takes place. One of its side effects is tricking us into thinking we need more oxygen, not less, so we start breathing more desperately, compounding the problem. If

SHOOTER AT FAR RIGHT TAKES solid cover as 3-D target manikin is engaged and shot to the floor at a Tactical Arts Group (TAG) match in Manchester, NH.

NATIONAL COMPETITION is a definite "stress laboratory." Author awaits draw and fire signal at IPSC National Championships, 1978.

career with LAPD that encompassed multiple shootings in the line of duty. Dave was a competitive shooter for most of that same period in his life, and a damn good one. I would always pick his brain when we shot together at a major IPSC match or at the Second Chance shoot "back in the day." Dave told me that every time he had to shoot a man, he felt a sense of palpable calmness that allowed him to stay steady and get the hit in time to win…and that he often felt more stress in a match than he felt any of the times he was aiming at an armed antagonist and pulling the trigger, with his own survival or that of a citizen on the line. Dave is one of the few men I know who ever actually shot a hostage taker out from behind a hostage. He did it with a single shot from his service revolver, and the shot was so perfect that the gunman and his weapon hand were both limp and dead before his corpse began to fall. The hostage survived unscathed.

Jim Cirillo figures prominently in this book. Jim and I shot on the same squad at the first Bianchi Cup event in 1979 at the Chapman Academy in Columbia, Missouri. Of all the matches I ever shot, Bianchi Cup was unquestion-ably the most intense pressure cooker. The first one was intended to be "the Wimbledon of handgun shooting," a championship of champions. That first year, you needed to have won at least one state championship or equivalent to even get an invitation. There was a bunch of money on the line – something like $30,000 for first place if I recall correctly, unprecedented at that time – and you knew that one bad shot could theoretically cost you every penny of that if you were hoping to win it. (Startling revelation: every one of us there hoped to win it.)

"SPACE GUNS" threatened to make Bianchi Cup irrelevant in 1989 when this photo was taken, but game was revitalized when Production gun class was later introduced.

Cirillo and I had just completed the Barricade Event up on the hill, and were walking down the trail together and over the little bridge on the Chapman Academy range to shoot the Moving Target event. Jim told me, "Jesus Christ, I never felt pressure like this in any of my (expletive deleted) gunfights!"

A bit surprised, I asked him why he thought that was.

"Because there wasn't all this (expletive deleted) time to build up to it! And there weren't all these (expletive deleted) people watching," he replied.

After I left the pro shooting tour I thought I had retired. It turned out to be semi-retirement. During the time I was away from it, I realized competitive shooting had become my personal "pressure laboratory" to gauge and maintain not only my ability to draw, fire, and hit, but my ability to do so under stress.

The beauty of competitive shooting, and the real reason it did far more to prepare soldiers like McBride and Marines like Hathcock and cops like Cirillo to win gunfights, was that in this seemingly sporting environment, handling their guns swiftly and surely under significant pressure had caused that expert handling to become a reflexive norm.

"FORCE ON FORCE" role-play can replicate "real world scenarios."

Cops who are known by their opponents to be skilled with guns have found that their reputation alone can prevent bloodshed. If you study the history of the aforementioned Jelly Bryce, you'll find that his reputation was so imposing that armed, barricaded felons surrounded by police and ready to shoot it out, were known to surrender when they realized that Bryce had arrived on the scene.

My time as a police officer has been entirely in the state of New Hampshire. I was proud to be a friend of Andy Cannon, one of the finest police marksman (and police instructors) the Granite State ever produced. New Hampshire's only statewide newspaper was and is the *Manchester Union Leader*, which continues its policy created by its famed publisher William Loeb, a member of the National Rifle Association's board of directors when he lived, that shooting was a legitimate sport and was therefore to be covered just like baseball or football in sports pages of his statewide newspaper. Therefore, whenever Andy Cannon won the state championship, or a lesser match of note, the story and his picture got in the newspaper.

Andy worked for the NH Department of Fish & Game. The night came when he was staking out a field where he

INSTRUCTORS UNDERSTAND the relevance of competition. Author, left, and Gunsite's then-director Richard Jee at National Tactical Invitational, 1995.

had a tip that jack-lighting poachers were going to show up. They did, and soon Andy was on them, in his patrol vehicle with lights and siren. The poachers jumped in their vehicle, and the chase was on. Andy radioed that he was in a high speed pursuit.

There were four suspects in the vehicle, two in front and two in the back seat. In his headlights, Andy could see that one of the two men in the rear compartment was raising what appeared to be an M1 carbine and trying to bring it to bear on him from the left rear window. Ducking down behind the dashboard for cover until he could barely see the road and the car in front of him, Andy broadcast on the radio that an M1 was in play and he was about to come under fire.

Suddenly, he saw a violent flurry of movement in the back seat of the fugitive vehicle. The carbine went sailing out the window, and seconds later, the car pulled over and parked, and three of the men inside raised their hands and sat meekly still. Cannon couldn't see the fourth. Opening his door and angling his engine block for cover, Andy parked behind them with his roof lights still flashing, cov-

GREAT CARE MUST be taken to prevent accidental shootings in force-on-force. Here, participants double check that only Sims guns will be "in play." An excellent safety guide is "Training at the Speed of Life" by Ken Murray.

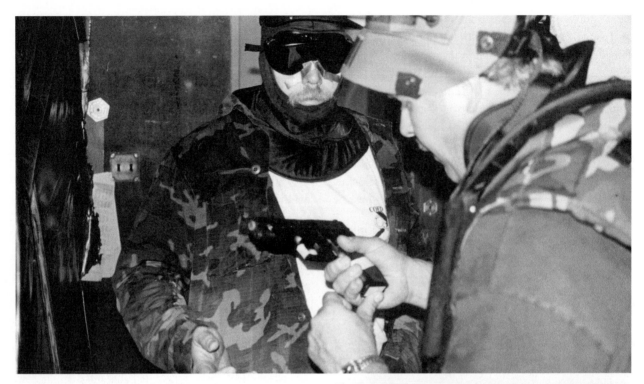

SAFETY PROCTOR ISSUES NTI participant a training gun pre-loaded with Simunitions™ projectiles. Dark goggles impair vision, add stress and challenge.

ered them with the same Smith & Wesson .357 Magnum Model 19 he used in competition, and ordered them over the cruiser's loudspeaker to remain still and not move. Soon, assisting units arrived, and the felony stop was completed without further incident.

The resultant tally was three meekly-surrendering game law violators, and one groggy and bloody suspect dragged semi-conscious from the left rear seat. He was the erstwhile gun-wielder, and turned out to be the brother of the man sitting to his right. The weapon that was thrown from the vehicle turned out to be not an M1 carbine, but a .30 caliber selective fire M2, fully loaded with a 30-round "banana clip" and its selector switch set on full automatic. The gun had been illegally brought back to the U.S. from the Korean War by the father of the two outlaw brothers.

Police soon learned what had happened. The violators were well aware that there was one particular conservation officer who patrolled that part of Moultonboro, New Hampshire…and they read the newspapers like everyone else. When the one brother raised the machine gun to fire at the pursuing officer, the other brother ripped it away from him and beat him unconscious, screaming at him

TACTICAL MATCHES reinforce the reality of preparing for a predictable fight. From left, Roger Lanny, author, and Lyn Bates go over strategy for NTI. Note that they're carrying extra pistols, allowed by the rules.

at the top of his lungs as he did so. What the desperate brother was yelling was, "You God-damned fool, that's *Andy Cannon* in that police car! You shoot at him, he'll kill us all!"

GETTING THE MOST "TRAINING" FROM MATCHES

Shooting bulls-eye pistol – standing in a rigid duelist's position, carefully thumb-cocking his revolver in the centerfire event, and firing no faster than five shots in ten seconds – Col. Charles Askins, Jr. developed skills and

THE ORIGINAL FEDERAL AIR Marshal's course is one of the most demanding law enforcement qualifications ever, makes an excellent competition stage.

SHOOTING A MATCH mirror image (i.e., lefty if you're right handed) is an excellent skill builder, particularly for instructors. Author is shooting an IDPA match with Glock 26.

confidence that saved his life and the lives of many other good people he was responsible for protecting. That tells us that any trigger time under pressure can be valuable in the training context.

Obviously, Askins didn't shoot that way when the chips were down. We recall that he was smart enough to move behind cover, firing as he went, in the incident where he was alone against three gunmen – one a proven cop-killer – and shot them all, decisively winning the battle.

That said, though, the more the match experience replicates good tactics – use of cover, tactical movement, etc. – the more valuable and "job-related" it's obviously going to be. With that in mind, it makes sense, if you only have limited time to devote to competition shooting as part of your training regimen, to give priority to the matches that will inculcate the most relevant possible skill sets.

For that, it's hard to beat IDPA, the International Defensive Pistol Association. Let me tell you about the most recent IDPA National Championship in which I competed before writing this book.

LESSONS FROM AN IDPA NATIONAL CHAMPIONSHIP[1]

We would probably all agree that a shooting match is not a gunfight.

However, *a gunfight is a shooting match!*

In either case, two people are testing their skill at hitting man-size targets that might be running, bobbing or weaving, or partially obscured behind hard cover. Each of those two people might themselves be moving, ducking, pushing someone out of the way, or attempting to keep awkwardly-positioned cover between themselves and incoming fire.

Does it not stand to reason that the person most experienced in doing those things, and in combining those skills while under some degree of pressure, might have some

WINNING THE SILVER PLATE or whatever strokes the ego, but that's not the main purpose of "competition as training."

advantage over the other when the stakes on the table are their own lives instead of trophies and plaques?

AN EXAMPLE IN POINT

In late September of 2010, a few hundred of us convened at the fabulous U.S. Shooting Academy range complex in Tulsa, Oklahoma, to compete in the fourteenth annual National Championships of the International Defensive Pistol Association (IDPA). Founded by IPSC (International Practical Shooting Confederation)/USPSA (United States Practical Shooting Association) veteran competitors at a time when those other games seemed to be more run and gun athletic marksmanship than anything else, IDPA's purpose was to return to the simulated gunfighting envisioned by IPSC founder Jeff Cooper.

Most stages, or shooting scenarios, require the gun to be drawn from concealment. All require the gun to be carried in a concealable, practical holster. All demand a "street-type gun" with no recoil compensator, and no optical sights. Ammunition must meet a power level of roughly 158 grain .38 Special +P revolver ammo for Stock Service Revolver, Enhanced Service Pistol, and Stock Ser-

vice Pistol divisions, and approximately that of a 185 grain jacketed hollow point .45 ACP round out of a short barrel pistol in the Enhanced Service Revolver or Custom Defense Pistol divisions. The complete rule book can be downloaded at no charge from the organization's website, www.idpa.com. *(Author's note: in early 2011, power floor in Stock Service Revolver was lowered to equal standard velocity 158 grain .38 Special ammunition.)*

The 2010 Nationals consisted of seventeen challenging stages. A few were pure tests of shooting skill. Some happened indoors in "shoot-house" format: moving in dim light, you had to grab a gun from a table and engage multiple targets at close range, or negotiate through a "building search" and shoot the bad guys without shooting the good guys.

Any match, any contest, is a skill test. The question is, are the skills being tested relevant to real-world needs? Take a look at some of the challenges created by the team led by Match Director Curt Nichols, himself a four-time National Champion IDPA shooter and an experienced street cop, and see for yourself.

"STANDARDS"
THAT GO BEYOND STANDARD

Stage 3, called "National Standards," was the longest course of the event. It encompassed 42 shots at distances

PPC MATCH FOR "off duty guns" limited barrel length to 2.5 inches. Author won this one with stock, snub-nosed S&W 686.

TACTICAL LESSONS: at NTI match, shooter can't see badge indicating "good guy" in armed target's other hand, and "shoots a friendly."

CHIEF OF POLICE BOB Houzenga, a six-time national champ, demonstrates his speed with department issue Glock .40 from Safariland security holster.

from six to twenty-nine yards. There was a lot of potential for missed shots, so it was a real "deal-breaker" for those more into speed than accuracy. Scoring was "Limited Vickers." In most IDPA stages, "Vickers Count" is your elapsed time, with half a second added for each point down from a perfect possible score, but you can fire extra shots to make up for bad ones. In Limited Vickers, you can fire only a specified number of shots, no make-up allowed.

This stage included "weak hand only" and "strong hand only" firing. It included speed reloads and tactical reloads, head shots, and firing from either side of a vertical barricade at the longest distance.

Lessons: Because we all like to look good and perform well, we generally shoot two-handed when we're practicing. Trouble is, real-world problems often require one-hand-only manipulation of the defensive sidearm. At longer ranges, supporting the firing grasp against the solid barricade gives you better hits. Many have confused "search techniques," where you stay well back away from the wall because someone might be hiding in that undiscovered territory to grab your gun, with pure cover techniques that maximize the protection of the barrier you're hiding behind, while simultaneously letting you deliver more accurate fire to extinguish the threat. It was my experience and observation that bracing on the barricade at long range was the most successful strategy.

The Standards weren't the only place where one-handed shooting proved effective, either, which leads us to…

"WEAK HAND" ONLY

The Nationals put significant emphasis on firing with the non-dominant hand only in 2010. In Stage 16, titled "Wrong Number," course designer Nichols at one point put you into a situation where you had to dial the phone for 9-1-1 with your dominant hand, holding your gun in your non-dominant hand. At that point, a target sprang up that you had to shoot multiple times. Those who regularly practiced with their "weak hand" were grateful for that experience in this dimly-lit scenario.

(Another lesson emerged from this stage: one was required to speak into the phone at the moment the target was attacking. Many who hadn't planned for this real-world need did not have time to transition from talking to shooting and still get all their hits.)

In Stage 1, "A Day At the Range," designed by former national champ Jerry Biggs, the shooter faces a scenario that in 2010 took the life of a gun club member in Pennsylvania: the bad guys attack a lone shooter on the range to steal his gun. At one point in the scenario, the shooter's

121

GLOCK'S CHRIS EDWARDS, an ex-cop, fires while backing up and using his own body to shield "baby" during an IDPA National match.

gun arm is presumed to be wounded, and he or she has to "finish the fight" weak hand only.

Relevant? Oh, yes. Tactical instructors call it "target focus" and expert on eyewitnesses Dr. Elizabeth Loftus calls it "weapon focus," but whatever you call it the fact is when someone is up against an armed person, they tend to focus on the weapon the other person is holding. "Where the head goes, the body follows" is a truth of physiology and armed combat alike, and since where the head is looking is where the shots go, people on either side of the fight tend to shoot one another in the gun hand or gun arm with a disproportionately high frequency. I recall a New York City officer who dropped his gun after being hit in the upper arm/shoulder area by his antagonist. He picked up the dropped gun and, using his weak hand only, shot and killed his assailant.

Lesson: In a gunfight, the gunfire goes in both directions. We all have to be prepared to take a hit and keep fighting. The single most likely place we're going to be hit may well be somewhere in the gun arm. It is imperative to a "full survival skill set" to be able to shoot fast and effectively "weak hand only." Kudos to IDPA for making that "part of the program."

DENNIS REICHARD WON multiple Indiana State Action Pistol championships with the same six-inch barrel S&W .44 Magnum he carried for decades as his police service revolver.

SHOOTING FROM VEHICLES

In recent decades, "carjacking" became an American crime phenomenon. More recently, so did "road rage." Each has resulted in a significant number of situations where good people who could shoot back saved their lives from modern "rustlers" who were prepared to murder them to steal their "ride."

This reality was well reflected in the 2010 IDPA Nationals. There were stages where we had to shoot from the driver's seat out the driver's window. There were stages where we had to shoot from the driver's seat to our right, out through the passenger's window. There were stages where we had to get out of the car to not only take maximum cover, but to get an angle of fire where we could aim and shoot the opposing "target" at all.

In 2010, there was a gunfight in middle America where a bunch of punks who had already become cop-killers were cornered in a parking lot. They were taken down by a courageous conservation officer who had responded to this high-priority scene and rammed the suspects' vehicle from behind with his own heavy-duty vehicle. Taking fire from the suspects' van, he unlimbered his own patrol rifle and simply fired through (his own) windshield, neutralizing the threat. This hero cop used successful out-of-the-box thinking that all of us can emulate if we're ever fighting car-to-car with multiple, heavily armed, homicidal criminals, as he was.

In one scenario at the Nationals, Stage 15 (another one designed by the redoubtable Curt Nichols), each of us was put in a situation where we were sitting center in the back seat of a full-size sedan and suddenly had to draw our guns and engage threats to the outside. This was a meaningful experience to me, since I had researched and written about the situation that occurred at the Little Bohemia shootout in the 1930s with the Dillinger gang. A coupe with three lawmen all jammed together in the front seat pulled up to question a suspicious person. Seated in the middle was a local constable who had a Smith & Wesson .38 Special in a shoulder holster, and should have been the one person in the car most capable of drawing from a seated position and neutralizing an attacker outside the vehicle.

The man they had stopped to talk with turned out to be perhaps the most psychopathic killer of the whole Dillinger Gang, known as Baby Face Nelson. When Nelson came up with a machine pistol and opened fire, the man in the middle seat was too cramped by the lawmen on either side of him to get to his gun. Everyone in the car got shot up, and the agent sitting to one side of the constable was killed. We can learn from this.

Lessons: If you're shooting out the left side driver's window and the deadly threat moves in front of the car, you'll have to lean out the window to keep line of sight and get a stopping hit. Put the car in Park, brace your right foot on the floorboard, and you'll be able to lean your head, shoulders, and upper body far enough out the open window to keep the threat in line of sight and put some fight-stopping bullets in it. Bracing the inside of your left arm on the outside of the door can help you pull your upper

JERRY BARNHART, one of the best shooting professionals action pistol competition ever produced. Here, he's geared up for an Open class event, with hardware that wouldn't be practical for the street.

body outward, to give you a good, continuing track of fire on such a target.

The vehicle might be one-passenger style, and that changes the dynamics. In Stage 13, "Motorcycle Mania," former National Champ Jerry Biggs' course design put us astride a recreational vehicle with a heavy pack on our back. Feet had to stay on the pedals as we shot an array of targets nearly 180 degrees apart.

Lesson: The ability to flow between a bent-arms Weaver and a straight arms Isosceles position from the waist up when pivoting from weak side to strong side was advantageous here. A one-punch fighter won't last long in the ring, and a one-stance shooter is handicapped when he can't step to face his target.

You might even be under the vehicle when trouble starts. Nichols' Stage 11 had you begin supine on a rolling mechanic's creeper under a jacked-up Jeep. (It was titled "Jeepers Creepers" – cute!) Remember that a man on his

THE GUN YOU CARRY is almost certainly accurate enough to win a combat match. This is a 25-yard group with 230 grain Gold Dot, fired from box-stock Kimber Custom II .45.

back under an obstacle is vulnerable to attack by standing men he'll have trouble seeing coming.

Lesson: Sometimes you have to get up before you can fight. Grabbing the undercarriage of the Jeep, lifting your feet, and pulling the whole rig with you on it quickly out from under the vehicle turned out to be the smart plan here. Whenever we're in a disadvantaged position, we need to have a plan for getting out of there quickly.

If you need to get to one side or the other of the car when you're on the wrong side or in the middle, *lean forward and then pivot your upper body "gun turret" toward the threat!* This can give you more range of movement and allow you to safely extend your handgun past a passenger on either side of you.

Use your feet, extending them sideways. This will allow you to push much more toward the window on either side, and give you far more range of movement with which to engage the threat. If the constable at Little Bohemia had been taught to lean forward and do this, he might have been able to shoot Baby Face Nelson before Nelson could shoot him and his brother officers. The foot pushed against the floorboard of the car extends both your body and your

DEPARTMENT ISSUE RUGER .45 service pistol...state champion trophy won with it...and state laws. Yes, they all fit together.

weight forward, toward the threat to give you more range of movement and toward the recoil of your own gun, to give you faster recovery time between shots.

WE AIN'T JUST WOOFIN' HERE

Cops and armed citizens alike are often required to shoot vicious dogs to keep themselves or other good people from being horribly bitten and mauled. There may also be times when the shooter is trying to keep his own dog under control with one hand, and having to deliver rescuing gunfire with the other hand.

Both of these scenarios were played out for the hundreds of contestants at the 2010 IDPA Nationals.

In Stage 14, "Who Let the Dogs Out," the shooter begins standing in the bed of a pickup truck, both feet on the lowered tailgate, and faces a dozen "dog targets," representing a whole pack of feral canines. The shooter is required to get one shot into each without hitting the innocent human targets mixed in, one of which is moving.

Lesson: Even a parked pickup is not the most stable firing platform. The vehicle's suspension means springs, and springs mean bounce. The winning strategy was to take a deep backstep to place your standing body over the rear axle, where bounce was least. In a real-life attack of this kind, it would also put the body far enough back to be better placed against a mad dog or wolf that was fast and strong enough to jump up onto a truck bed.

The flip side of this situation was perhaps the most ingenious of the match. In Stage 5, "Can I Bite Em? Can I Bite Em Now?" the shooter began holding the leash of his own agitated dog, represented by a cantilevered weight on the other end of the leash. The mission was to maintain control of the "dog" while shooting the bad guy targets. That shooting is not easy when something is pulling on your support hand!

As I fired it, I was reminded of a friend of mine who worked K9 for a southern Sheriff's Department, who had to kill an armed fugitive one-handed with his SIG .45 while holding his lunging dog's lead in his other hand. Yes, this sort of situation does happen.

Lesson: The winning strategy proved to be simply holding the leash in one dedicated hand, and firing the pistol with a dedicated strong-hand only grasp. I discovered that too late, midway through the stage. Learn from those of us who did it poorly, and have a plan for this situation beforehand. That's one of the things IDPA competition is all about.

BOTTOM LINE

A gunfight simulation match that's based on things that have been known to actually happen gives the participant authentically replicated experience. Those lessons stick. A friend of mine in the Carolinas is a street cop and an avid IDPA competitor. He feels that the competition did more than his training to make use of cover second nature to him. Some months ago on a routine call he was confronted by a man who raised a Mossberg 12-gauge at him. He reflexively dove to the side, evading a shotgun blast that otherwise would have killed him, and firing from cover

AS MUCH AS POSSIBLE, compete with the gun you carry. Author wins a state shoot for cops with department issue Ruger P90 .45, here firing from the 50-yard barricade.

with his Glock 21, he shot and killed his attacker. This lawman credits IDPA in part with saving his life.

Like I said … the shooting match isn't a gunfight, but the gunfight is a shooting match. The more experience you've deposited in your "long term muscle memory bank," the better your chances of successful outcome in either scenario.

# # # #

IPSC/USPSA

In the 1950s, Col. Jeff Cooper created a sport of simulated gunfighting that drew in some of the defining champions and great teachers of the era that followed, men like Ray Chapman and Ken Hackathorn. In the mid-1970s, a coterie of those who believed in the concept came from all over the world to meet at Ray's school, Chapman Academy, in Columbia, Missouri. Known as the Columbia Conference, that conclave marked the birth of IPSC, the International Practical Shooting Confederation. In time, a specific governing body for the sport in the U.S. would evolve, the United States Practical Shooting Association (USPSA).

From golf to automobile racing, it is human nature to evolve equipment which will give the competitor an edge in winning the game. This equipment will not always be practical for the original use from which the sport built around it evolved. Just as an Indy race car bears little relation to a vehicle for everyday transportation, some of the "race guns" that evolved to win IPSC were too unwieldy and impractical for even a police officer's uniform holster,

MAKE SURE MODIFICATIONS that improve match performance won't impair street performance. This altered Colt Python mainspring gave a smooth, one-stage pull, but did not compromise ignition with Magnum primers.

let alone an armed citizen's concealed carry rig.

Disappointed by this evolution, some disaffected leaders of the sport broke away and created new organizations, hoping to return to Cooper's original concept of simulated gunfighting with practical combat handguns. One such evolution, in 1996, was IDPA. Another, slightly earlier, was the creation of the Single Stack Classic, led by pistolsmith Dick Heinie. For the Single Stack, rules would be those of IPSC, but the holster had to be concealable and not worn ahead of the hip, and the same was true of magazine pouches. (Guns and ammo would not have to be actually concealed in every stage, however.) The match would be devoted to 1911 pistols of any make, but with only single-stack magazines. Moreover, there would be no recoil compensators or optical sights, the bulky add-ons that had led to "space guns" dominating the sport in the first place.

The result was one of the most popular matches in the country. USPSA's management was seeing the handwriting on the wall. Not only did they add categories of competition for stock guns, ranging from Limited Ten (no comps or optics, no more than ten rounds in the magazine) and Production, but circa 2006 USPSA adopted the Single

COMPETE WITH WHAT YOU CARRY. Author wore this Moran-tuned Python on duty at times, won several state titles with it.

"ONE SHOT, ONE CENTER HIT" is a winning formula. After author's personal best on six five-pin strings, each moon clip from Al Greco Custom S&W 625 had one live round left.

Stack Classic into its repertoire of matches, making it the USPSA Single Stack National Championship.

Come back with me for a little bit, and take a look at the shakedown cruise of the Single Stack.

SINGLE STACK CLASSIC[2]

In the gray morning drizzle of Thursday, May 4, 1995, Ken Cramberg stood with his back to three IPSC targets. At the signal he spun toward them, clearing his Colt National Match .45 auto from under the mandatory jacket, and we watched as he punched a .452-inch diameter hole through the A-zone of the leftmost of three targets in an *El Presidente* array 10 yards distant.

The rest of Ken's run was smoothly executed, but we who watched him knew we'd seen an historic moment. Cranberg had just fired the first shot of the first 1911 Single Stack Classic in Milan, Illinois.

The brainchild of pistolsmith and long-time IPSC competitor Dick Heinie, the Classic was ramrodded by Bob Houzenga, a career cop and perennially high-ranked competitor in the sport.

Springfield Armory was the lead sponsor, joined by

BOB LLOYD TUNED this S&W 686 for the street, but it has won one state and one regional IDPA championship in Stock Service Revolver division. Properly approached, the competition range can be relevant to the street.

Colt. Sponsoring stages were Caspian Arms, Competition Electronics, Ed Brown Products, Hellweg, JP Enterprises, K.C. Hilites, Rack Systems, and Smith & Alexander.

A growing number of action handgunners are learning that, sometimes, the timely thing is to go back in time. In this case, the concept was a return to "original IPSC," the first five or six years or so before the equipment race began in earnest. The rules were simple. You could use:

• A 1911 pattern pistol, with single stack magazines of the length standardized by the gun factory,

FOR A FEW YEARS AUTHOR carried Glock 22 on duty, with NY-1 trigger, used it to win three state shoots. "Compete with what you carry" to get the most out of "competition as training."

S&W 686S BECOME IRRELEVANT "race guns": Left, snub with scope; right, Andy Cannon Ayoob/Cannon Street L revolver mounted with red dot sight and Jarvis barrel weight for Bianchi Cup open class shooting.

- A barrel no longer than five inches,
- No recoil compensator,
- No optical sights, and
- The holster must be behind the edge of the hip (International Concealed Carry Rule).

"Russell Cluver, the Illinois IPSC Section Coordinator, and I," says Heinie, "had been listening to new shooters complain about high capacity guns, even in current Limited Class, which leaves the standard 1911 at a great disadvantage in most courses.

"We knew the same guys were going to win, but it puts people on a more level playing field. People would enjoy it more this way, we thought. And I think the match proved us right."

Four 10mms and at least one .40 S&W and one .38 Super were used; all the rest were .45 autos, according to Heinie, who shot a 10mm along with Walt Rauch, Arnt Mhyre, and Ray Hirst.

Rob Leatham used a .40 S&W (with ammunition) loaded to 10mm length by seating the bullets out farther, allowing the use of 10mm magazines, which some believe function better in a 1911 than the stubby .40 S&W loaded

ULTIMATE IN "GAMESMANSHIP": 2.5-inch 686 fitted with telescopic sight to get around local club rules for "off duty gun" match.

to standard OAL (over-all length). Presumably, .40 S&W brass for practice is much more plentiful than 10mm, making this expedient worth the effort.

Most of the pistols were full Government Model length with five-inch barrels. However, more than a few 4¼-inch Commanders were in the field, and at least one determined old boy on my squad shot his carry gun, a neat little street-tuned Colt Officers, and shot it very well indeed.

COMPLIANCE FACTOR

There were no trick sights. No sneaky weasel tricks. There

were more than a few pistols with trigger jobs that brought them down to pull weights that were suited better to meets than streets, but was it not Jeff Cooper himself who said of duty 1911 triggers, "Three pounds, crisp, is the word"?

Holsters were another matter. It was the only thing anyone whined about. The rule had been that the rig must ride no farther forward than the edge of the hip, and when people started asking, "Where's that?" it was clarified to read no farther forward than the seam on one's pants.

There was still whining, but the moaners were few in number. Houzenga and Heinie have been warned that next year, at least one shooter may show up wearing pants with seams located at the front trouser leg crease.

Holster choice seemed to break down into thirds. One well-represented contingent wore their street leather – inside-the-waistband holsters and the Milt Sparks Yaqui Slide or equivalent. A smaller number went with the speed rigs of the past – the Hackathorn Special that Sparks popularized, or Bianchi's Chapman Hi-Ride.

The third category wore 1995-class match gear – Riley Gilmore's slick plastic puppy designed for raceguns, and the same Safariland and Ernie Hill stuff you'd see in IPSC Limited.

The Team Safariland contingent had an experimental new race holster that they dutifully wore in the mandated position, behind the ileac crest of the pelvis.

The trick holsters were perhaps the one discordant note in the whole "back to basics theme" of the 1911 Single Stack Classic. Houzenga and Heinie and company are wondering what to do about it for 1996.

My own suggestion would be to stay with the "classic" format and require an inside-the-waistband holster. Let's see the gamesmen trick that one out.

AUTHOR, LEFT, AND RAY CHAPMAN go over lesson plan for advanced officer survival course at Chapman Academy, 1980s. Both felt that, properly approached, competition could be a relevant adjunct to training.

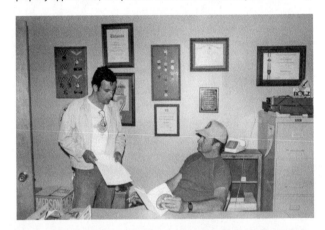

LEARN FROM THOSE who beat you. If two guys outshot you, find out how they did it.

THE FOUNDERS OF THE NATIONAL TACTICAL INVITATIONAL, displaying the NTI motto. From left: Skip Gochenour, Chuck Davis, Walt Rauch.

HELLUVA COURSE

Houzenga has shot well in many IPSC Nationals, and routinely wins the Chapman Academy's annual Missouri Police Practical Pistol State Championships, the only such match in the country to my knowledge that is fired with the officer's departmental duty gun and leather, with each event replicating known gunfights instead of merely a "stage of fire."

He knows how to build challenging scenarios, and in the Single Stack Classic, I think he outdid himself. It was one of the most challenging events I've shot in more than 40 national and international matches I've entered.

Consider the second stage, what used to be called "schoolhouse exercises" in the early days of IPSC, titled here "Double Duty Standards III." Thirty-six rounds were fired in a total of 33 seconds, which wouldn't have been bad at all except for the breakdown.

Try six rounds in six seconds, from the leather, standing...at 50 yards. The single toughest stage of a PPC course, by contrast, is six shots under the same circumstances in 12 seconds at 25 yards; at the Classic, we had half the time at twice the distance.

Or, from 15 yards, five seconds to draw, hit each of three targets twice, including the transfer to weak-hand-only which does all the shooting. Or, from the same distance in the same five second space, draw and fire one on each, reload, and one more on each of the three IPSC Brussels targets.

I've shot the Bianchi Cup 10 times, and let me tell you, this one made the Practical Event at the Cup seem like NRA slow fire. And remember – it's done with a five-inch Government Model.

"Possible" on this was 180 points. Smart money was that it wouldn't be "cleaned," and anyone who scored over 170 points would win the stage. As I was coming off the line, someone yelled, "Mas, did you break 170?"

"Only in power factor," I replied.

GEEZER FACTOR

You'd think guys who'd been shooting this sort of stage when Robbie Leatham was too young to chase cheerleaders – me and Ken Hackathorn, for instance – might've had an edge. Naaah.

Ken and I tied for 15th place on this one. Ted Bonnet won it – with a 154 out of 180 possible. I have to say it was the toughest such practical pistol stage I've shot in my life, and that ain't the age talking, kids, it's the mileage. The "best of the best," Bonnet had scored only 85.56 percent of "possible."

Consider also the fiendish last stage, "Snooze and You

A SHOOTER RUNS the daunting course at one of the first big money matches, the Shoot For Loot in Laramie, Wyoming, circa 1976.

REMOTE CAMERA catches the author, then a member of the HK factory pistol team, shooting the moving target event at Bianchi Cup, 1981. Pistol is HK P9S Sport Target 9mm.

Lose." It looked simple enough: shoot a steel target that triggered a gravity turner when it fell, and then shoot the turning target; do a mandatory reload; and do it again on the second set.

The semi-surprise match bulletin didn't say how long we'd have to engage the turner, but since six hits were called for, we assumed it would be at least a two-second exposure.

Wrong, 1911-breath. We all got a "walk-through" in which the exposure time of the gravity turners was demonstrated. I figured I'd just do the mental count thing – "one thousand and one" equals about one second for me – so I'd know how to pace myself.

With only a slight hint of a Cheshire cat grin under his blond mustache, Bob Houzenga tipped over the first Pepper Popper to trigger the first turner. The Brussels spun. "One-thousan…"

The target was gone.

He tripped the next. "One thou…"

Gone.

It was the first time I can recall that my jaw dropped while observing the walk through of a match.

SMOKIN' RUN

I thought at first that I'd done okay. The sweet-trigger stainless Colt Government, tuned with Dick Heinie's Ultimate Defense Package, hammered four Black Hills 230 grain hardballs into the first turner, which I estimated to have been exposed barely more than half a second, and three into the next, which couldn't have exceeded half a second total exposure.

I felt pretty good about that – until Robbie Leatham smoked the thing in less than 6½ seconds, with six hits on each of the gravity turners, and losing only two points in hit value.

There were a total of 10 stages in the Single Stack Clas-

BACK IN THE DAY, bulls-eye pistol was all the competition most cops could find to shoot. This is Jerry Wilder of the Indiana State Police, one of the great champions, in his heyday. He once outdrew, shot, and killed a gunman pointing a Luger at him.

sic. An *El Presidente* was done true to the old rules, with the three targets the full distance apart – and from concealment. This may be the quintessential "IPSC Course of Old," along with the Cooper Assault Course.

Arnt Myhre edged Leatham on this one with 58 points out of 60 possible, using 6.78 seconds to react, turn, draw from concealment, shoot each of the three targets twice, reload, and do it again.

In third place was Merle Edington, whom I consider to be the man who established the U.S. Army as a force to be reckoned with in practical shooting, with 59 points scored in 7.42 seconds. Colt provided their excellent sportsman's jackets for the mandatory concealment in this stage, to "keep everyone equal." (Kept us warm and dry, too.)

PASSENGER 45

In "Passenger 45," you started seated and reading a magazine when the signal came to pivot out of your seat, take mandatory cover, and engage four "terrorists" a considerable distance behind you in a laboriously constructed airliner simulation.

A planeload of hostage targets ducked (partially) after

DOCUMENTABLE QUALIFICATIONS can help you in court. From left: County Attorney Mark Hathaway, Capt. Ayoob, Chief Russ Lary.

you dropped the first one. Leatham captured this one with a brilliant 4.48 second run.

"Courtroom Defense II" was a crowd scenario in which your pistol and the mag(s) you'd need for the mandatory reload were in a closed attaché case on a desk in front of you. Arnt Myhre romped this one in 6.99 seconds, taking eight targets in an environment rich in "no-shoot" zones, and nailing six shoot targets at least twice.

"Don't Stop 'Til They Drop" put the shooter against six big poppers, six little ones, and a stop plate. No tactics, just shoot fast-straight-hard. Leatham won it in just over 7.5 seconds.

TACTICAL THINKING

"Embassy Incident" required the most tactical thinking as you moved between cover points, and, in the most crucial moment, faced a "truck that had you in the headlights." You had to shoot out the headlights (Bianchi plates) which set the opposing targets in motion for you to engage. Bonnet won this one too, edging out Leatham and Edington.

"Tri-Plex" was very well designed, forcing the shooter to engage from multiple positions at multiple angles behind all heights of cover. Jack Barnes, an ace in Open IPSC but unclassified in Limited, blew the big kids away, capturing this stage a third of a point ahead of Leatham.

"Wall of Shame" messed with your head. As you moved down a catwalk, you didn't just have to take the shoot targets out from behind the no-shoots, you had to shoot through wooden lath laid like bars across the shooting ports.

You knew consciously you could just shoot through them since they were wood, but something told you to move 'til you had a clear shot between them – and the clock was running the whole time. Bonnet won this event, followed closely by Merle Edington.

IF YOU WEAR CORRECTIVE LENSES, shoot for the record without them occasionally, to prepare for predictable real world situations. Dark glasses drawn on target show this qualification was "shot blind" without visual correction.

OFFICER DOWN

"Officer Down" was my personal favorite, because it demanded multiple skills and was true to the tournament's concept of, "It's the shooter, not the gun."

The scenario was the rescue of a wounded cop. You had to move through three positions, taking down a total of 10 targets. By the time you reached end game, you had to secure your own 1911, pick up a Mil-Spec Springfield Armory .45 on the ground by the uniformed dummy of the officer, reload it from slide lock with a magazine of hardball that you snatched from the pouch on the officer's duty

HERE'S A WIDE TARGET array that must be engaged from astride a two-wheeler, IDPA Nationals 2010.

THE HEAVY BACKPACK on your shoulders, and remaining balanced on the bike, both complicate shooting greatly. IDPA Nationals, 2010.

belt, and take down the last four Pepper poppers. Leatham took this one like Grant took Richmond, almost five percent ahead of second place Arnt Myhre.

HELLUVA MATCH

Only the experienced competition shooter knows the difference between "Helluva Course" and "Helluva Match." The course is the challenge, the "shooting problem" itself. The match is the totality of hospitality, fairness, sportsmanship and camaraderie that makes or breaks the entire experience.

I shot on the first day with the hard-working, uncomplaining legion of Range Officers who made it work the rest of the time. We had the only bad weather. For the registered shooters, the gun gods smiled and decreed perfect climate.

There were no complaints, no protests, no beefs. At the end of the first day of scheduled shooting, things were running ahead of time-table, and by the time it was over – with the awards ceremony completed at the time it had been slated to start – Houzenga's splendid crew made the thing operate like the movement of a Patek Phillipe wristwatch.

That may be a poor analogy. Unlike that Rolls Royce of Swiss watches, the 1911 Single Stack Classic actually ran faster than it was supposed to, leaving 88 supremely satisfied competitors.

RICH PRIZE TABLE

You heard about this match, and you didn't come? "Oh, ye of little faith…"

Eighty-eight shooters vied in what first the sponsors and now the contestants feel was not over-confidently titled the first annual Single Stack Classic. None went home empty-handed.

No fewer than eight superbly customized Springfield Armory, Colt, Caspian and Baer 1911 pistols were awarded to the winners. Dick Heinie, a heavy hitter in the Pistolsmiths Guild, had called in a whole lot of chips to make this happen.

The winners, and the prizes, were:

• Match Winner: Rob Leatham (Larry Vickers custom pistol)

• 1st Grand Master: Arnt Myhre (Richard Heinie custom pistol)

• 1st Master: Doug Boykin (Jim Garthwaite custom pistol)

• 1st "A": Marvin Fair, Jr. (Bill Wilson custom pistol)

• 1st "B": John Gangl (Les Baer custom pistol)

TACTICAL COMPETITION can hurt. Author points to paint marks from Simunitions™ at NTI event, one reason he wore Second Chance vest and groin guard under his clothes.

- 1st "C": Mark Collazos (Dave Stagg custom pistol)
- 1st "D": Larry Pearson (Kim Ahrends custom pistol)
- 1st Unclassified: Jack Barnes (Mark Krebs custom pistol)

This game isn't winner take all. Note that one $2,000+ prize gun was taken by a score that was only 42.15 percent of Leatham's winning tally. Note that Merle Edington's powerful third place overall finish didn't win him a custom gun at all. Big dogs run with big dogs here, a fact not lost on Heinie and Houzenga who realize that little guys are the backbone of the sport.

WHAT IT ALL MEANS

We all wondered how we'd do if the playing field was leveled and we all had the same type of gun. The 1911 Single Stack Classic showed us two things about that, two things we had long suspected would be true.

First, the same people would win. Second, those of us who shot against them would feel a whole lot better about it nonetheless.

One of the great things about participating in events like the Bianchi Cup, Second Chance, the IPSC Nationals and, now, the 1911 Single Stack Classic, is the great people you meet. None of today's big name shooters have the egos you'd expect of a superstar. Ours is the most egalitarian of sports.

In a society that enjoys its sports vicariously on TV, we handgunners can shoot in the very same match as superstars like Leatham, Edington, Bonnet, et al. Not in a "pro-am" thing, not in a "we'll let you tag along if you give us money" thing, but in an "if you beat Leatham you're the champion and we'll damn well give you the chance to do it" thing.

This, in the last analysis, may be what so terrifies lightweight yuppie elitists when they look at shooters, their values, and the so-called "Gun Culture."

It's a place to learn things about yourself. I borrowed Dick Heinie's own Ultimate Defense Package Colt .45. This $2200 pistol (that you have to wait five years to have built on your own base gun) worked splendidly with the flawlessly functioning, match-grade Black Hills 230 gr. .45 hardball I fired through it.

RUN WITH THE BIG DOGS

It just seemed appropriate to shoot Heinie's match with a Heinie gun. I couldn't resist the chance to go for broke and try to beat the World Champion; I went too fast and crashed and burned. So did a lot of others.

"It ain't about the gun, it's about the shooter," and the point is, the 1911 Single Stack Classic gives you a format where you can do that. You can't race against an Unser or play tennis against a Connors or golf against a Nicklaus, but you can shoot against Rob Leatham. And this says something good about you and Robbie both.

You can do it with a top-grade, out of the box 1911 and hardball – and, with the equipment issued on site, wouldn't that be a helluva match? – and whether or not you win, you'll know for the rest of your life that you got up off the porch and ran with the big dogs.

You may even have a moment like I had with Nyle Leatham, father of the winner. "This is where it started," Nyle told me softly as we walked together across the impeccably-groomed ranges of the host facility, Milan Rifle Club Inc.

"My son won his first national championship here some 12 years ago. I pictured it in my mind often. It's good to see it now," Nyle reflected.

IDPA ACE DAN BURWELL engages from astride two-wheeler, IDPA Nationals 2010.

It was good for Nyle, too, to watch his son win this particular tournament. Like I said, it ain't about guns, it's about people.

# # # #

OTHER "CARRY GUN" EVENTS

Heinie and company were a bit ahead of IDPA chronologically, but neither group was the first to work to bring "combat shooting" sports (which soon came to be called "practical shooting" instead) away from specialized guns that were suited for winning matches and not much else, and back to the sort of firearms people actually carried.

In the mid-1970s, Richard Davis created the sport of bowling pin shooting: "plinking for grownups," if you will, only instead of knocking tin cans off the back fence with a .22, you were blasting heavy tenpins three feet back off a big, rugged table, and whoever "cleared the table fastest" won. The whole "space gun" thing with auto pistols had started there, with master gunsmith (and former WWII sniper and national bulls-eye pistol champion) Jim Clark, Senior, creating the first 1911 "pin gun" for John Shaw of Tennessee. Richard was the founder of Second Chance

HERE'S THE BROAD and somewhat distant array of targets that must be engaged from vehicle at left, IDPA Nationals 2010.

Body Armor, and the inventor of the soft, concealable "bullet-proof vest." Ironically, the man who "bullet-proofed America's police" was never a cop himself: Rich was an armed citizen whose inspiration to create his brainchild was a shootout he won against a trio of armed robbers, in which he was wounded twice himself. What he wanted to promote was an event that tested skill with the real-world handguns that armed citizens and cops carried daily.

Accordingly, he soon divided his prize-rich annual Second Chance Match into a "space gun" division where recoil compensators and red-dot electronic sights were al-

SHOOTER ENGAGES "armed carjacker" targets from passenger seat, IDPA Nationals 2010.

lowed, and a "stock gun" division in which they weren't. Like competed against like.

The National Rifle Association had long since included a side event for off duty guns with short barrels in their PPC events for police. From the beginning, IDPA provided for a BUG category. BUG stood for Back-Up Guns, the sort of short-barrel pistols and revolvers that a serious user might carry as a second gun, and that many in the interests of concealment would carry as their primary weapon in the real world.

A core tenet of "combat shooting" is that the more time one has shooting under pressure *with the gun one actually carries*, the better one will be with it. A streetwise ex-cop and current police trainer named Lance Biddle under-stood that better than most. He also understood that a whole lot of the armed citizens he trains now, and the cops he trained then and now, carried little five-shot revolvers or subcompact semiautomatic pistols on their own time. Yet, he noticed, they'd carry big ol' service pistols to shoot concealed carry matches.

Lance decided to do something about that. Here's the competition he created to test good people's skill with those little guns they wore every day to protect themselves and others.

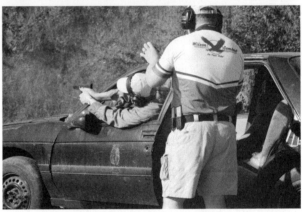

THIS LADY RUNS a Glock 34 out the driver's window in a counter-carjack stage, IDPA Nationals. Dynamics from two sides of the front seat are distinctly different.

LESSONS FROM THE BACKUP GUN CHAMPIONSHIPS[3]

How do the various small handguns fare against each other in realistic combat competition? An ex-cop/current police trainer decided to find out, and a unique and in-structive shooting match was born.

If you've competed in the National Championships of IDPA you've probably met Lance Biddle. He would have been running one of the stages you shot. As IDPA's Florida State Director, Biddle has been an ambassador for this re-ality-based handgun sport. As a match director and safety

FLORIDA/GEORGIA REGIONAL woman champ Gail Pepin exits driver's seat, uses engine block for cover to engage far right targets with her Springfield XD(m) 9mm.

officer alike, he's a stern taskmaster, but a fair one when he arbitrates the rules. (Whoever said "It's easier to ask forgiveness than permission" has never shot a match under the watchful eye of Lance Biddle.)

That attitude comes from 22½ years as a street cop in a busy municipality adjacent to Columbus, Ohio. When Biddle designs a CoF (Course of Fire), he builds in street reality. A while back, cognizant of the fact that in his Florida stomping grounds even off-duty cops often carry small "pocket guns" instead of the full-size competition-grade handguns that often show up in regular IDPA matches, he decided to create an unofficial state championship for the truly small handguns that IDPA calls BUGs, or Back-Up Guns. He was inspired by Mack Rudisill, an IDPA regular who always competes with his daily carry J-frame snub and Speed Strips. Because you'll find a little bit of a smartass in anybody who's done police work as long as Lance and has psychologically survived, he jokingly called it the National Championships, and then the World Championships, of the BUG. When another smart-ass with a badge suggested he extend it to the rest of the known galaxy, Lance planted his tongue firmly in his cheek and titled it

ANOTHER OPTION for driver to engage target on right: leaning over and firing out of passenger window.

the BUG Championship of the Universe.

I heard about his second such match, and hit it in 2010 at The Gun Shop in Leesburg, Florida. Owner Gordon Schorer's wonderfully eclectic gun shop encompasses a state of the art indoor range where he and Biddle host regular IDPA matches, bowling pin shoots, and of course, the now-annual BUG event. Naturally, Pocket Pistols 2011 was there for this year's event, as well.

THE RULES

It was made clear from the outset that this was not an

2010 IDPA NATIONALS had ample "weak hand only" shooting. Here, author engages from behind cover with Wilson CQB and .45 hardball.

IDPA match, and in some ways it departed from IDPA rules. The rules for this independent event mandated revolvers with barrels no longer than 2.5 inches, and true *subcompact* auto pistols. Basically, it was 3.5-inch 1911, yes; 4.25-inch Colt Commander, no. "Baby Glock" G26 or G27 si, compact G19 or G23 with four-inch barrel, no. In deference to the hugely popular J-frame revolver, all guns had to be loaded with only five rounds, and reloaded only once with only five rounds, per stage. Because so many real-world pistol-packers have gone with Crimson Trace LaserGrips on snub revolvers or that company's Laser-Guard, or the LaserMax unit (which replaces the recoil spring guide) on subcompact autos, Lance decided to allow such devices in a separate "laser" category.

In the first couple of matches, Lance had noticed that for those who went with the spirit of the game and shot with what they actually carried, the pocket carry and fanny-pack carry hugely popular in Florida were distinctly disadvantaged when the shooter began with the usual IDPA position of hands relaxed at side. He had long since realized that an advantage of either the pouch or the pocket was that a hand could surreptitiously be placed on the gun

without anyone else being aware of it, and therefore the 2011 event allowed a shooter so equipped to start with the hand on the gun in the pocket or the fanny pack, so long as the gun itself was not exposed to view. And, because the whole theme was, after all, backup guns, each shooter was given the choice of reloading or going to a second small handgun after the first ran dry.

CHALLENGING COURSES OF FIRE

Biddle retired to Florida, which has seen many home invasions in which the felons tie up or handcuff their victims. In one stage the shooter began seated at a table, handcuffed, and had to access his hidden gun(s). (Yes, you can shoot that way. Yes, you can even reload that way. But having a second gun *really* helps if you have to *defend* yourself that way…)

In another, you find yourself at a poker table in a game gone bad, and realize the other players have set you up for armed robbery. There's time to sneak your pocket-size gun out and get it leveled on the opposition "under the table" before they go for their weapons. In nearly 40 years of competitive "combat shooting," I've never had the chance to try this tactic at a match. We all did at the 2011 BUG Championships. (You can do it with this kind of gun. You can't do it with Dirty Harry's 6.5-inch barrel .44 Magnum in a shoulder holster.)

DAN BURWELL RUNS between cover points at IDPA Nationals, Safety Officer with timer running to keep up. Pistol is S&W M&P 9mm.

The "Bill Drill," combat shooting icon Bill Wilson's practice regimen of drawing and trying to put six shots into the center zone of a silhouette target at seven yards in two seconds, is particularly challenging with small, short-barrel handguns. We had to do it at the BUG Championships, and a second time at three yards with all head shots! Any shot outside the head at three yards or the eight-inch diameter center chest zone on the IDPA target at seven yards, was considered a miss. No, we didn't make the hits clean in two seconds with "belly guns" from concealment, but some shooters came surprisingly close.

In one stage the shooter is in a pitch-dark narrow hallway with a flashlight in one hand and the pocket-size handgun concealed. Suddenly, he becomes aware that a crazed man with a sword is charging him from 25 yards away. He has to draw, illuminate the target, and fire five shots. This stage reflected the reality that criminal attackers don't give you "handicap points" for having a short-range gun. There isn't room here to list each of the ten stages, but let it suffice to say that all were challenging!

USING REPLICATED COVER and supposedly wounded in gun arm, Gail Pepin sweeps an array of targets "weak hand only."

LESSONS FROM THE BUG CHAMPIONSHIP

The 2011 match saw far more subcompact autos in 9mm and .40 S&W in play than snub-nose .38s, but it was the latter that won the overall championship. Retired USAF pilot Dave "The Blaze" Blazek was overall winner with a pair of LaserGripped lightweight S&W Centennials firing 130 grain .38 Special ammunition. Lesson: The old wisdom that "a second gun is faster than a reload" seems to hold some water. Further Lesson: When there are several dim-light situations involved, as in real life, a laser sight comes into its own.

A SCRAP CAR DOOR and some inventiveness create a stage replicating use of part of vehicle as cover.

Having your hand on the gun speeds the draw. A draw breaks down into "access" (getting past the concealing garment(s) and placing the hand onto the gun – the toughest part) and "presentation" (ripping the gun out of the holster and bringing it on target—the somewhat easier part). Blazek in first place with his J-frame S&W .38s, and me in third place starting with hand on a Springfield Armory XD(m) subcompact 9mm fitted with InSight X2 laser/white light unit in an Uncle Mike's fanny pack, proved that at the match. Lesson: If circumstances allow you to surreptitiously grasp your concealed handgun "before the balloon goes up," DO IT!

While lasers help, you don't necessarily need them to shoot well. First place in non-laser category and second place overall was IDPA Five-Gun Master John Strayer, working a Springfield XD9 subcompact auto out of a high-ride Blade-Tech hip holster. He felt that the Dawson night sights on his pistol definitely helped him in the many dim-light stages at the event. That said, however, Strayer employed his own "backup to the backup" S&W 340 M&P on at least one stage; placed second in the BUG Championship in 2010 with multiple Crimson Trace equipped

STOCK SERVICE REVOLVER National Champ Craig Buckland begins stage "asleep in a tent."

S&W J-frame snubs; and used a bone-stock S&W 642 with Crimson Trace laser to win the famous Snubby Summit match hosted by Andy Stanford in Titusville, Florida, in 2005.

Utter reliability remains paramount. I watched one shooter with a low-priced .380 who was doing quite well, but dropped out of contention to win when his budget pistol jammed repeatedly. The top five shooters were using utterly reliable guns: Blazek with J-frame S&W revolvers; Strayer with the XD9 and the S&W 340 for backup; me with an XD(m) 9mm subcompact and, on one stage,

THIS SHOOTER FIRES from rear passenger seat. In a motorized society, IDPA uses a lot of vehicle situations in its quest for realistic stages.

a backup S&W 340; David Brackett in fourth place with a Glock 26 9mm subcompact; and Chris Christian, a Master IDPA shooter, rounding out the top five with a Smith & Wesson M&P 9mm Compact auto and a Taurus Model 85 .38 snub for backup.

Backup to the backup makes sense. Note how many who made the "top five" used a second gun at some point. Dave Blazek, the overall winner, did so every time he ran past five shots, and beat everyone else. There is a lesson here.

Thanks to Lance Biddle for running this instructive event, and to Gordon Schorer at The Gun Shop (www. gunrange.net) for hosting it, and to range safety officers Dave Chandler, Dale Gikiere, Bert Medlin, Dave Rodgers, and John Grubb, who made it happen.

Shooting challenging scenarios under stressful, difficult conditions is some of the best defensive training you can get. Biddle's ground-breaking work with these "pocket guns" teaches useful lessons to all of us who use them for lawful purposes, whether as our primary armament or our "backup." If you're interested in attending next year's "Backup Gun Championship of the Known Galaxy," send an email to onthebeep@yahoo.com and ask to be put on the list for notification.

\# \# \# \#

Because of its emphasis on "street guns," concealment holsters, and tactical elements such as use of cover, IDPA serves my personal "competition as an element of training" needs right now, better than any other single shooting game. As they say on the Internet, your mileage may vary. However, there are many competitive shooting disciplines that can sharpen relevant defensive skills for you. The trick is knowing what you're getting out of each, and putting together the right training recipe: a pinch of this, and a soupcon of that. Here's one approach…

FIRING OUT THE LEFT REAR of the car at a forward angle is more difficult: you can see shoulders supported on window frame, but inside the car, right leg is exerting pressure to hold the shooter stable in this awkward position.

THE COMPLETE DEFENSIVE HANDGUNNER[4]

The polished all-around wingshooter would want a slap of trap, a spray of sporting clay, a fleet of skeet, and a smidgeon of pigeon on his or her shooting development schedule. Let's consider an optimum regimen of skill tests and learning experiences for the trained defensive handgun shooter.

A NEED FOR SPEED

When your life's on the line, a couple of fast "8"s can beat a slow "10." Pilots say speed is life, and some gunfighters agree. Jeff Cooper made this element one third of his three-part formula for success: accuracy, power, speed. We recall that Bill Jordan said "Speed's fine, but accuracy's final." I'll buy that, but Bill's saying "speed's fine" isn't exactly out of context by itself.

IPSC, the International Practical Shooting Confederation, offers practical shooting matches at venues nationwide through its arm in this country, USPSA (United States Practical Shooting Association). Coarse accuracy delivered with lightning speed is what wins in this game. Ross Seyfried, the second American to win the world champion-

WHEN SHOOTER BEGINS in middle of rear seat...

ship in this discipline, is famous for saying "You can't miss fast enough to win." That's true of most things, but I've seen some IPSC courses in the last few years where the emphasis was so much on speed that you could miss fast enough (every now and then) to at least place first in a stage.

IPSC is notorious for "race guns and space guns," but if you shoot in the increasingly popular Limited Stock Class, a "street" Government Model .45 or Glock .40 service pistol will do just fine. My favorite tournament in this vein is the superbly managed 1911 Single Stack Classic.

Steel plate shooting is another high speed game, with more of a premium on accuracy. It reaches its apotheosis

...more movement is required to get into firing position. From 2010 IDPA National Championships.

in the famed Steel Challenge, subtitled the World Speed Shooting Championships. There's no "D-zone" margin of error for sloppy hits; if you miss the plate you have to shoot at it some more while the clock is running. It's a "pass/fail" kind of deal.

For a while, you needed trick guns to be competitive here. Now, however, Steel Challenge wisely offers classes for IDPA-type service guns so people can compete on a level playing field with the guns they carry for protection. There's even a category for single action "Cowboy" revolvers.

WEIGHTED LEASH represents straining dog; this shooter tries to control both that and his gun at a particularly challenging IDPA stage.

AN INCISION OF PRECISION

"But accuracy's final," said Jordan, the veteran of many a lethal shooting encounter. Bill was an enthusiastic supporter of PPC, the Practical Police Course that NRA has thus far limited to cops and security personnel, but which many local clubs offer to all law-abiding citizens.

The shooting pace is slow. For example, you have 20 to 25 seconds to draw, fire six, reload, and unleash six more from the seven yard line. The slowness is the bad news. The good news is that the regulation PPC target, the B-27, has a center ring the size of a human heart, even if it's located more toward the solar plexus of the target than it

should be. Courses are heavily laced with kneeling, prone, and standing barricade stages, which give PPC more emphasis on shooting from cover than any other handgun sport. These elements are all to the good.

Once solely the province of the sixgun, PPC is now offered by NRA for autopistol shooters as well. Long defined by ridiculously heavy "PPC guns" firing light wadcutter midrange .38 Specials with the recoil of a mouse burp, the game got a bad rap for practicality in terms of hardware. Fortunately, that has changed.

My inclination today is toward PPC matches I can shoot

CINDY BOWSER, one of IDPA's top female contestants, needs all her considerable skills to control both "lunging dog's leash" and her SIG 9mm.

in the Service and Distinguished classes. NRA Service Revolver requires a four-inch factory barrel and sights produced by the factory. NRA Off-Duty Revolver has the same rules, with a 2½-inch barrel demanded. NRA Distinguished is done to the same tune with up to six-inch barrels allowed. In all cases, 158 grain lead service loads are required. No +P or Magnum ammo are allowed, because what it might give the shooter in more practical training is overcome by the unfair distraction to the competitor on either side of you from the louder blast. Remember, it's a skill test and the rangemasters have to keep a level playing field. Recoil reduction modifications like muzzle brakes, Hybridizing, or Magna Port are also forbidden.

In NRA Service Auto, similar rules are in play. Factory barrel and slide, no recoil control devices, and of course, iron sights from the factory that made the gun. In Police Distinguished Automatic, they'll allow a BarSto service configuration barrel and BoMar sights. Duty loads are required in each case, with 147 grain Winchester subsonic 9mm and Federal Match 230 grain .45 hardball being among the most popular choices.

In Service events, sixgun or auto, the course goes from three to 25 yards, and consists of 48 shots with 480 points possible. In Distinguished, both pistol and revolver will fire 60 shots with 600 points possible from seven to 50 yards, with some 24 rounds unleashed at the latter, demanding distance.

Needless to say, a perfect 600 score in Distinguished is extremely rare, though it does happen on occasion. Even the 25-yard service courses are tough. Only one of the more than 500 of us who shot the Service Revolver event at the National Police Shooting Championships in Jackson, Mississippi, this year posted a clean 480: Defending national champion Clay Tippitt of the U.S. Border Patrol. (I was a distant ten points behind him with a four-inch Python I used to carry on duty. Funny… the "480" score had worked in rehearsal…)

A DOLLOP OF WALLOP

A tenet of competitive shooting is to work up the load with the least recoil that the rules will let you get away with. This is in direct contradiction to the conventional wisdom of survival in the street, which is to use the most powerful round you can control. Sure, I can shoot bone-jarring .45 Super ammo in the S&W 4506 Gary Hindman converted for me and go against guys with 147 grain subsonic 9mm in a service pistol match, but I like a level playing field as much as the next guy. We all need to work on controlling hard recoil in rapid, accurate combat fire, but

DAN BURWELL DEDICATES support hand to weighted leash, and gun hand to S&W M&P 9mm in this challenging stage at 2010 IDPA Nationals.

it's better to use the heavy stuff in a match where it does you some good.

Pin shooting is hard to beat. The "Handgun Bowling" game was created (in the 1970s) by soft body armor inventor Rich Davis of Second Chance, whose company hosted the premier such event. To blow the heavy wooden tenpins off the table faster than the other guy, you need a bullet with some smack to it. Hang all the compensators you want off the business end, you're still going to have to absorb some recoil. That goes double in local events that require you to use un-ported, un-compensated Stock class guns.

Triton's hot 10mm 165 grain JHP at 1300 feet per second (fps), Black Hills's full power 230-grain .45 Auto JHP, and Cor-Bon's +P .45 have all worked well for me at Second Chance. I won the New England Regional pin shooting championship a few years ago with a Smith & Wesson Mountain Gun firing Federal 180 grain .44 Magnums rated for 1600 fps. It was a "pins from Hell" match, and that's the kind of power it took to get the wood off the table. See why I feel that at a pin match, you'll get your "monthly recoil requirement"?

Most pin shoots have shotgun events, too, which are ideal for the buckshot-loaded twelve-bore that is so popu-lar as a final resort for home defense. You don't need to be a bear to control this kind of power, you just need to be smarter than the shotgun. A good example is petite Bonnie Young, who wielded a 12-gauge Remington 11-87 with Double-O with her husband Sam and myself to finish in the money in the three-person team event at Second Chance '98.

A WHACK OF "TAC"

Building search tactics, use of cover, movement patterns, use of light in dark situations and other elements of tactics are often more important to survival than pure shooting skill. "Tactical shooting" is what I would stick with if I could apply but one competitive shooting discipline to my own training regimen.

Ken Hackathorn started it all when he designed the "Hackathorn Invitational." His friend and colleague Rick Miller picked up the ball with the Paladin System, an example or match from which traditionally appeared for many years in every issue of *Combat Handguns* magazine. Emphasis is on tactical movement, taking cover when possible, engaging threats in tactical order, etc. Naturally, only "street guns and gear" are allowed.

Numerous gun clubs around the country have picked up on Rick's Paladin concept. I remember shooting a Paladin match in Miami years ago, and being pleased that I

IDPA STAGE DESIGNERS can be sneaky. As author fires from cover toward target at right…

could win First Class A honors with the gun I was legally carrying there, a five-inch Colt .45 auto that I then wore on police patrol as well as for concealed carry. We all had to draw from concealment, too.

Some groups have branched off the Paladin concept in their own direction. A good example is TAG, the Tactical Arts Group in Southern New Hampshire. More than once, these streetwise gunnies have taken a homicide case I was working on and made it into a match. Their shooters got up to date "fresh from the street" skill testing and problem solving, and my client and I had the benefit of watching a number of people relive his incident to see what we could learn from it.

Perhaps the best "home grown" tactical event I've seen is that run by street-wise police officer Marty Hayes at his school, FAS, the Firearms Academy of Seattle. These "FASTactics" events, as I've come to think of them, are some of the most treacherously cunning I've ever experienced …and, therefore, some of the most valuable for learning survival on the street.

Tactical shooting reached its height with the National Tactical Invitational, created in 1990 by Walt Rauch, Chuck Davis, and Skip Gochenour. (The event ran through

…another target pops up just off his left shoulder. "Tunnel vision in action" was experienced by most who shot this stage at IDPA Nationals, 2010.

the year 2010 before disbanding.) I shot it for the first six years, but feedback from later years indicated it was always instructive.

All true tactical shooting events require the gun to be concealed or worn in a secured uniform duty rig. Full power ammo, practical iron sights, and no recoil control devices seem to be universal rules also.

FINDING THE BALANCE

Some shooting disciplines are pre-balanced for you. Former IPSC national team member Bill Wilson brought in Hackathorn and Rauch from the tactical side to form IDPA. The result was a shooting discipline that might be called "Street IPSC," and which strikes me as a welcome return to the precepts upon which Jeff Cooper founded IPSC (in 1976).

Some are delighted with where IDPA is going. Some don't think it goes far enough. I was at a tactical match recently where a contestant who had shot IDPA said loudly, "For God's sake, IDPA says being 50% behind your cover is acceptable! Mas, you're a tactical guy. What do you think of that?"

"Well," I replied, "I think that's 50% better than IPSC."

With a much smaller maximum point zone on the target than IPSC, and using a "Vickers Count" scoring system that is more accuracy-driven than the speed-driven "Comstock Count" most often used in IPSC, IDPA is going in the tactically correct direction. I invoke Jordan one more time: "Speed's fine, but…" Well, you know the rest.

That said, IDPA is not entirely accuracy driven. My first year or so of shooting it, I strove to deliver maximum five-point hits as fast as I could. I would be near the top, but never first place. "Always the bridesmaid," as it were.

In mid-1998, I changed my strategy slightly and began shooting IDPA as fast as I could stay in the four-point zone, which is not dissimilar to the upper part of the K5 zone on FBI's old Colt silhouette target. I started winning the local matches, and have thus far garnered three IDPA state champion titles. (One for revolver, one for team, and one, bless me, for state champion "Senior." The breath of mid-life crisis grows hotter at the back of my neck…)

Requiring concealment in some stages and a concealable holster in all of them, IDPA wisely demands engaging multiple targets in tactical order and puts a much heavier penalty on hitting an "innocent bystander" target than does IPSC. Naturally, the "no comps/no optics" rule is in effect. IDPA may not go as far toward street reality as I might like, but it's coming closer all the time, and I think it's a very relevant test of survival shooting skills.

NRA Action Pistol, a discipline whose flagship is the famous Bianchi Cup, took a turn back toward reality in 1998 when director Russ Stott wisely put in a new and heavily rewarded "stock gun class." An accurate 1911 or other service pistol or a Smith & Wesson 686 revolver could easily win it, and in fact, the latter did. With equal parts barricade shooting, falling plate shooting, moving targets, and a demanding Practical event closely modeled after Jeff Cooper's famous Advanced Military skill test, the Bianchi

Cup is remarkably "street relevant" so long as you shoot it with street relevant gear! I shot the '98 event after an almost ten-year layoff, using a stock HK 9mm and a Ted Blocker LFI Concealment Rig. I didn't score well, which galvanized me to train harder, and that's one of the things skill testing in a match environment is about.

I'm particularly partial to GSSF (Glock Shooting Sports Foundation) matches. I've never seen a course of fire that is so effective at simultaneously challenging the master shooters and being a great experience for the novices, each of whom shoot against their own classes. Yes, you have to use a Glock, but a bunch of you carry that brand anyway. GSSF's Chris Edwards did a splendid job of creating a good test of pure defensive firing ability, though cover, swift draw, and other tactical elements are not addressed in this sporting environment.

There are other matches that will test your skill. Combat shooters say old-fashioned bulls-eye shooting is irrelevant, but a disproportionate number of the top combat shooters I've seen had bulls-eye as their foundation. It's always easier to get faster once you're accurate, than to get more accurate once you're fast. And the one-handed shooting skills of bulls-eye pistol are needed more often in the real world than any of the people who shoot exclusively two-handed want to believe.

Not all practical real-world shooting is combat. I once had to shoot an impala in the Eastern Transvaal, 117 yards off the muzzle of my four-inch .44 Magnum, or eat dried mutton that night. Skill developed earlier in long range shooting gave us fresh venison instead of old sheep. It wasn't a "preservation of life" thing, but it sure was a "quality of life" thing at the time. A hunter or police officer might need a long range shot to humanely dispatch a crippled animal that has limped a distance from an accident scene. And the rule on defensive pistol shots at long range isn't, "They don't happen," it's just "They don't happen often," which is a different thing entirely.

My gun club has an NRA Hunter Pistol metallic silhouette match every month. If I'm around, I'll shoot it with my carry gun. I'll never be open winner against scoped, single shot T/C Contenders. But each time I shoot a half-size steel ram (about the size of a small dog) off its pedestal a hundred meters away, I'm reminded that the same pistol/cartridge combination would have nailed a gunman in the chest at the same distance. It's a validation of technique and equipment, and therefore, a confidence builder.

IN THIS TOUGH IDPA Nationals stage, shooter had to scoot the "creeper" out from under jacked up vehicle, then get to gun and start shooting.

BOTTOM LINE

The defensive use of the handgun is a multi-dimensional discipline. A pistol match shot by someone who carries a gun for serious business should be seen more as a training experience and a skill test than as a sporting event. The object of the exercise isn't necessarily to win (though it's that much better if you do); the object is to find your weak points in time to shore them up, and also to validate the techniques and equipment you're relying upon to keep yourself and other good people alive and well.

# # # #

The above speaks to the handgun, since that's the topic of this book. You don't want to neglect the increasingly popular sport of "three-gun": pistol, rifle, and shotgun. It's basically IPSC with longer ranges, and a good bit of running with your gunning. If you think that's more suited to soldiers than home defenders, keep in mind that you may have to sprint from the entertainment center to where the household protection long gun is stored when the intrusion alarm goes off. Heck, the Cowboy Action shooters have been doing three-gun all along: a couple of Frontier-style single-action sixshooters, a double barrel or Winchester '97 style scattergun, and a lever action Winchester or equivalent. A friend of mine who taught officer survival and combat shooting for many years at a state level police academy points out that unlike most forms of combat shooting, Cowboy Action often requires you to verbalize as you're bringing your old-fashioned guns to bear…a definitely "street relevant" skill, even if the hardware is a bit dated for modern purposes. Any kind of trigger pulling under pressure puts something positive for defensive use in your "long term muscle memory bank," or my Single Action Shooting Society handle ain't "The Camelback Kid."

While the National Tactical Invitational has been discontinued, master defensive instructor Tom Givens of Rangemaster in Memphis, Tennessee, has for some years run an annual Polite Society Match in conjunction with his yearly National Tactical Conference in venues from his home base to Tulsa, Oklahoma, at the excellent U.S. Shooting Academy facility. The Polite Society Match, named after Robert Heinlein's famous quote "an armed society is a polite society," is a side event to the training conference, a smorgasbord of the best and the brightest in areas ranging from hand to hand combat, to combat shooting, to professional psychologists briefing you on the nature of the opponent you can expect to confront. I've made it an annual stop on my schedule.

PERSPECTIVES

Keep the combat shooting disciplines in perspective. Former world IPSC champ Frank Garcia now teaches some excellent programs at his Universal Shooting Academy in Frostproof, Florida. I enjoyed the heck out of his three-day, three thousand round advanced pistol course, and recommend it enthusiastically. Frank makes the point that if your collective training is your education, the match is the test that determines how well you've absorbed what you learn. If you ever need your firearm as a survival tool, that will be the final exam as it were, and if you haven't fine-tuned those skills you've learned, it could be a "final" exam in more ways than one.

Competitive shooting certainly isn't the be-all and end-all of training. Rather, it is a component of your training. It conditions you to shoot under stress, with your hands shaking and your knees knocking and your mouth as dry as Jim Cirillo told me his was when he faced three armed robbers with only his S&W .38 Special in his hands…and shot down every one of them in what was later determined to be approximately three seconds.

If you study the work of police psychologist Alexis Artwohl, perhaps our leading authority today on altered perceptions as they occur in gunfights, you'll find some interesting similarities to what match shooters experience at every tournament if they're taking it seriously. Dr. Artwohl notes that the most common such phenomenon is *auditory exclusion*, in which even gunfire may go unheard, along with shouts of comrades or witnesses, with an 84% occurrence rate. Almost every match shooter has experienced stages of fire where they don't recall hearing their shots, or hearing a range officer say or even shout something.

Tunnel vision is next, with 79% of those survivors she studied experiencing it. Ever shoot a practical match and not see one of the targets, or miss an identifier such as a badge that one of the targets was "holding"?

Tachypsychia, a sense of things going in slow motion? It happened to 62% of the gunfighters she studied, and if you've shot a match, you've probably experienced it there.

Memory distortion, such as events being recalled out of sequence? 21% of her study group experienced it in gunfights, and probably something close to 100% of action pistol competitors have experienced it after a complicated IPSC or IDPA stage.

Being familiar with these things beforehand makes them easier to handle when they occur in the real world.

All these things taken in context contribute to making the match a microcosm of the gunfight and, therefore, useful live-fire preparation for such an encounter.

Competition is part of an on-going skill test, a personal laboratory in which you can acclimate yourself to using your defensive firearm swiftly and accurately under pressure. Track from McBride in WWI to George in WWII to Hathcock in Vietnam to a generation that has come back from the Middle East as I write this with stories of how practical shooting competition before they went made them more formidable fighters and helped them come back.

History tells us that the person with more experience in fast, accurate shooting under stress has an edge when the stress goes all the way up to life-or-death stakes on the table.

Which is why I keep saying that a shooting match isn't a gunfight, but a gunfight damn sure *is* a shooting match.

[1] First appeared as "Lessons From the 2010 IDPA National Championship," in *Complete Book of Handguns 2011*, by Massad Ayoob

[2] First appeared as "Single Stack Classic" by Massad Ayoob, *American Handgunner* magazine, September/October 1995.

[3] First appeared as "Lessons From the Backup Gun Championships" by Massad Ayoob, first quarter 2011 in Harris Publications' electronic journal, *Tactical Life*.

[4] First appeared as "The Complete Defensive Handgunner" by Massad Ayoob, *Complete Book of Handguns 1999*, Harris Publications.

THIS S&W MODEL 28 .357 and department issue duty gear were carried by one of author's brother officers in the 1970s. Many still rely on this technology.

CHAPTER FIVE

CHOICES

T here are lots of choices to make in this matter. The trick is making the right ones for the right reasons.

CHOOSING THE GUN

The gun? In the military it will be issued to you, and in police service or security work it might be picked for you, and that's that. If the gun you're likely to be fighting with is, say, an issue Beretta 9mm, that's the gun to be both training and competing with, to best hard wire your abilities to reflexively use that weapon when your life is on the line. (And you've got a fine gun to do it with, anyway. I've seen champions like Ernest Langdon and David Olhasso win major titles shooting the Beretta 92 against everything else out there in IDPA, and have seen the Beretta in the hands of military aces like Marine Gunnery Sergeant Brian Zins win the Distinguished and the President's Hundred against the most finely tuned 1911s at Camp Perry. I won the next-to-last PPC match I shot, a Police Service Pistol event, with a 92G.)

You can live with the "company gun," but wish it was more finely tuned to better win a match with it? Consider buying your own "match version." I know lots of cops who carry a Glock 22 on the street, but use a longer barrel Glock 35 for IPSC Production Class competition. In the police revolver days, it was common for officers to carry a four-inch service revolver on the street, and maybe use it in Service competition… to get a six-inch version for Distinguished matches…and perhaps to have a custom gun made up on the same frame and action with a heavy Douglas or Apex six-inch bull barrel and a sophisticated BoMar or Aristocrat sight rib for open class competition.

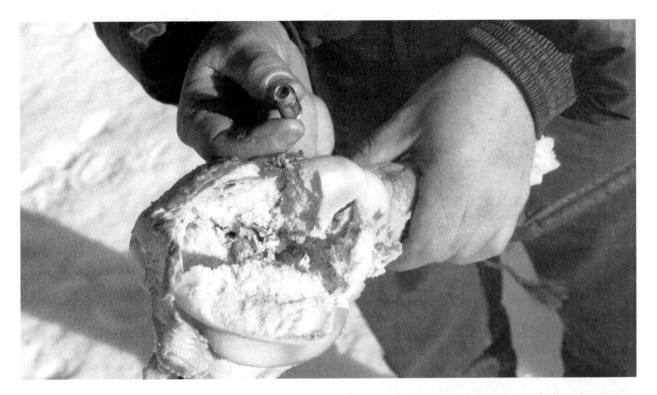

BULLET TESTING ON MASSIVE COW femurs is predictive of whether a bullet is likely to smash a human pelvis or not.

Each modification – lighter trigger, heavier barrel, sights – changes the match gun a little bit more from the street gun. The individual shooter has to balance his or her particular needs or goals. If a slightly lighter trigger, longer sight radius, or sights more suitable for ranges than dark alleys give that particular shooter a better score…and winning the match is more important than perfect replication of the street gun's handling and shooting characteristics…the battery of "similar but not the same" guns may make huge sense.

But if you're shooting competition purely to improve your skills with your home defense gun or carry gun and could care less about winning a prize, shooting with the exact same gun you're likely to be carrying "on that day" makes the most sense of all.

Only you can make the "which gun" choice.

CHOOSING THE AMMUNITION

If caliber isn't chosen for you, pick for your needs: the person giving you advice may have found the best choice for him, but not necessarily for you. The four-inch-barrel Smith & Wesson .44 Magnum was the gun the great Elmer Keith carried until the end of his days: he had helped

MSC (MAXIMUM SUB-CALIBER) AMMO, designed by Ed Sanow, was probably the best load ever developed for a .25, but history still shows us that a .25 auto is a poor choice for self-defense.

develop it, over a lifetime of hunting big game, working cattle, and living outdoors with large things to shoot. Ross Seyfried, the second American world champion of the combat pistol, won the title with a Pachmayr Custom Colt .45 auto, but carried a Model 29 .44 Mag identical to Keith's when working a cattle ranch, and for some of his career as a big game hunting guide, for exactly the same reasons. When I hunted big game in Africa, I carried a four-inch S&W .44 Magnum, because in that time and place, my needs were much like theirs. As an old guy who

OLD-STYLE JHP (jacketed hollow point) (left) didn't always expand in flesh, but its flatter meplat (frontal surface) still did more damage than round nose ball, right.

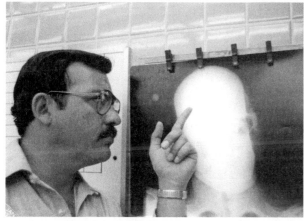

X-RAYS CAN SHOW what to look for during autopsy.

spread as fact. We're talking here about defensive ammo, not competition ammo.

MYTHS ABOUT DEFENSIVE HANDGUN AMMUNITION[1]

Most private citizens who carry guns or keep them at home for self-defense don't get to debrief many police officers or other citizens who've been in gunfights. Most of them don't get to talk with homicide detectives who investigate shootings in detail, or surgeons who treat gunshot wounds, or medical examiners who perform the autopsies when those shootings prove fatal. Nor do they generally get to have long, detailed discussions with the engineers who design and test today's ammunition, using ballistic gelatin and various barriers in the course of their extensive research.

My work does allow me to speak in detail with all those people. Researching gunfight results, going over the detailed reports of fatal shootings and discussing them with the people who put them together, and picking the brains of industry professionals have been part of my job for decades. Nineteen years as chair of the firearms committee of the American Society of Law Enforcement Trainers,

spends less time outdoors than I once did, that gun no longer suits my needs, and the .44 Magnum is certainly not the best choice for your elderly grandmother with osteoporosis. Choice is based on individual need and individual capability.

Once you've decided on revolver or auto, chosen all metal or polymer construction, picked the platform and the brand and the caliber, it's time to choose the ammunition. There again, you want to make the choices for the right reasons. There's a lot of myth on this topic that's

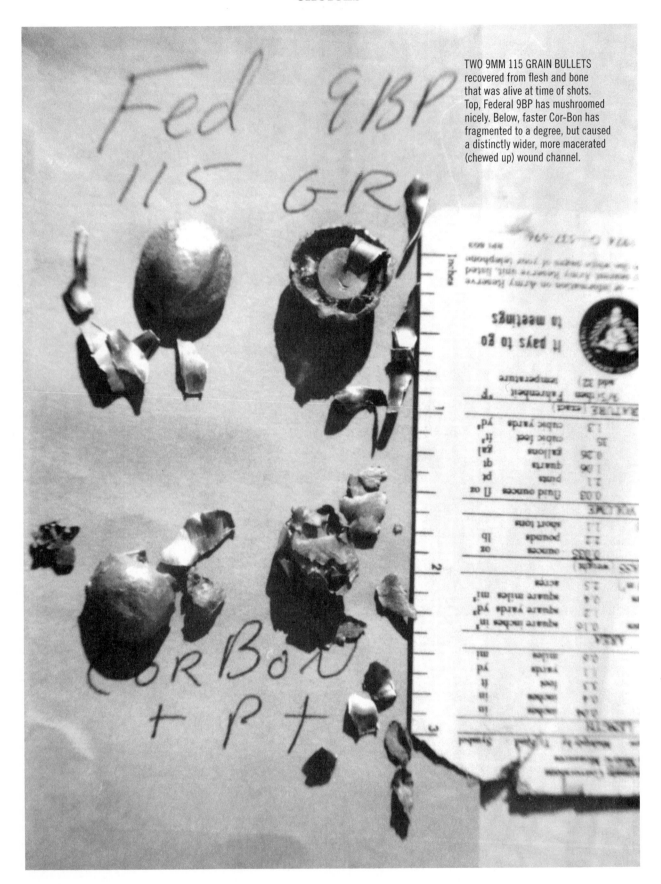

TWO 9MM 115 GRAIN BULLETS recovered from flesh and bone that was alive at time of shots. Top, Federal 9BP has mushroomed nicely. Below, faster Cor-Bon has fragmented to a degree, but caused a distinctly wider, more macerated (chewed up) wound channel.

CALIBRATED BALLISTIC gelatin is today's ballistic testing medium of choice.

and the last several years on the advisory board of the International Law Enforcement Educators and Trainers Association, have given me an uncommon opportunity to access lots of people in lots of law enforcement agencies large and small, to get the inside story on how assorted guns and ammunition have actually worked in real-world gunfights.

The collective input from those real-world sources causes me to shake my head at some of the myths and magical thinking about defensive ammunition that have appeared to some degree in the firearms press, and flourish to a much greater degree on the Internet. Let's look at a few of those.

Myth #1: "Hollow points won't expand anyway, so why use them?"

Reality: Unless you're using old – or old-fashioned – hollow points, that's just not true. The modern high-tech hollow points such as Federal HST, Remington Golden Saber, Speer Gold Dot, or Winchester Ranger-T, almost always expand in actual shootings unless they've gone through something like steel first (tends to crush the nose cavity shut) or plaster wallboard (fills the cavity with inert matter and prevents expansion). And even then, sometimes these bullets will still expand after they've pierced the given barrier to strike flesh.

Myth #2: "9mm and .45 have the same effect."

Reality: Not necessarily. Let's look at one department where that does in fact seem to be the case. Las Vegas Metro gets involved in a lot of shootings. They issue Gold Dot ammunition for all three of their authorized service pistol calibers: 230 grain .45 ACP, 180 grain .40 S&W, and 124 grain +P 9mm. During a visit there early in 2010, LVMPD's firearms training staff told me they were getting equally fast stops with all three loads, assuming hits in the same areas.

However, look at their ammo list carefully. Their .45 is a standard pressure load under 900 foot-seconds velocity, and their .40 is likewise standard pressure, under 1,000 fps. Their 9mm is a +P, rated for 1250 feet per second. This same 124 grain +P Gold Dot 9mm has worked famously well for NYPD for a decade or more, and Chicago PD was very pleased with its improved performance (and that of the similar Winchester 124 grain +P) after they switched to that formula due to disappointment with the performance of previously issued 147 grain JHP.

When you mix like with like, subsonic with subsonic, field experience generally results in an upgrade in caliber. FBI began the trend to the 147 grain subsonic 9mm in the late 1980s. A little more than a decade later, the Bureau

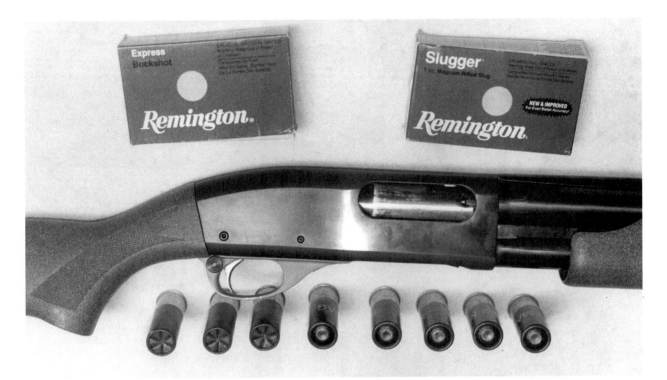

WHETHER LOADED with buckshot or slugs, the shotgun is universally agreed to be a more powerful man-stopper than a handgun, within appropriate range. This is the ubiquitous 12 gauge Remington 870.

adopted the Glock pistol in *.40 S&W* as their standard issue. FBI still authorizes 9mm as an optional round, using a high-tech 147 grain JHP, but also authorizes the .45 ACP, for which they issue the 230 grain JHP. This policy has resulted in solid confidence in their equipment among the estimated 10,000 FBI Special Agents.

We can't ignore the simple laws of physics. A 230 grain +P .45 caliber Winchester Ranger-T or Federal HST bullet, striking at 950 feet per second, and expanding to virtually an inch in diameter after thirteen inches of penetration, is simply going to cause a larger wound than a 147 grain .36 caliber 9mm bullet that expands to only perhaps two-thirds of an inch at the same velocity and penetration depth. Anyone who believes otherwise has never shot test animals and dissected the wounds with those loads, as I have … or perhaps just needs a refresher course in Physics 101.

Myth #3: "Over-penetrating bullets that could strike innocent bystanders don't matter, because statistics say you're going to miss more than you hit and cause more danger with un-slowed bullets, anyway."

Reality: Not true at all. The bystander struck by a missed shot, and the one wounded or killed by a bullet any

WITH THE SAVAGE RECOIL of this 11-ounce S&W 340 and full power .357 Magnum ammo, the recoil reducing glove makes huge sense.

reasonable person would have known was likely to over-penetrate its intended target, are entirely different things. Apples and oranges.

If your "shoot-through" of a legitimate target tragically injures or kills an innocent person, the defense cited in Myth #3 will be torn apart in mere seconds by the opposing attorney, with a single devastating cross-examination question. "So, Mr. Defendant, you disregarded this obvious danger your chosen ammunition presented to innocent people, because you admit you *expected* to be presenting *a different and much greater danger* to those same innocents?!?"

It goes to an element called *mens rea*, which translates literally to "the guilty mind." *Mens rea* means an intent to commit a crime, or a level of negligence so gross that it rises to a culpable (i.e., guilty) standard. The good person who fires a gun at a violent criminal in good faith, making their best effort to hit that criminal and stop the threat he presents to innocent human life, clearly has justifiable in-

102 GRAIN REMINGTON Golden Saber does as well as any .380, but there's still no .380 the author trusts for "stopping power."

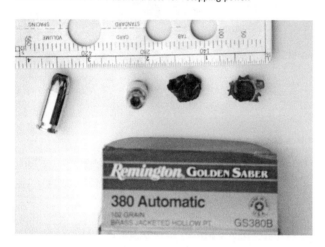

tent. If he misses, it should be easy to prove that he missed because of the stress induced by the criminal shooting at him, or by the criminal ducking and bobbing and weaving as he fired. In other words, it's not hard to show that the proximate cause of the bystander's injury was the action of the criminal, not the defendant who fired at him.

But when that good person loaded his gun with ammunition he knew or should have known would go through and through the criminal – the only "backstop" for the bullet, even if he placed the shot perfectly – everything has changed. He has recklessly disregarded the safety of people who might predictably be behind that criminal, unseen by the shooter because of the tunnel vision that we know is more likely than not to occur in such an encounter, or because the body of the criminal who had to be shot simply blocked the shooter's view.

Anyone who believes that over-penetrating bullets are nothing to worry about in a gunfight owes it to himself (and to his loved ones, who will be affected by the post-shooting ordeal in court) to go to a legal library or online and look up "deliberate indifference." While doing so, he should also look up "reckless and wanton disregard for human life."

WINCHESTER'S NEW HOLLOW point designs create .380s that expand, but the .380 doesn't have the power to both expand well and still penetrate to what FBI considers adequate depth.

158 GRAIN LEAD HOLLOW POINT +P made cops much more secure with the stopping power of their .38 Specials such as S&W Model 10, right, but quest for more firepower led them to autos like 14-shot 9mm Beretta 92 Compact, left.

There is a reason virtually every police department in this country uses expanding bullets that are designed to stay inside the body of the violent offender who may force officers to shoot him. All who keep or carry defensive firearms would be wise to consider the vast pool of collective institutional experience in studying gunfights that led to JHP ammunition becoming the national standard for police handguns in this country.

Myth #4: "Only the permanent crush cavity of the bullet wound track contributes to incapacitation. Temporary stretch cavity around the bullet's path only bruises tissue, and has no effect on incapacitation."

Reality: This belief seems to be an early warning signal that the believer has been paying too much attention to ballistic gelatin test results, and not enough to actual gunfight dynamics, not to mention Logic 101.

If you have ever seen someone take a hard solar plexus punch from a competent fighter, you have seen "temporary wound cavity" in action. As the blunt force of the impact temporarily paralyzed the diaphragm and caused a short-term inability to breathe, the recipient of the blow probably stopped or at least slowed his own aggression, and very likely even doubled over or collapsed to the floor. The blow created a substantial and violent temporary displacement of internal organs – "temporary wound cavity" – but no permanent wound cavity at all. The blow may or may not have caused internal bruising, but it certainly stopped or profoundly mitigated aggression…"stopping power in action," you might say.

Something similar has been widely observed with handgun bullets. Consider the .357 Magnum with 125 grain jacketed hollow point. When this round was introduced in the 1970s, and through the 1980s when it became hugely popular in American law enforcement, the 125 grain Mag load had ample field testing. Coast to coast, reports were almost unanimous as to its ability to stop fights suddenly and dramatically, often with a single solid torso hit. In Indianapolis, the first big city to adopt it to my knowledge, the lieutenant in charge of firearms training told me back in the '70s that the first ten shootings with it were all instant one-shot stops, including three violent perpetrators who sustained only arm or leg wounds. At a nominal velocity of 1400-1450 feet per second from a four-inch barrel, this round also seemed to work well with the 2.5- and three-inch barrels of the weapons then commonly issued to detectives.

It wasn't just Indianapolis. Surrounding Marion County Sheriff's Department had similar experiences. As the con-

FAIRBURN STUDY of ammo effectiveness based on street results, undertaken for Police Marksman Association, showed much the same results as Evan Marshall's research.

cept spread, so did others: Indiana State Police; the Kentucky State Police (some of whose troopers nicknamed the round "the magic bullet"); and Texas lawmen, who coined the term "lightning bolt effect" to describe the results on the other side of the gun when they had to fire in the line of duty.

By the 1990s, when police were going *en masse* to high capacity pistols and disenchantment with standard pressure 9mm JHP loads had already led to the introduction of the .40 S&W cartridge in a joint effort between Smith & Wesson and Winchester, SIG and Federal joined corporate hands to create an auto pistol cartridge that would duplicate the terminal ballistics of the 125 grain .357 Magnum revolver round. The result was the .357 SIG cartridge, with a 125 grain jacketed hollow point in the 1350 to 1400 foot-second velocity range. It quickly proved itself to live up to expectations. The Delaware State Police were the first to adopt it, followed shortly by Virginia State Police and the Richmond, VA Police Department. In the gunfights that followed, the departments unanimously reported *dramatic* performance improvement over the early 147 grain subsonic 9mm rounds they had used prior to the .357 SIG transition. A senior officer of the Virginia State Police told me they were particularly impressed by how many suspects were instantly stopped by hits to areas of the body such as the abdomen, which did not usually result in immediate one-shot stops with other calibers.

Bear in mind that not all scientific ballistics researchers conclude that only permanent wound cavity matters. Many years ago Dr. Bruce Ragsdale, of the Armed Forces Institute of Pathology, determined that a 115 grain +P+ 9mm bullet at 1300 feet per second could tear apart a pig aorta embedded in ballistic gelatin, inches away from being touched by the bullet itself. The 9mm 115 grain +P+, such as the Winchester load or the Federal 9BPLE, established a very solid track record as a "man-stopper" over the decades and remains a viable defensive choice in its caliber today.

Myth #5: "The 147 grain subsonic JHP is the best/ worst 9mm load ever."

Reality: Neither is true, and with some of *today's* high-tech ammo, the truth is more toward the middle.

The first-generation 9mm subsonics, simple copper-jacketed lead hollow points, often but not always produced spotty results in actual gunfights. I saw case after case where it failed to expand and punched through and through. When NYPD went to hollow points, it had ample data on 147 grain subsonic JHP from the city's Transit Authority and Housing Authority police, which NYPD had absorbed, and from other agencies; NYPD chose instead the 124 grain

+P Gold Dot, whose performance they've found most satisfactory. Chicago PD went to 124 grain +P 9mm after multiple failures with 147 grain subsonics. San Diego had some success with the original 147 subsonic, but when they authorized larger calibers, a great many of their officers voted with their feet and their wallets and bought bigger guns out of their own pockets. Ditto LAPD and Los Angeles County Sheriff's Department. As already noted, the agency that started the whole 147 grain 9mm trend, FBI, has long since switched to issuing .40s. The list goes on.

FIRST GENERATION 180 grain subsonic ammo for .40 S&W worked better than expected, but some lighter, faster loads proved even more dynamic in the field.

However, over the years much better 147 grain loads, all using modern high-tech bullets, have emerged. LAPD and LASD report strong satisfaction with the Winchester Ranger version of the 147 grain. Portland, Oregon has been very satisfied with the Federal HST in 147 grain, and that's also the load in San Diego for officers who stayed with the 9mm. I've not heard any complaints about it from there.

If I was required to carry a 9mm with 147 grain subsonic, I would load it with either Federal HST or Winchester Ranger-T, and not lose any sleep over it. However, I would definitely prefer something like the 124 grain +P Gold Dot, and I personally load my 9mms as a rule with the Winchester Ranger-T 127 grain +P+. In dozens of shootings in Orlando out of 9mm SIGs, that Winchester load has performed splendidly, and out of all proportion to its "paper ballistics" (1250 feet per second).

BASIS OF CHOICE

Rather than basing defensive ammunition choice solely on ballistic gelatin lab testing or solely on anecdotal gunfight reports, the best approach seems to be a combination of an experiential base and a laboratory testing base.

AUTHOR EXPERIENCES recoil of full power .357 at its height in 11-ounce S&W. Trigger is being reset as he starts to bring the gun back down. There's such a thing as too much recoil!

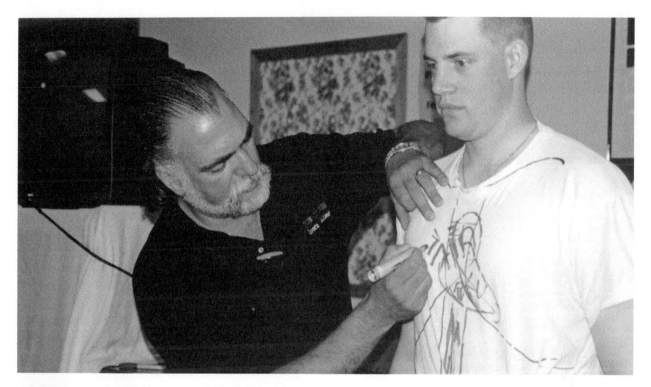

DR. JIM WILLIAMS shows students where the vitals are in his acclaimed Tactical Anatomy class, strongly recommended by author.

RECOIL-INDUCED INERTIA effect seen in 158 grain handloads in 11-ounce S&W .357. Standard round is at far right. Bullet in center cartridge has pulled forward after one or two shots. By three or four shots, round at left has pulled so far forward it will protrude from cylinder face and lock up the gun.

When a round that earns good field reports does not perform consistently in lab testing, it raises understandable doubts. When lab test indicators fly in the face of repeatedly observed reality in the field, it is an early warning that junk science might be in play.

Retired Detroit Police sergeant Evan Marshall and his colleague Ed Sanow are widely seen as the most audible voices from the experiential side, while Dr. Gary Roberts is probably the most prominent spokesman from the laboratory side today. Both cross over into both domains in their analysis of defensive ammunition. If you can find a round both sides agree on, you have all the validation you can possibly get from authoritative sources.

In **.45 ACP**, both sides seem to agree on high-tech 230-grain JHP. In **9mm Luger**, both endorse the "NYPD load," the 124-grain +P. In **.40 S&W**, 165 grain JHPs at 1140 fps that have worked famously in the field from Tulsa (Remington Golden Saber) to Nashville (Winchester Ranger-T) are on the "approved list" for both sides. In **.357 SIG**, the 125 grain Speer Gold Dot that worked so well for Texas DPS, VSP, and Richmond PD are likewise "on both lists."

Once the end-user has a load in which he or she can be confident, it's now easier to focus on the things that are more important to winning gunfights. Alertness. Tactics. Skill at arms.

It's more a software matter than a hardware one, but the hardware is an obviously indispensable part of it, and one of the few elements of the fight that the defender can control beforehand. It's important to make solid choices. And to make sound choices, we have to be able to sort the many myths from the very complicated reality.

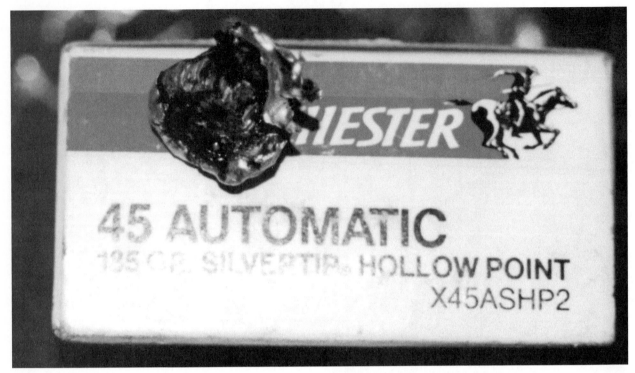

EXPANSION OF WINCHESTER Silvertip 185 grain .45 ACP was ragged but reliable.

CHOOSING WHERE TO AIM

One area where the street and the range sharply diverge is that in a match or a qualification shoot, you'll be told where to aim. "Center-X ring, of course!" (PPC) "Two to the body, one to the head!" (IDPA) On the street, your targets will be limited by what parts of his body the opponent hasn't shielded behind cover, and exactly what it is you have to do with your gun to stop him. He's standing over a downed victim, his upraised knife about to violently descend? If you're sure you can make the shot, a hit in primal brain will stop him faster than anything else, and that part of his body is more distant than any other from the victim you're trying to save, reducing the likelihood that you'll hit the victim instead of the perpetrator. The usual contraindication to the head shot is absent here: visually tunneled on his victim, the criminal can't see your gun coming up to aim at his head, and can't "duck the shot."

You're taking him at gunpoint for whatever reason? I would strongly advise you to aim pelvis high on him: any higher, and your own hands and gun will block your view of his hands, which means you very likely won't see him

DESIGNED FOR DEEP penetration, this 230 grain Remington Golden Saber recovered from flesh has not expanded much. Reduced velocity from three-inch barrel pistol is at least partly responsible.

go for his gun until he's already whipped it out and shot you with it.

He's coming at you with a knife? A deep brain shot is unlikely on a facing man, because while he can't duck your bullet he very likely will reflexively duck away from the shot when he sees your gun coming up to aim at his eyes and head. If his brain is fully oxygenated, you can vaporize his heart and he still has up to fifteen seconds of conscious, purposeful physical activity left before he becomes unconscious…and it only takes him one and a half seconds to reach you from seven yards away, a fact long proven by master gunfight survival

CHRONOGRAPH TESTING for velocity readings is one piece of the ammo selection puzzle.

instructor Dennis Tueller. But if you bust his pelvis, any orthopedic surgeon will confirm, he'll be down in the next step because the cross-member of his skeleton's support will no longer be able to hold him upright.

They don't have pelvic shots in combat matches as a rule, and even a lot of the "head targets" give equal value to a hit that would have instantly dropped a man, and one that might have merely broken his jaw or even only shot off his earring. It's important for the combat shooter looking for real world results to seriously consider points of aim on his opponent's body.

TACTICAL CONSIDERATION: POINTS OF AIM[2]

I'm not sure where the phrase "aim for the center of mass" came from in the world of defensive shooting. It had already been in common use for a long time when I came along, and I'm pretty old. But however ancient the advice is, there are those of us who believe it is obsolete.

WHERE IS "CENTER OF MASS"?

It's generally understood that a "center of mass" (COM) hit means that you've landed a bullet somewhere in the

LONG THE GOLD STANDARD for .45 ACP defense loads, Federal 230 grain Hydra-Shok gave this result in living tissue. Test pistol was short barrel Glock 30.

trunk or torso of the humanoid threat. But where exactly is that center? And of what particular "mass"?

If you (or the person you're teaching) should perceive center of mass to be the center of the human body standing vertically, well, we're probably looking at a "gut shot." Historically, these tend to be highly lethal in the long term, but death is often delayed for many days. The purpose of firing is not to kill a man with a slow-acting bullet wound; it is to make that person *stop his violent attack immediately*, irrespective of whether or not he dies subsequently from the injuries you inflict upon him.

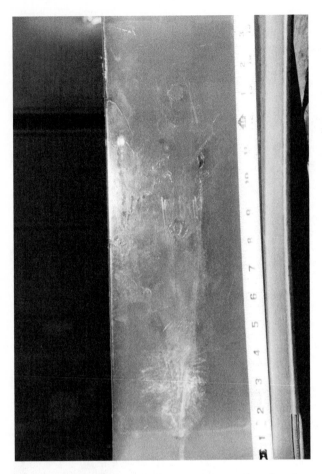

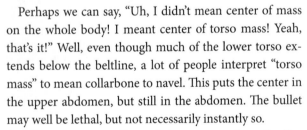

BALLISTIC GELATIN is testing is only one piece of a complicated puzzle when it comes to selection of defensive ammunition.

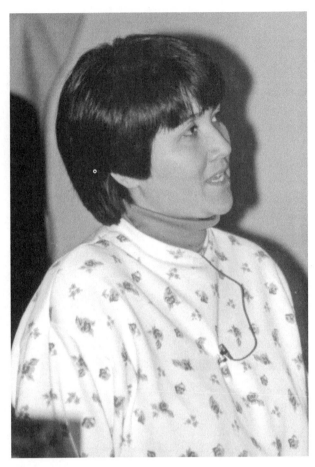

HERO COP STACY LIM OF LAPD addresses one of the author's classes. Shot in the heart with a .357 Magnum, she returned fire with her 9mm and killed her assailant…and obviously survived.

Perhaps we can say, "Uh, I didn't mean center of mass on the whole body! I meant center of torso mass! Yeah, that's it!" Well, even though much of the lower torso extends below the beltline, a lot of people interpret "torso mass" to mean collarbone to navel. This puts the center in the upper abdomen, but still in the abdomen. The bullet may well be lethal, but not necessarily instantly so.

Talk to experts in Tactical Anatomy, such as Dr. Jim Williams, who wrote the highly acclaimed book of that title. Dr. Williams is a gunshot wound survivor himself, and as an emergency room physician he has treated a great many gunshot wounds in others. Cross-trained in combat shooting and the use of lethal force as a sworn police officer and police surgeon, Williams also understands what it takes to deliver "surgical accuracy" from a handgun in a fast-breaking life-or-death situation where the assailant has to be stopped immediately to keep him from crippling or killing the shooter or some other innocent person. Wil-

liams is a competitive shooter who has won state championship titles shooting the service type handgun.

Williams and other experts with his level of medical knowledge recommend a point of aim that centers on the heart. Basically, you are aiming at the point where you would apply pressure if performing CPR. From a square-on frontal angle, this can create a wound track that damages both heart and thoracic spine, an injury likely to result in rapid incapacitation. A bullet that's misplaced a bit high can still hit aorta or thoracic spine. A few inches off to either side still at least gets a lung hit and may cut a pulmonary artery, and low left or right can produce massive hemorrhage in liver or spleen. Low center may put the bullet through the diaphragm, robbing the opponent of his ability to breathe, and may reach mid-spine to drop him in his tracks.

The cardiac point of aim therefore gives the greatest likelihood of a stopping hit, given the fact that we know

166

.357 SIG ROUND, particularly this 125 grain Speer Gold Dot, has delivered awesome performance in shootings from Texas to the east coast.

marksmanship degrades under stress for several reasons. However, we all have to remember that while instant one-shot stops *sometimes* occur from heart shots, *sometimes they don't.*

The heart shot "works" by stopping the supply of oxygenated blood to the brain, resulting in unconsciousness. However, if the brain is fully oxygenated, even if the bullet has completely shut down cardiac function, the individual can "stay up and running," performing conscious physical action, for fourteen or fifteen seconds or so. And, there is no guarantee that a gunshot wound to the heart will result in complete cessation of heartbeat.

Trauma docs will tell you that there are a lot of former patients walking around who have survived being shot in the heart. Many of these wounds involved small caliber bullets, but there are cases where the round was something like 9mm ball or .38 Special. I've not personally run across a case of a human being surviving a .45 caliber gunshot wound through the heart, but I do know of one with a .357 Magnum. She – yes, she! – responded by shooting her assailant twice through the chest with her 9mm Beretta. He turned to run, still pointing the gun dangerously, and she shot him two more times, killing him. She survived to

WINCHESTER'S NOTORIOUS Black Talon didn't proved inconsistent in its 9mm 147 grain subsonic variation. Today's Ranger-T from same maker seems much more reliably effective.

become a role model instructor. Stacy Lim, LAPD, taught us all some lasting lessons that night.

THE PELVIC SHOT

The pelvis is the cross-section of skeletal support. You can shoot a guy in the leg and he may still stay up, but if your bullet smashes the pelvic girdle – the big ring of bone that encompasses our hips – the body can no longer stay upright or ambulate, and the man you've shot will probably collapse within the next step he attempts to take. If you doubt that, ask any trauma surgeon or orthopedic surgeon.

167

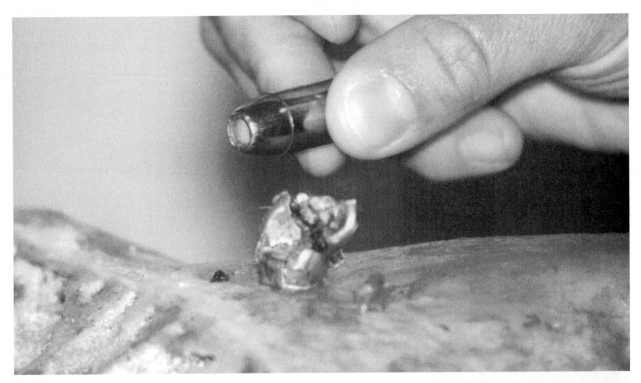

WHEN RECOVERED from actual flesh and bone, many hollow points don't expand to the same shape they do in homogeneous ballistic gelatin.

In a famous gunfight in Baton Rouge, Louisiana, many years ago, a violent felon attacked two police officers and managed to gain control of one cop's service revolver. He shot her in the heart, and she fell, dying – the first female police officer to be murdered in the line of duty in the state of Louisiana. Her male partner entered an epic struggle with the man, shooting him nine times with .38 Special bullets. Yes, he had to reload during the fight, and was seriously injured himself. An award winning competitive police combat shooter, he hit the cop-killer with every shot he fired, most of them center-mass. One of his bullets, aimed intentionally at the killer's head, opened up his skull and exposed brain matter…and the man got up from the floor and kept fighting.

At the end, the embattled cop, Officer Steve Chaney, fired his tenth shot into the man's pelvis, and the manic cop-killer dropped like the proverbial rock. Unable to regain his feet, he bled out and died on a carpet saturated with his life's blood. Chaney would say later that the shot to the "hip-bone" was the only one that kept him down… and ended the terrible death battle.

History shows that the pelvic shot tends to immobilize the recipient of the wound, so long as a serious fracture

ACCURACY IS ANOTHER piece of the puzzle. Old Pro-Load .45 ACP ammo gave this excellent 25 yard group from author's Glock 30; the stray hit in the 8-ring was probably human error.

occurs in the pelvic girdle. That area of the body also encompasses some major blood vessels and "nerve centers." Men hit with bullets from powerful guns in this area of the body tend to fall to the ground, often "jack-knifing" – doubling over – as they go down. Survivors of these wounds often describe excruciating, debilitating pain, and inability to stand after sustaining the injury.

In the 1960s, NYPD created the famed Stakeout Squad, a group of thirty-some hand-picked marksmen who were placed in robbery-prone places of business, or locations

A COLT .45 AUTO issued to the Shanghai Police in the 1920s, from the collection of Wayne Anthony Ross. Note that grip safety and thumb safety have both been pinned. Shanghai cops carried them hammer down on empty chambers, and racked the slides when trouble reared its head. Not a good plan today, in many respects, author believes.

where detectives had gotten tips that a robbery was going to go down. The duty handgun round at that time was the 158 grain solid (non-expanding) .38 Special bullet at standard pressure, which meant relatively low velocity. The Stakeout people went to famed pathologist Vincent DiMaio, Senior, then the chief medical examiner for the city of New York. (His son, Vincent DiMaio, Jr., would later become the chief ME of Bexar County, Texas, and write the authoritative text titled *Gunshot Wounds*.) Dr. DiMaio, Sr. told the squad that their best chance of dropping a man in his tracks, if they could not guarantee the difficult task of a deep brain shot, was to shoot him in the pelvis.

The Stakeout cops took him seriously. Of the three Stakeout Squad members who amassed the largest number of shootings in the controversial history of the unit, one shot so many men in the pelvis that he earned the nickname "The Proctologist," because as one member of the squad put it, "Everybody he shot in the ass hit the ground." Obviously, that officer was not aiming for the gluteus maximus, the muscle structure of the buttocks where children were traditionally spanked because it would hurt but wouldn't

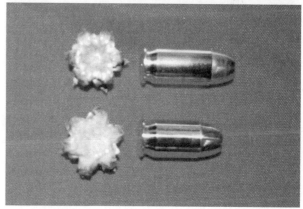

STANDARD PRESSURE .45 ACP, top, and .45 GAP seem to have identical performance with identical bullets, in this case Winchester Ranger SXT.

injure; he was aiming for the pelvic girdle, which also encompassed the coccyx, the "tailbone" of the spine.

THE DEEP BRAIN SHOT

There is much bad advice out there about where to specifically aim a shot to a lethal opponent's brain cavity. It's not just a "head shot." Much of the human head does not contain vital areas. I know one officer who was shot in the chin at point-blank range with a 230 grain .45 Auto hardball round, on course to his brain stem. However, the bullet glanced off the heavy, curvilinear bone of his lower

DON'T FALL FOR THE MYTH that double action autos can't be shot well. S&W 4013 put 60 timed shots into this tight qualification group, using full power .40 S&W ammo.

mandible (jaw), and took a path safely away from the part of his body "where he lived." To make a long story short, that officer – shot seven times total with a .45 – shot back with his Glock .40 and nailed his assailant seven times in return. The last three 180 grain jacketed hollow point police bullets hit the gunman's head, one tearing through the brain and leaving the would-be cop-killer dead on the ground. The officer has since recovered, after many surgeries, and returned to full duty status. I've had the privilege of shooting pistol matches with him since. (He's a helluva good shot. "It's all in the motivation.")

MORE VISIBLE SIGHTS, easier-operating thumb safety, and modern-shaped grip safety fit the needs of the owner of this 1911 pistol.

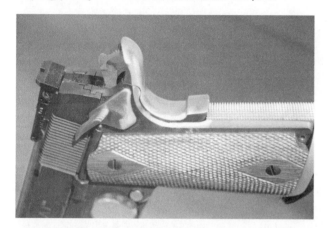

Some of the prevalent bad advice includes, "Shoot him between the horns!" A famous instructor, no longer with us, advised to aim for the center of the forehead. Gun-wise physicians, including neurologists and neurosurgeons whom I've discussed this with, disagree emphatically. They will tell you that this part of the head is in front of the upper brain, and a hit there can trigger what they colloquially call "an electrical storm in the nervous system." That is, the body will tend to tighten its muscles spasmodically when the brain is injured here.

This is why we see people shot in the upper brain appear to stand up on tiptoes, then topple over; the strongest muscles in the legs are the anti-gravity muscles, and when they spasmodically tighten, that "up on tiptoes effect" is the result.

When you're under fire from someone trying to kill you, his standing on tiptoes won't make or break your survival. What does matter is, if he is pointing his gun at a hostage and has his finger on the trigger, a shot to upper brain may well cause him to reflexively fire the gun! This is because, as those muscles tighten throughout the body at the instant he receives the wound, the flexor muscles of the fin-

THIS S&W MODEL 640 has had its cylinder latch turned into a Murabito thumb safety by Rick Devoid, www.tarnhelm.com. It's shown here in "on safe" mode.

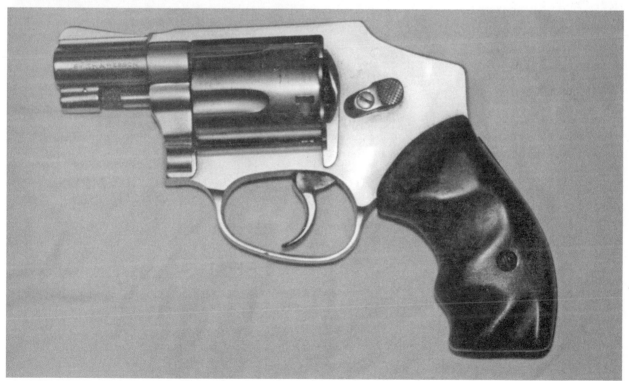

CUSTOM SIGHTS, reshaped and stippled grip better suited this Glock to its owner's needs.

gers are stronger than the extensor muscles.

Carlos Hathcock, the Wimbledon Cup Rifle Champion who went on to become the most famous Marine Scout-Sniper of the war in Vietnam, well understood this. In Charles Henderson's biography of Hathcock, *Marine Sniper*, you can read of a case where Hathcock saw an enemy soldier pointing a 7.62X39 rifle at American lines. Hathcock threw his scoped bolt-action to his shoulder and cracked off a shot as soon as his crosshairs hit the enemy soldier's head. At the moment the bullet hit the man in the brain, he reflexively fired his rifle. Fortunately, he did not hit anyone. The brain-shot man then staggered several yards, like a zombie, before he collapsed. Forever after, including his second career training American police SWAT snipers, Hathcock emphasized the importance of shooting the bad guy lower in the head – in deep brain.

Even the famous "between the eyes" shot may hit too high – at least if the killer's head is erect as you sight your gun on him – to keep him from firing a reflexive, deadly shot when he is hit. Study of anatomy shows us that if the head is erect, the *deep brain* area – the pons and the medulla oblongata – will be situated behind the nose if the killer is facing the shooter who is firing the rescue shot.

GHOST RING rear sight on Glock.

The nasal cavity, unlike much of the rest of the skull – and remember, doctors call it the "cranial *vault*" for good reason – is not likely to cause the bullet to ricochet. There is only relatively soft, honeycombed sinus material between the bullet and the part of the murderer's brain that you have to short-circuit to rescue the victim.

EXTERNAL ANATOMIC LANDMARKS

Surgeons use markers to draw lines and spots where they will insert the scalpel as the operation begins. The term they use is "external anatomic landmarks." This means the spot on the outside of the body that aligns with the spot inside the body where external intervention needs to take place.

For the surgeon, that landmark "marks the spot" where the "benevolent knife" will begin the surgery that will heal the sick. For the armed rescuer, it marks the point where the rescuing bullet must enter a malignant human being's body to shut down the organism and render it incapable of killing or crippling other, innocent human beings.

For the head, picture a headband pulled down over the ears, and now wrapped around those ears, and the nose, and in the back, the occipital protuberance, that bump you can reach up now and feel at the base of your skull. With the head erect, that will guide the bullet into the brainstem and turn off the human being with instant collapse. While lesser mammals may convulse with "post-agonal response" – what the layman calls "death throes" – from such an injury, the more sensitive and highly evolved human simply collapses from with totally relaxed muscles. It happens instantaneously. This is why Hathcock, and the master snipers in both the police and military worlds, followed his advice to aim there.

If the head is thrown back as the attacker looms over the victim who is about to fire in self-defense, the orientation of the external anatomic landmarks vis-à-vis the underlying deep brain changes. Now you would be wiser to aim your bullet through the open mouth, or under the chin if the mouth is closed, to lace it into deep brain. And if the opponent is facing you with his head bent forward in the frequently seen body posture of aggressive assault, now the "between the eyes" aiming point, sometimes called "the Lone Ranger Mask" or the "cranio-ocular shot," will be perfectly in line with deep, primal brain.

For "body work," forget that nebulous "center mass" terminology. You are aiming for the heart, and from the front, heart into spine. Between the nipples is the aiming point on an erect human torso. If you are firing upward or your target is leaning backward, aim lower; if the target is bent forward in an aggressive "I'm coming to kill you!" posture, set your sights lower to angle the shot upward and into the "fuel pump." Two friends of mine were involved in a cataclysmic gun battle with two violent, heavily armed robbers. The first perp, a very large man, fell into the smaller partner and knocked him down, his corpse atop him like a human sandbag. As the two officers poured fire into the threat, one had the presence of mind as he dropped his empty gun and reached for a loaded one to yell to his partner, "Bill, you're hittin' high!" In moments, the bullets had

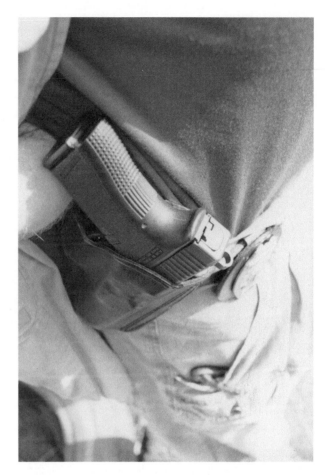

OLDER EYES need more visible sights. Ghost ring on this Glock works well for some.

gone to the right place, and both gunmen were dead on the floor.

For decades now, I have taught my students that they should have a copy of the classic textbook *Grey's Anatomy* on their bookshelf next to their firearms manuals. I remind them, as I remind you now, to memorize the diagrams until you can visualize the internal structures automatically from any angle.

As you study this topic, analyze whether the proponents of any given point of aim have actually studied gunfights in which people were shot in those parts of the body, or whether they are just reflexively parroting old training mantra of "center of mass" or "two in the body, one in the head." In a recent internet forum discussion on this topic, some folks said, "The pelvis will be harder to hit than the heart."

Dr. Jim Williams, the police surgeon and tactical anatomy expert cited earlier, recently told me he had calculated "the target area (in frontal plane) of the vulnerable bony

DOUBLE ACTION first shot autos proved to work well in gloved hands. S&W 9mm Model 3913 is shown.

area of the average (70 kg./150 lb) adult male pelvis as 110 square inches, and the vulnerable neurovascular area of the pelvis at 45 square inches, vs. approximately 30 square inches for the high-chest (mediastinal) target zone (again, the frontal plane)."

THE BOTTOM LINE

Anyone who has studied this ugly discipline comes to the same conclusion: placement of the shot is more important than any other factor in stopping the threat posed by the homicidal human. Knowing your target is every bit as important as knowing your weapon. Head shots fail when the bullet doesn't reach deep brain. "Center mass" shots fail when the bullet doesn't reach vital internal structures. Pelvic shots fail when they don't strike the actual pelvis with enough power to cause major fracture; pre-fragmented "frangible" bullets are notorious for this, as are round-nose bullets that ricochet off hard, curvilinear bone structures, just as they do with skull hits.

It is an ugly topic to have to discuss. But failing to stop a murderer who can be stopped with no other means but gunfire is an even uglier and more unacceptable outcome.

COMMONALITY OF TRAINING. Little Colt .380, below, has exact same manual of arms as full size .45, above.

CHOOSING HOW TO AIM

Debates between different camps on ammo choices have approached a level in some quarters that reminds you of religious fanatics, right down to one side declaring a *fatwa* against their perceived "enemies" and attempting to destroy their careers. You see a similar fervor in the debate over "point-shooting versus aimed fire" on the technique side of the combat shooting house. This stuff is not a belief system, folks, it's an evolving art and science.

ALL ABOUT AIMING[3]

We'll never know how many forests have died for printed media arguments, or how much bandwidth has been consumed for Internet arguments on the issue of aimed fire versus point shooting. As the late Dave Arnold wrote and often said in private, much of the heated argument comes from people misunderstanding one another's terminology. I've come to think of that aspect as "Combat Semantics."

One side says that if you don't use a sight picture you won't hit well enough to save your life. The other side says that you won't be able to see your sights in a high-stress situation, and thus only point shooting can save you. Who is correct?

Within those limits of terminology, both and neither. The first thing we need to do is establish a working definition of what is "aimed fire" and what is "point shooting." Without such definitions to establish clear baselines, we will continue going in circles over this issue.

DEFINITIONS

For purposes of understanding each other, let me state at the outset the definitions I work within on this issue.

THIS SPRINGFIELD 1911 .45 tuned and recoil compensated by Mike Plaxco won several matches for author, but is not a practical "street gun."

But first, two concepts need to be understood: index and coordinates. The index is what lines up the firearm with the intended target. The coordinates are what must be accomplished to achieve index.

For instance, a Gunsite graduate firing from a classic Weaver stance is using a visual index, and his coordinates include a boxer's stance, a two-hand grasp, and an isometric push-pull on the handgun.

There are basically two kinds of indices: a visual index is one in which the shooter can see where their gun is located in relation to the target. A body position index is one

WALTHER .380 in Thunderwear worn beneath pants, while not optimum in power, serves the concealed carry needs of some.

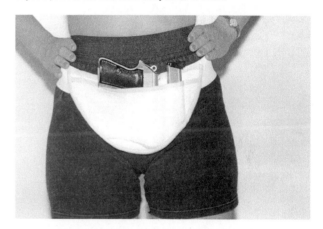

NOT EVERYONE has the same choice factors. For many years, when going overseas, author took this 9mm Browning Hi-Power, because ammo, parts, and magazines were easy to find in most countries. Today, a Glock 9mm might better suit same needs.

where the shooter can see the target but not his own gun. For example, the popular "speed rock" technique uses a body position index. Inspired by Western-style fast draw competition of the 1950s, adapted to combat pistol doctrine by Jeff Cooper during the same period and popularized in modern defensive usage by my colleague Chuck Taylor later, the speed rock's coordinates are: the shooter square to the target, upper body rocked back at hips to elevate gun muzzle, and gun fired from hip level with one hand only. Optionally, the upper portion of the handgun is rolled slightly outward to allow recoiling slide to clear body, holster, and outer garments, and to direct the shot more toward the centerline of the target.

As I define it in training (and here), a visual index would be some degree of aimed fire, the degrees of aim in question ranging from very coarse to very precise. A shooting method that relied totally on body position index would be true point shooting.

WHAT YOU NEED TO SEE

World-class practical shooting champion Brian Enos said it best: "See what you need to see." What he meant was, how big is your target and how close is it? On a very close target in a competition where you can accept a four-point hit instead of a maximum five-point score in the interest of faster time, simply seeing the gun in secondary focus superimposed over the target will suffice. As distances increase, you can "shoot through" unfocused sights, as described by Enos and one of his contemporaries, another great champion named Michael Plaxco, and still hit at fairly close range. Almost everyone experienced in the field agrees that by the time you reach the 25-yard line, a sharply focused sight picture will be essential to an assured hit.

The shooter needs to be able to flow between these techniques as the situation unfolding in front of him changes unpredictably, as it can be expected to in actual combat. Point shooting advocate Roger Phillips calls this concept a "sight continuum."

As you determine your own best sight continuum, keep a realistic idea of target size in mind. If your opponent is six feet tall, and you are attempting to stop him with a shot to the torso, you are not looking at a target that is six feet high. You are not even looking at a target that's 18 inches high from navel to top of sternum. To shut him off quickly, you will have to hit the spinal cord or at least his heart. His spinal cord is about as thick as the little finger, and

HIP-LEVEL SHOOTING is strictly for close range, author believes. These shooters are probably pushing the envelope.

his heart is about the size of his closed fist. In short, the actual target is much smaller than most people think, and more precision will probably be called for than is generally recognized in the "conventional wisdom" of the combat shooting disciplines. The maximum point "A-zone" of an IPSC silhouette measures six by nine inches. The maximum point "down zero" zone of an IDPA target is a circle with an eight-inch radius. Each is overly generous when compared to actual human anatomy, and can give a less-dynamic lung shot the same maximum value as a much more decisive heart-into-spinal-cord hit.

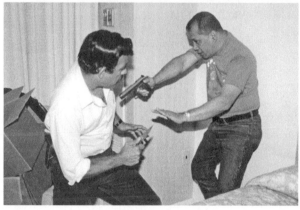

RAY JAYLO, RIGHT, re-enacts his most recent point-shooting encounter with author. Despite close distance, he has extended gun and brought it to eye level. Fast chest shots instantly killed his attacker in the incident.

BODY POSITION INDICES

Hip-level shooting methods (the Bill Jordan technique, the speed rock, and some interpretations of the old FBI crouch) are totally reliant upon body position indexing. They tend to be practiced on static targets, and do not fare well against moving targets. Therefore, they are at their best against targets within touching distance and not moving laterally: i.e., the situation of a lethal attacker within punching or choking distance and intent on delivering a forward blow with a weapon or otherwise attacking straight forward.

As a rule, the higher the weapon gets toward eye level, the more likely the shot is to strike the upper part of the opponent's body. Mid-torso techniques such as the "protected gun position" tend to do this better than methods which hold the gun lower. This is recognized by many responsible advocates of the lower positions, such as Chuck Taylor, who teaches to angle the gun upward from the speed rock to put the bullets into more vital zones in the upper torso.

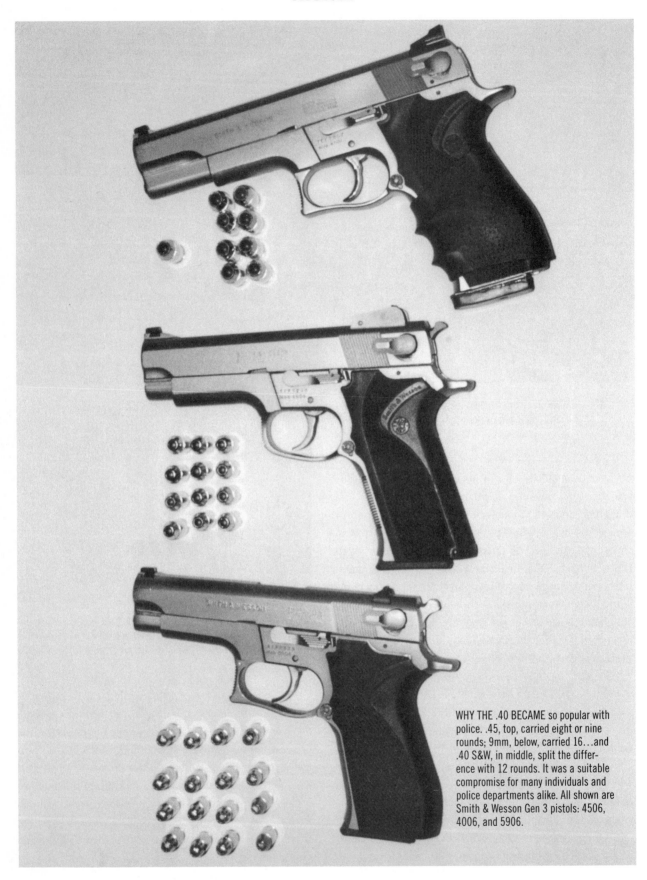

WHY THE .40 BECAME so popular with police. .45, top, carried eight or nine rounds; 9mm, below, carried 16…and .40 S&W, in middle, split the difference with 12 rounds. It was a suitable compromise for many individuals and police departments alike. All shown are Smith & Wesson Gen 3 pistols: 4506, 4006, and 5906.

CIRCA 1991, author shoots below line of sight as required by a stage in the demanding Hackathorn Standards course at National Tactical Invitational. Pistol is Middlebrooks Custom Colt .45 auto.

Some of the point-shooting techniques that are more effective at greater distances bring the gun up level with the shooter's face. Point shooting advocate Julio Santiago suggested that the barrel should be parallel with the chin. Perhaps the most famous of the point-shooters, the late Col. Rex Applegate, brought it even higher. I once unloaded the Beretta 92 I happened to be carrying, handed it to Rex, and asked him to demonstrate his technique. Rex's arm snapped up and locked the 9mm on the imaginary target. You could have drawn a straight line from the pupil of the good Colonel's eye, to the front sight, and it would have continued on to the target. I asked him the obvious: Could he see the sights? He replied yes, of course, but he wasn't looking at them or for them.

One point made by Applegate's contemporary, the late Col. Jeff Cooper, a proponent of sighted fire, was that if the gun was brought to the normal aimed fire position with the sights level with the eyes, even if the shooter couldn't see the sights, long term muscle memory would bring the gun into line as the body had learned to do in visually aimed fire.

VISUAL INDICES

Obviously, for the sense of sight to take part in the firing

AUTHOR DEBRIEFS Reynaldo Jaylo, said by Filipino newspapers to have won more than twenty line-of-duty gunfights. Though he described his method as point-shooting, Jaylo told author he always brought the gun to eye level in shootouts.

process, the gun has to be up high enough where the eye can see it and register in the brain the gun's position vis-à-vis the target. The higher versions of the protected gun position can allow this to a degree. When I personally shoot from "protected gun," I index the inside of my wrist against the pectoral muscle. The gun can barely be seen here. It works in practice and in matches, but I fear that in a life-threatening situation, the cone of tunnel vision will close in over the gun and render it invisible for practical purposes. The same is true with positions in which the gun is extended at chest level.

NYPD FIREARMS instructor Frank DiMario shows author the department's approach to hip-shooting at arm's length distance, circa 1990.

When the gun is extended at a level with the shooter's face, the gun itself intrudes into the cone of tunnel vision and can be seen superimposed over the target's body, even under the greatest degrees of stress. This allows a coarse degree of "aiming" that can be good enough at reasonably close range.

The late, great Jim Cirillo did a lot of work in point-shooting and in developing what he called "alternate sight pictures." He felt that even with the shooter focused on the target and threat, the brain was subliminally picking up a coarse sight picture. Though virtually all of Jim's many shootings with the NYPD Stakeout Squad found him using a conventional sight picture, he realized that in many reactive situations the average officer would be focused on his target instead of the gun and would not be able to get that same precise sight focus. He taught three such techniques: geometric point, nose-point with the gun level with the shooter's nose, and gun silhouette. The latter proved most effective for the students when I saw Jim teach, and I found the same to be true in working with his techniques later.

Brian Enos, Mike Plaxco, and other great competitive shooters spoke of the next level of progression as "shooting through the sights." The gun was extended, and the shooter looked through the sights while focused on the target, seeing a conventional sight picture in the fuzzy "grayed-out" perspective of secondary focus. In close, it was and is enough to assure good shot placement. It also fits the concept of "flash sight picture," as defined decades earlier by Col Cooper: a quick glance at the sights to verify that they are more or less on target, in the instant before the shot breaks.

A technique that will give very good shot placement at high speed out to about seven yards is to stay focused primarily on the target, and watch for what appears to be a front sight sitting atop a rear sight. I called this "sight-point index" when I started teaching it to people in the 1970s, because we were pointing the sights more than the whole gun, but it became known as StressPoint Index after I published the technique in my book StressFire in the early 1980s. The technique was later rediscovered by the great world practical shooting champion, Todd Jarrett, who gave it what I think is a more descriptive name: "shooting out of the notch," called so because the front sight is up and visible to the eye completely above the notch of the rear sight. The eye's primary focus is on the threat, and in secondary or tertiary visual focus, the front sight is still readily visible because it is up where you can see it, and not hiding in that tiny notch.

Next up is the conventional sight picture: front sight all

GOULD & GOODRICH BOOT HOLSTER makes baby Glock concealable backup gun for many police officers.

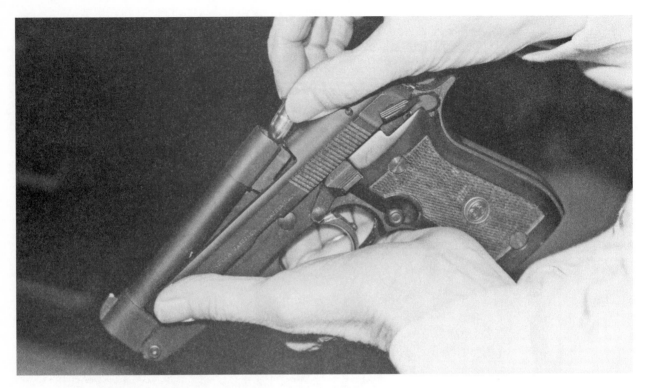

(2nd of 6): THE TIP-UP BARREL of the Beretta 86 allows the user to manually insert or remove the "chamber round."

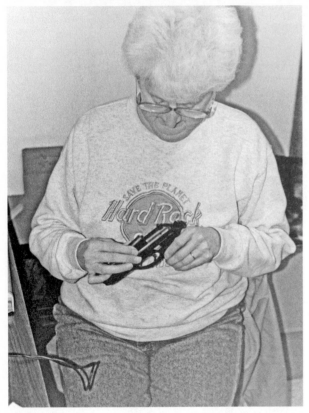

(1st of 6): COMPROMISES CAN be made for unique needs of individuals. Afflicted with arthritis, this older woman has difficulty with regular autos, but not with the Beretta 86.

the way down into the rear notch, its top edge level with the top edges of the rear sight, equal light visible on either side, and with the eye's primary focus directly on the front sight. This is the sight picture used by Jim Cirillo and his partner, Bill Allard, to stack up the bodies of bad guys in numerous gunfights in New York City.

Finally, if the shooter needs to "draw a fine bead" as old marksmen used to say, one can take the conventional sight picture and focus, not just on the front sight, but on the very top edge of that front sight. This was the sight picture taught by John Skaggs, the protégé of world combat pistol champion Ray Chapman, and for many years after Ray's retirement, lead instructor at Chapman Academy. John taught this trick for long range shots, 50 to 100 yards, or for when you had to put the bullet into a gunman's ear canal at a distance of, say, 25 yards.

Only the last two techniques are "sight-focused." All the rest are, to use a term popularized by point shooting advocates, "target-focused" or "threat-focused."

SIGHT AND DRAW CONTINUUM

Tom Kohl's concept of the "sight continuum" is, I submit, absolutely valid. It works very well with a parallel

(3rd of 6): THE BERETTA 86 can be kept and carried "cocked and locked." Easy-operating thumb safety buys her time if someone gets it away from her, and short single-action first shot means she doesn't have to struggle with heavy double action trigger pull.

concept that might be called "draw continuum," a presentation of the gun that flows upward and outward from the holster to better allow the shooter to fire from all the various index positions depending on the distance of the threatening target and the immediacy of the need for the given shot to be fired.

Let's say the attacker is right on top of you, one hand already on your throat and the other raising a knife. As the muzzle clears your holster, throw your shoulders rearward and perform a speed rock, angling the muzzle upward to put the bullets in the thorax or, if you want to drop him fast, perhaps just firing right into his pelvis. The top of the gun should be rolled slightly outward, which turns the muzzle more inward to the center of the opponent's midline. This also keeps the slide from fouling on an overcoat (or on protruding body parts, as can happen with the seriously obese).

If you're within arm's reach but the opponent's hands aren't on you yet, you might wish to keep your torso upright and go to the protected gun position, with your gun hand at your ribcage. This reduces the chance of your opponent grabbing your gun, but easily puts bullets into his

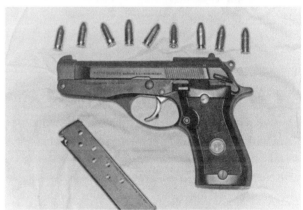

(4th of 6): IT'S ONLY A .380 caliber, but the Beretta 86 carries eight in the mag and a ninth in the chamber.

upper body. Again, the top of the gun should be rolled out somewhat toward your gun hand side. It will keep an autopistol's slide from jamming when due to hitting clothing or body parts. I have seen pistols jam when their slides hit the breasts of well-endowed women shooting from the protected gun position. As noted above, I've found that, at least for me, a felt index of the inside of the gun hand wrist against the pectoral muscle works best. You have to experiment and find out what works best for your body shape and range of movement.

Warning: Do not do either of the above techniques with

(5th of 6): THE DESIGN OF THE 86 is such that barrel is most unlikely to tip up by accident.

guns that are Magna-Ported, Hybrid-ported, or otherwise compensated in such a way that they vent burning gases and gunpowder particles upward. The burning powder particles and hot gases can strike the shooter in the eyes, temporarily blinding and disorienting them, and possibly causing permanent loss of some degree of vision.

In the above techniques, the gun comes straight up out of the holster and the shooter rocks its muzzle forward toward the target. Once that forward movement of gun hand and gun are underway, the gun is thrust straight forward to the target. As this is done, the hand will naturally rise upward with its barrel parallel to the ground and on target. The support hand can come in, always from behind the muzzle for safety, of course, to form a two-hand grasp at any point once the handgun is completely forward of the shooter's torso. Once the handgun's muzzle is oriented to the target, the shooter can fire at any point from close to the body all the way out to full arm extension.

Before the firearm has reached eye level, the shooter will have the option to fire with the gun about the same level with his chest. This might be the geometric point position, which generally requires a two-hand hold, or the old NRA police point shoulder stance, which was really

(6th of 6): ON THIS GUN, if she presses the mag release and drops mag, chambered round can't fire, another advantage for a physically weak person who might have to struggle against a disarming attempt.

more of a "point diaphragm" technique and could be done one-handed or two. However, my personal experience with this, and what I've seen over decades on police firing lines and in other instructors' classes with it, is that this will only work if the shooter's chest is square with the opponent's. It does not lend itself well to real world conditions, where the opponent can easily duck to either side and the shooter will be required to track his movement while pulling the trigger. Nor does it work well when the shooter and target are on different levels, as when firing up

FAMED GUNFIGHTERS of history Lone Wolf Gonzaullas (1911, top) and Tom Threepersons (Colt Single Action, below) obviously appreciated the "front sight" concept. Note enlarged sights on their guns in this photo from Larry Wilson's excellent book, "The Peacemakers" (Chartwell Books, 2004).

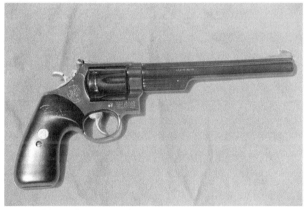

AUTHOR USED this "consciousness raising gun," 8 3/8" S&W Model 29 .44 Magnum with huge Jordan stocks, to show instructors how difficult it was for small-handed students to skillfully operate handguns that were too large and powerful for them.

or down a staircase or shooting at a supine gunman.

As the gun comes up to the level of the shooter's face, one can use more effective techniques. This is because the eye can now confirm for the brain whether or not the weapon is on target. Cirillo's gun silhouette concept is absolutely valid. Jim taught the shooter to recognize what the silhouette of his handgun looked like when superimposed over the target and aligned for a perfect shot. To do this, you take a conventional sighted aim, then hold the gun immobile and memorize what the outer silhouette of your gun looks like from a shooter's eye view. When you see that the rear of the cylinder of your revolver is perfectly round and not oval; when you see that the rear silhouette of your Glock seems perfectly square, or when you see that the twin wings of your slide-mounted Beretta, Ruger, or S&W autopistol's safety are parallel, you know that you are ready to fire and get a fairly well-centered hit.

Next up on the continuum of coarse aim to precise aim is the StressPoint Index of the StressFire defensive shooting system. Here, as Jarrett put it so descriptively, the front sight is up "out of the notch." The bottom of the front sight should appear to be resting on the top of the front sight or the top of the triangle. This aiming technique is accurate enough to assure heart and brain hits at close range if the shooter has good trigger control. Because the line of the shooter's vision is above the line of the bore, this introduces an element of triangulation, so the shots will start going high after about seven yards. However, greater distance should equal lesser threat and less fear, making it more likely that the shooter can successfully transition to the next level, true sight-focused fire.

THE LEGENDARY REX APPLEGATE demonstrated his point shooting technique for author, who took the picture. Note relationship of Col. Applegate's eye to the front sight.

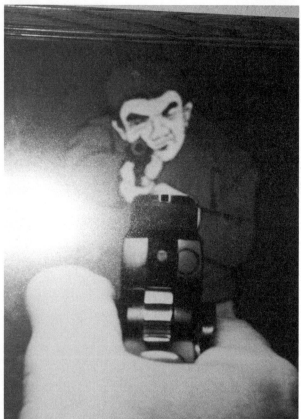

AIMING FOR HEART on this target, bullet will have to go through perpetrator's hand.

When distance or other circumstances demand a precision shot, the conventional sight picture is generally conceded by professionals to be the way to go. Remember, the primary visual focus is on the gunsights now, and particularly the front sight. For a very precise shot, as Skaggs recommended, a focus on the top edge of the front sight may give the best results.

How we determine what is or is not a "precise shot" requirement is determined by circumstances, and by the value system of the shooter. A top West Coast law enforcement trainer famously said, "When police fire guns in public with bystanders present, every shot should be a precision shot." This is no less true for the armed citizen, whose family members are likely to be in some proximity when he fires to fend off home invaders, carjackers, or an attack on himself and his family on the street. The situation dictates the technique: the job dictates the necessary tools.

Note that for true point shooting, a laser sight can be a lifesaver. The Crimson Trace or LaserMax unit projects a red dot on target and gives your brain confirmation that the gun is positioned where it needs to be, and the shot can be fired, now. And remember that, no matter how you index your firearm, trigger control will make or break whether the gun stays on target at the instant you discharge your shot.

One good self-testing medium is "combat competition." No, it's not a gunfight, but it's a microcosm of the gunfight in that "the pressure is on." You'll notice that some of the photos accompanying this article were taken in high-level IDPA competition, at the 2007 Wisconsin State Championships. You'll notice that those who do well point shooting there do it only at close range, and with their guns up at face level. This was true of D.R. Middlebrooks, the highest achieving point shooting advocate I've seen in such competition, when he was winning major matches with his Fist-Fire system. D.R. is good enough to make it work at 25 yards. That's not true of everyone.

DETERMINING YOUR OWN CONTINUUM

All of the above techniques are useful. Each can be a lifesaver depending on the nature of the attack. However, since attacks are by definition unpredictable, the more tools you have in the toolbox the more effectively you'll be able to accomplish the job.

A lot of big egos, my own included, have become involved in the heated debate over aimed fire versus point shooting, over body position index versus visual index. If you can accomplish both, and have both types of response instantly accessible, you are already past the argument.

AUTHOR DEMONSTRATES drawing/sighting continuum in action en route to winning Stock Service Revolver Championships at Wisconsin IDPA State Shoot, 2007. On signal for one-hand-only stage, Ruger GP100 blurs as it comes up to pectoral position…

THE MOST IMPORTANT CHOICE

…AND THEN HEAD IS DOWN for hard conventional sight picture on targets 7-10 yards distant.

CORRELATING DRAW continuum with sight continuum. 5-Gun Master Dave Maglio fires from the hip with his Glock 17 (note slide turned slightly outward), and will be unable to see his gun in relation to the target as he fires.

CHOICES

The most important choice in the matter of combat handgun shooting is one you've probably made already, or you wouldn't be reading this book to begin with. It's the choice to be armed and ready to protect your own life and the lives of those who count on you to protect them from the worst that can happen.

I for one thank you for making that choice. It is one that has been made by all four generations of my family since we made the United States our home. It saved my grandfather's life, and my father's. Without those abilities on both their parts, neither I nor my children nor my grandchildren would have been born. It worked for me, or my kids and grandbabies wouldn't be here. And it has already worked for one of my kids, or my handsome grandson would not be toddling upon this earth.

So, obviously, I think you made the right choice.

You've seen that my research taught me early on that those who compete in combat shooting have a higher survival likelihood when they have to use their skills "for real." When you debate the choice to try competition for the first time, remember that you're looking at it as a very affordable way to practice and evaluate your skills. A local IDPA or IPSC match will cost you about the price of a 20-round box of good carry ammunition for the entry fee. That buys you several stages that it would have taken you hundreds of dollars of investment in targets and props, and the better part of a day, to set up for yourself. You'll be able to watch top local shooters run through it, and talk with them afterwards; most will be happy to give a newcomer tips. It's a "best buy" in terms of the self-training dollar.

And if you worry about bruising your ego by shooting your first match and coming in dead last, remember two things from an old man who's been shooting in competition for more than four decades.

First, you probably *won't* come in dead last. That will most likely be some show-off bozo who didn't really know what he was doing, or some edge-of-the-rules cheater who got disqualified…not a safety-conscious, responsible gun owner shooting his or her first match to see what can be learned from it.

But, second…even if you *do* come in dead last, *you still beat a few thousand honchos in the area who think they're pretty cool with a gun but didn't have the guts to test their skills in public in front of fellow shooters, as you just did!*

The choice to be responsibly armed was the big thing, and since if you're reading this you've either made it al-

BY RAISING THE GUN to a retention position pectoralis-high, David has now brought it to where it is at least possible to see the gun in relation to the target.

With the gun extended and head up, watching the threat over the gun, the shooter can see the StressPoint Index, a.k.a. "out of the notch" sight picture. If a precision shot is deemed appropriate, head comes down for precise sight picture…

…which will look like this.

ready or are on the cusp of making it, I doubt that you'll have a helluva lot of trouble making the rest of the choices responsibly, too.

Good luck. Thank you for caring sufficiently about those who count on you to delve into this deeply enough to be reading this book in the first place.

I wish you Godspeed.

[1] Originally written as "Myths About Defensive Handgun Ammunition" by Massad Ayoob, 2010, for *Complete Book of Handguns*, Harris Publications.

[2] Originally appeared as "Points of Aim" by Massad Ayoob, *Complete Book of Handguns 2011*, Harris Publications.

[3] Originally appeared as "All About Aiming" by Massad Ayoob, *Complete Book of Handguns 2008*, Harris Publications.

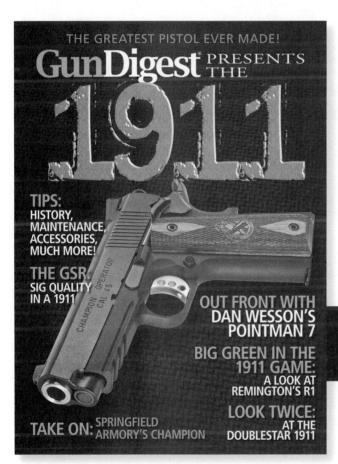

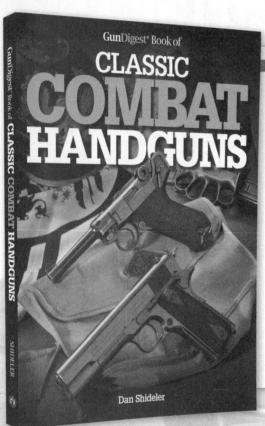